2008
THE BEST 10-MINUTE PLAYS
FOR THREE OR MORE ACTORS

SMITH AND KRAUS PUBLISHERS
Short Plays and 10-Minute Plays Collections

Christopher Durang Vol. I: 27 Short Plays

Frank D. Gilroy Vol. II: 15 One-Act Plays

Israel Horovitz Vol. I: 16 Short Plays

Romulus Linney 17 Short Plays

Terrence McNally Vol. I: 15 Short Plays

Lanford Wilson: 21 Short Plays

Act One Festival 1995: The Complete One-Act Plays

Act One Festival 1994: The Complete One-Act Plays

EST Marathon 1999: The Complete One-Act Plays

EST Marathon 1998: The Complete One-Act Plays

EST Marathon 1997: The Complete One-Act Plays

EST Marathon 1996: The Complete One-Act Plays

EST Marathon 1995: The Complete One-Act Plays

EST Marathon 1994: The Complete One-Act Plays

Twenty One-Acts from 20 Years at the Humana Festival 1975–1995

Women's Project and Productions Rowing to America & Sixteen Other Short Plays

8 TENS @ 8 Festival: 30 10-Minute Plays from the Santa Cruz Festivals I–VI

30 Ten-Minute Plays from the Actors Theatre of Louisville for 2 Actors

30 Ten-Minute Plays from the Actors Theatre of Louisville for 3 Actors

30 Ten-Minute Plays from the Actors Theatre of Louisville for 4, 5, and 6 Actors

2004: The Best 10-Minute Plays for Two Actors

2004: The Best 10-Minute Plays for Three or More Actors

2005: The Best 10-Minute Plays for Two Actors

2005: The Best 10-Minute Plays for Three or More Actors

2006: The Best 10-Minute Plays for Two Actors

2006: The Best 10-Minute Plays for Three or More Actors

2007: The Best 10-Minute Plays for Two Actors

2007: The Best 10-Minute Plays for Three or More Actors

2008: The Best 10-Minute Plays for Two Actors

2008: The Best 10-Minute Plays for Three or More Actors

To receive prepublication information about upcoming Smith and Kraus books and information about special promotions, send us your e-mail address at info@smithandkraus.com with a subject line of MAILING LIST. You may receive our annual catalogue, free of charge, by sending your name and address to catalogue@smithandkraus.com. Call toll-free to order (888) 282-2881 or visit us at SmithandKraus.com.

2008
THE BEST 10-MINUTE PLAYS
FOR THREE OR MORE ACTORS

Edited by Lawrence Harbison

CONTEMPORARY PLAYWRIGHT SERIES

A Smith and Kraus Book
Hanover, New Hampshire

Published by Smith and Kraus, Inc.
Hanover, NH 03755
www.SmithandKraus.com / (888) 282-2881

First Edition: April 2009
10 9 8 7 6 5 4 3 2 1

Manufactured in the United States of America
Cover and text design by Julia Hill Gignoux, Freedom Hill Design
Production editing and formatting by Electric Dragon Productions
Cover photo by Debra Gilbert
Rodney T. Moore, Joseph Mallon, and Genai Corban in *October People* by Mark Lambeck

ISBN-13 978-1-57525-710-5 / ISBN-10 1-57525-710-6
Library of Congress Control Number: 2009923520

Contents

Foreword

What makes a good ten-minute play? Well, for one thing the characters have to be interesting and the story compelling. Most importantly, though, the play has to have a beginning, a middle, and an end. It has to be a complete play. Many of the ten-minute plays I have read have interesting characters embedded in a good story; but they come off as scenes rather than plays. Perhaps some of them are.

I think all the plays in this volume have interesting characters and stories. Here, you will find fine new plays by established playwrights, such as Lisa Loomer, Gina Gionfriddo, Wendy MacLeod, Lisa Soland, and Don Nigro, as well as equally good plays by newcomers, such as Paola Soto Hornbuckle, Patrick Gabridge, Mark Troy, Robin Rice Lichtig, Nora Chau, Vanessa David, Laura Cotton, Jami Brandli, and Larry Hamm.

I hope you enjoy reading these plays; but more important, I hope you produce them.

Lawrence Harbison
Brooklyn, New York

PLAYS FOR
TWO MEN
AND
ONE WOMAN

The Adventures of . . .

KATHLEEN WARNOCK

Originally presented at Wings Theatre, New York City, October 2006, as part of 24-Hour Gay Play Insanity. Directed by Jeffery Corrick. Cast: Maggie Day—Jamie Heinlein; Commander Zorbod—Will Clark; Prince Dorga—Memo. A revised version premiered in Emerging Artists Theatre's Fall EATfest 2007, New York City, October 2007. Directed by Deb Guston. Cast: Maggie Day—Jennifer Joy Pawlitschek; Commander Zoron—Will Clark; Prince Kal—Nick Lazzero.

CHARACTERS

MAGGIE DAY, an adult now (midthirties on up), a young girl some years ago.

COMMANDER ZORON/DRAKE DARLING/YOUNG SANDY, thirties, star and leading man of a science-fiction TV series, *Atlantis: One Million Years BC.*

PRINCE KAL/FRANK GALLAGHER/YOUNG MAGGIE, mid- to late twenties, second lead of *Atlantis: One Million Years BC.*

SETTING

A living room/Atlantis.

TIME

The present, thirty years ago, one million years BC.

NOTE: Concerning pronunciations of the oaths and gods and goddesses of Atlantis, they can be pronounced as the actor sees fit, as long as he *means* them.

•   •   •

Lights up on Maggie, sitting at a desk, completely focused on whatever she's writing. In a moment, she stops working and addresses the audience.

MAGGIE: When I was a little girl, there was this wonderful show on TV. It came on every day at four, and I'd rush home from school, and I'd throw my books down, and get way too close to the TV . . . *(She does that. Calling off.)* NO, Mom, I'm not too close to the TV . . . I'm not going to ruin my eyes . . . Shhh! It's coming on now!

ZORON: *(Off.)* . . . in a time beyond recorded history, there once was a land, where princes ruled from golden castles and warriors conquered all they surveyed. This was the ancient land of Atlantis, once the most powerful kingdom ever known. Then one day . . . Atlantis was no more. All that remains are the myths, the legends, the heroes of . . . Atlantis! One million years BC!

MAGGIE: Starring Drake Darling as Commander Zoron. *(He enters, dashingly, as though in the opening credits of a TV show.)* And Frank Gallagher as Prince Kal, heir to the throne of Atlantis. *(He makes his entrance and stands by Zoron. They do some kind of elaborate salute/handshake.)*

ZORON: By the Sacred Scrolls of Fah-Kazur, I swear I will protect you, Prince Kal, if I must give up my own life.

PRINCE KAL: Will you show me how to be a warrior, commander? Will you show me what it's like to be a man?

ZORON: You are still young, unformed, like a mound of clay . . .

PRINCE KAL: Aching to be molded, shaped into a king, by a sure and strong hand.

MAGGIE: It was an old show even then. In black and white from the fifties. Really lousy special effects. But there was something about it . . . something that drew me to the TV every day and moved me in a way I didn't understand. The plots were simple—

COMMANDER ZORON: The Prince has been taken prisoner? By the Sword of N'Gok-thoon! Woe betide anyone who dares harm him! Kal! I'm on my way.

MAGGIE: And then Zoron would brave great perils and fight warriors who outnumbered him by the dozens, but who could never beat him. And finally . . .

(As she speaks, Zoron fights off his attackers, makes his way to the prince, who is bound and gagged on the floor. He frees the prince, and lifts him up, supporting him in his arms.)

PRINCE KAL: *(Faint.)* Is it you, Zoron? Am I dreaming? I knew you would come.

COMMANDER ZORON: Never doubt it for a moment, my prince.

MAGGIE: And they looked at each other. Their eyes met, and then the screen went black, and there was a commercial for cereal or something. Cereal! *(To mother, off.)* I will set the table when it's OVER, Mom! It's not over yet . . . but five o'clock came. And Zoron and Kal were gone. But I thought about them a lot. And they were always in danger.

COMMANDER ZORON: *(He is tied, back to back, with the Prince, struggling to free himself.)* Well, Kal, this may be the end of us. We may not make it out this time.

PRINCE KAL: Then let us end like men, Commander. If today is the day· of my death, then let me die with you, with bravery and honor.

COMMANDER ZORON: Must . . . break . . . free . . . Just . . . a little . . . bit more . . . *(He breaks his bonds.)* Thank Dorgos! Come, Kal!
(He pulls Kal up, and the two embrace.)

MAGGIE: Then what? THEN what? I drew pictures of them in my notebook, and when they seemed to stop the story too soon, I finished it, making up the ending that I wanted. Except I wasn't sure what that was. It was very frustrating. I talked about it with my best friend, Sandy. She was just as crazy about the show as I was. And we'd talk about it at recess and even act out scenes from our favorite episodes. She was always Zoron, because she was much taller than I was, and she had broad shoulders and blond hair like Drake Darling. She was always picked first for basketball. And I was Prince Kal, because I was smaller. I took gymnastics, though, so I was pretty strong, like the Prince. We took it very seriously.

(The actors playing Zoron and Kal become Sandy and Maggie playing Zoron and Kal. They go back and forth between talking like twelve-year-olds and as their TV characters.)

ZORON: *(As Sandy.)* OK, so like what do we do next?

KAL: *(As Maggie.)* Um, I think we should try that part again, where I've been wounded by the poison arrow, and you have to like, try to save me.

ZORON: *(As Sandy.)* OK. So, you're, like, lying there, all bloody and unconscious and stuff.

KAL: *(As Maggie.)* Right . . . let me get wounded first.

(He pretends to be shot by an arrow, clutches at it, staggers, groans, falls to his knees, begins to collapse.)

Zoron! Zoron! I am shot! The arrow pierces me, and its poison thickens my blood. I faint, I die . . .

(He begins to lose consciousness.)

ZORON: *(As Sandy.)* Wow! That was like, really good! *(Kal glares at him.)* Oh, sorry! Um . . . By the Shield of the Goddess Morda, I will save you. *(He drops to his knees and puts his arms around Kal.)* I will suck the very poison from your veins! *(Starts to lean over and put his mouth on Kal's chest.)* Um, Maggie, do you think we should be doing this?

KAL: *(As Maggie.)* Shut up, Sandy! I mean Zoron! Do you WANT Kal to die?

ZORON: *(As Sandy.)* No! No . . . of course not. But I . . . I what if someone sees us?

KAL: *(As Maggie.)* The light fades . . . my eyes grow dim. Save me, Zoron. You are my only hope. *(Pause.)* I SAID: SAVE me, Zoron. You are my ONLY HOPE!

ZORON: *(As Sandy.)* Oh, all right.

(Makes sure no one is looking. Begins to suck the poison out.)

KAL: *(As Maggie.)* Oh, Zoron, I feel as though . . . as though my soul is coming back. As though my body is filled with light and power. Oh, Oh, Oh . . .

ZORON: *(As Sandy.)* Are you all right, Maggie? I mean, Kal. How do you feel?

KAL: *(As Maggie.)* Kinda weird. *(Gasps.)* Kinda good.

MAGGIE: Kinda good? Very good! It was . . . closer to what I needed to know. Hot on the trail, as it were. But Sandy didn't want to play any more. At recess, she said she had other stuff to do and she didn't have time for baby games. Then they started showing something else on Channel 10 at four o'clock. Speed Racer. Huckleberry Hound. I wondered what happened to Zoron and Kal. Much later I learned that Drake Darling, the actor who played Zoron, had died of an overdose in the seventies. He found he couldn't get other acting jobs after *Atlantis*, and gradually he fell apart. He was living alone in a studio apartment in West Hollywood. I read that Frank Gallagher, who had played Kal, paid for the funeral. Frank bought an avocado farm near Fresno. You'd see him every now and then on those "Where are they now" specials, and people looked him up again when they started running *Atlantis* on cable. Sometimes he plays grandfathers on family dramas. He held up pretty well.

ZORON: Come with me, my young friend. Together we will explore the mysteries of the world, and none shall defeat us or separate us.

KAL: I will go with you always, Commander. Side by side, our swords in our hands, we will overcome all who attempt to stop us.

MAGGIE: That didn't happen in one of the real episodes, of course. But it did in one of the stories in my notebook. I asked my mom to call Sandy's mom and invite her over for my birthday. My mom made a beautiful cake, chocolate with butter-cream icing. My favorite.

KAL: What is it, Zoron? Why do you turn away from me? Do you not care for me anymore?

ZORON: Care for you? I care for you more than any other man! By the Serpent of Sordon, I see your face before me always.

KAL: Then why, why are you so obstinate? You go far from me, and do not answer when I call, and tell me I must leave you.

ZORON: It is your destiny, my prince. One day you will be King of Atlantis, and you must have the proper companion. I am but a rough warrior, who has served his purpose, and been glad of it. My time with you is done.

KAL: No! One day, my dear Commander, Atlantis might crumble and fall into the sea; one day, our armies might be defeated. One day, we will all be dust. And it will all mean nothing. Unless . . . unless . . .
(He kisses Zoron, who at first resists, then kisses him back.)

MAGGIE: And Sandy and I were Zoron and Kal, and the prince kissed the commander, and suddenly I knew what they wanted. What I wanted. I could finish the stories without endings, and write more of them. A lifetime's worth.

KAL: From this day forth, I decree that none shall part us, and that we will rule together, in peace. And let it be known in Atlantis, and forevermore that none shall ever be parted from the one he loves.

ZORON: I hear and obey, my king. My love.

KAL: Tell them to make ready the feast, Zoron, as I come of age today, and there will be much rejoicing and birthday cake.

ZORON: With butter-cream icing!

MAGGIE: I guess . . . no, I KNOW, that was the most important day of my life. I found out who I was and what I was meant to be. It was the day I knew I was a . . . writer.

END OF PLAY

Antarctica

GEORGE FREEK

Originally produced by Theatre One, Middleboro,
Massachusetts, May 3–6 and 10–13, 2008.
Directed by Dorothy Boroush. Cast: Bruce—Jerry Morse;
Ellen—Karen Gustafson; Ruth—Kathrine Gilpin.

CHARACTERS

> BRUCE, thirties, an attorney.
> ELLEN, thirties, his wife.
> RUTH, thirties, a family counselor.

SETTING

> Bruce and Ellen's living room.

TIME

> Recently.

•   •   •

A middle-class living room. However, everything is strikingly white. Also, from off, we can hear rap music playing. Bruce sits, a bit uncomfortably, with Ruth. Ellen is pouring them coffee.

ELLEN: *(Suddenly looks around, sighs.)* I feel like I'm in Antarctica. And I don't know where to go. Everywhere I look there's nothing but snow and ice. I mean there ISN'T anywhere to go. But the really strange part is, I know I'm having a dream, and I say to myself, "It's a dream, Ellen. Wake up." But I can't. I can't seem to wake up.

BRUCE: But eventually you do.

ELLEN: I'm really afraid some day I won't!

> *(Pause.)*

MALE VOICE: *(From the TV.)* Some side effects of Senalis may be dry throat, headache, nausea, and, rarely, cancer of the pancreas; also, if an erection lasts longer than three days, see a doctor.

ELLEN: I don't think we need that. *(She turns off the TV.)* I think I should try Taylor again. *(She goes behind the rear wall into what is presumably a hallway and speaks, presumably into a bedroom.)* Taylor, Ms. Wortham is here. I think it would be a good idea if you came out and spoke with us. *(Pause.)* Well, could you please turn that music down a bit so your father and I can talk to her? *(No change. Both embarrassed and irritated, Ellen returns to the living room.)* Personally, I think we should be more assertive in disciplining him. It doesn't seem like a good idea simply to let him do whatever he wants. Of course, Bruce thinks I'm wrong about that.

BRUCE: I just think since he's a teenager we ought to give him room to learn from his mistakes. *(Uncertainly to Ruth.)* What do you think?

RUTH: I'm not here as a marriage counselor, Mr. Gilbert.

BRUCE: No, of course not, I'm sorry.

ELLEN: *(Not quite imploring.)* We just want to know if we're doing the right thing, Ms. Wortham.

RUTH: I don't think it's wise for me to be judgmental, either.

BRUCE: Anyway, my point is that Taylor is sixteen.

ELLEN: And that's MY point, too.

BRUCE: *(Uneasy.)* The thing is I really feel we ought to be discussing these issues with our son.

RUTH: Naturally, that's a good idea, Mr. Gilbert. Opening up communication is an excellent beginning.

BRUCE: *(Awkwardly.)* Unfortunately, he doesn't seem to want to communicate with us.

ELLEN: Well, I think we should MAKE him!

RUTH: Ah. And Mr. Gilbert, what do YOU think about that?

BRUCE: *(Diffident.)* Well . . . I don't think we should actually force him.

ELLEN: But this is really all about him.

RUTH: Mrs. Gilbert, don't you think it's about ALL of you?

ELLEN: True, but he's part of it, a big part!

RUTH: I probably shouldn't be committing myself like this, but I really think his natural curiosity will eventually bring him into the discussion without any need for force.

BRUCE: *(Confident now.)* And that is exactly what I think!

ELLEN: But what if it doesn't?

RUTH: *(After a short pause.)* Look, there are a few things I think I can tell you from my experience as a family therapist. This is an incredibly stressful period for your son. And I do not simply mean going through the teenage years. I am also talking about today's society as a whole. We are living in a period of great uncertainty—

ELLEN: But isn't every time a little uncertain, Ms. Wortham?

RUTH: *(Condescending.)* Excuse me, but I don't think we want to get into a historical discussion here, do you? My point is that, along with this additional societal stress, teenagers want to think of themselves as independently functioning units. They are, however, at the same time, desperately in need of belonging to some kind of social group to which they can identify. Now perhaps you both can understand that?

ELLEN: *(Thinks.)* Yes, I guess I can.

BRUCE: Oh boy, I sure can! When I was about ten I was irate when my parents refused to let me wear my hair like my favorite pop star. And now that I think about it, I'm not sure I ever really got over it.

RUTH: *(Nods knowingly.)* Did you feel as if your integrity was somehow violated?

BRUCE: That was it!

RUTH: Therefore, you see what I am getting at. A teen's sense of self-esteem is rather fragile. And to damage that could cause irreparable harm to his developing sense of self.

BRUCE: My God! That sounds serious!

ELLEN: *(Not quite so sure.)* All right, but then, what should we do?

RUTH: Let me ask you, Mrs. Gilbert. What HAVE you done?

BRUCE: *(When Ellen now looks at him for help.)* Well, we bought him a new car for his sixteenth birthday. *(Quickly.)* Oh sure, I know that was only a material object, but we felt like it was a beginning.

RUTH: And how did, uh . . . Topper respond to that?

BRUCE: *(Collar tugging.)* Well, initially . . . Taylor was very pleased.

RUTH: *(Raised eyebrows.)* Initially?

ELLEN: *(When Bruce passes the buck.)* Unfortunately, he hasn't been driving it recently. He was in an accident the second week he had it. It needs repairs and they're rather expensive, so we haven't had them done yet.

BRUCE: I'm afraid he's a little angry with us about that, too.

ELLEN: *(Taking the initiative again.)* And since the accident was entirely his fault, I felt like he should get a part-time job to help cover some of the expenses.

BRUCE: Um, I'd like to add I'm against that. His grades already need a lot of improvement.

ELLEN: *(To Ruth, once again more uncertain of her ground.)* Mrs. Wortham, tell me. Do you think I'm way out of line expecting him to accept some of the responsibility?

RUTH: *(Thoughtful.)* Nooo . . . Not exactly—

BRUCE: *(Assuming Ruth is secretly on his side.)* Look, please, Ms. Wortham. We want you to tell us EXACTLY what you think.

RUTH: Frankly, Mr. Gilbert, I don't think that is the best way to handle this situation. After all, what really matters is how you and Mrs. Gilbert decide to confront these issues, isn't it?

BRUCE: Well, er, yes, of course—

ELLEN: *(She suddenly sniffs.)* Oh God!

RUTH: *(Now turns on Ellen somewhat imperiously.)* Do you disagree with that, Mrs. Gilbert?

ELLEN: No, no, certainly not. It's that smell! I really think it's—

RUTH: *(Sniffs.)* It does smell like marijuana, doesn't it?

ELLEN: Oh My God, this is so embarrassing! *(She rises angrily and heads to the hallway.)* Taylor! Taylor Gilbert, what in the world are you—

RUTH: *(Stands up and restrains Ellen.)* Mrs. Gilbert, think! PLEASE! Calm down! Do you really believe it's a good idea to try and deal with a situation like this when you're angry?

ELLEN: Well—

RUTH: I mean what do you think anger will accomplish?

BRUCE: That's exactly what I try to tell her!

ELLEN: I know. I'm sorry. But—It's against the law! *(Now shouting, to Bruce.)* I mean you're his father, don't you think YOU should do something!

BRUCE: *(Jumps up, shouting at her.)* Well, what do you want me to do, for God's sake! Take him out to the woodshed!

ELLEN: You probably should have done that years ago!

BRUCE: Oh! Now it's all MY fault! Well, let's not forget that you were the one who—

RUTH: *(Sharply.)* Mr. and Mrs. Gilbert! *(They immediately shut up and look at her, embarrassed and guilty.)* May I please get a word in here?

ELLEN: Yes, of course—

BRUCE: We're sorry, very sorry. *(Surly, at Ellen.)* At least I am—

RUTH: Please! Is this any time for the two of you to begin arguing with each other?

ELLEN: *(Humbled.)* No. You're absolutely right.

RUTH: This is not the time to begin accusing each other.

BRUCE: *(Hangdog.)* No, of course not. I'm sure we're both terribly sorry.

RUTH: All right then, why don't we all sit down again and try to examine this with cooler heads?

BRUCE: That's a good idea. *(He sits down.)*

ELLEN: *(Meekly.)* Would you like some more coffee, Mrs. Wortham?

RUTH: No, thank you. *(She stares at Ellen, who looks uncomfortable, then sits down.)* Now then, I think we need to face some hard facts here, wouldn't you agree?

ELLEN: Yes, definitely.

BRUCE: *(Thoroughly cowed.)* Whatever you say. I mean you ARE the professional.

RUTH: So, on the negative side, as you pointed out, Mrs. Gilbert, marijuana is illegal. On the other hand, let's face it: these days it is readily available to every teenager and, therefore, in common usage. Now, experts tell us there are numerous reasons for this, aside from the pleasure it purportedly affords. *(Rapidly reciting a litany.)* There is also peer pressure, the fear of failure, the need to escape from an oppressive and overwhelming sense of reality, even sexual inadequacy—

ELLEN: What!

RUTH: But there's no point in going on with this list until you discover exactly which of these reasons is motivating, um . . . Trainor—

ELLEN: *(Softly.)* Taylor.

RUTH: *(Irked at having been interrupted.)* Excuse me?

ELLEN: Nothing. Sorry.

RUTH: What I am getting at here is this: have you discussed this with him?

BRUCE: Well, no—

ELLEN: I guess we felt a little hypocritical. I mean we both smoked some pot when we were in college.

RUTH: It's true that some of our generation seems to have a difficult time dealing with adulthood. But forget that. Let me point out the positive side of things. I think it's a good sign that, er . . . Taylor . . . feels comfortable enough to indulge his habit at home with you present—

BRUCE: I understand. You're saying that's better than if he were doing it while he's off joy riding with his friends.

RUTH: Well, naturally, he might be doing that, too.

ELLEN: Oh God!

RUTH: *(Restraining hand in the air.)* But, Mrs. Gilbert, I am also saying that in a fumbling, perhaps even a desperate way, he could be reaching out to you.

BRUCE: *(A ray of hope!)* You mean you think he's trying to communicate with us!

RUTH: It's a definite possibility.

ELLEN: *(Dim ray of optimism.)* So then . . . that's a good thing.

RUTH: To use a metaphor common in therapeutic circles, he has thrown you the ball, now it's your turn to run with it.

BRUCE: Well now, that is very encouraging! *(To Ellen.)* Don't you think so, honey?

ELLEN: Yes, I guess so.

BRUCE: I mean this is our son, our only child we're talking about here. We want him to grow up to become a decent, responsible citizen. We don't want to . . . to lose him.

RUTH: Well, I really think this is a first step towards meaningful contact. Now, of course, the two of you need to follow it up.

BRUCE: We understand that. *(To Ellen.)* Don't we, honey?

ELLEN: Yes. *(Nervously.)* But there's one more thing I think we should mention—

RUTH: *(Looking at her watch, rising.)* I'm afraid my time is up for today.

BRUCE: I really think we've accomplished enough for one afternoon, honey.

ELLEN: *(Outburst.)* But I think we should mention that he has a girl in there with him!

RUTH: *(Pause; calmly.)* Do you mean locked in his room with him?

BRUCE: OK, now come on, honey, so Taylor has a girlfriend.

RUTH: I mean you're not talking about kidnapping here?

BRUCE: No! Good God no!

ELLEN: No. Nothing like that. But she did spend the night. And, well, frankly, we did consider calling the police.

BRUCE: I was totally against that! I'm assuming it's all just harmless fun.

ELLEN: And I assume you've discussed sexually transmitted diseases with him and the necessity for protection.

BRUCE: *(Uncomfortable again.)* Well, we figured he pretty much knew all that.

RUTH: *(To Ellen, who seems much more disturbed than Bruce.)* I'm afraid I don't have much more time, but really I suggest you don't react precipitously to this development. There is at least an even chance it's not as serious as you think.

BRUCE: Yes. That's exactly what I've been telling her!

RUTH: Naturally, there is a possibility that it IS a criminal matter, but for the moment, let's hope not, and I suggest you consider that there are positives as well as negatives to this situation. For one thing—*(Suddenly, her cell phone rings its catchy tune.)* Excuse me. Hello? *(Pause.)* Well, I warned you she might become suicidal. *(Pause.)* Yes, of course! Immediately! *(To Bruce and Ellen.)* I'm sorry, I really must leave now. I have a small emergency to deal with. We will talk again next week. In the meantime, I truly believe we have made some serious progress today. Good afternoon. *(She quickly exits.)*

ELLEN: But—

BRUCE: I don't know about you, but I feel pretty good. *(Ellen does not look quite so good.)*

ELLEN: *(The music now rises a few decibels.)* I really hate that music.

BRUCE: You know our parents said the same thing about OUR music, honey.

ELLEN: *(Sighs.)* Maybe you're right.

BRUCE: *(He smiles at her.)* You know I am. Now smile! And how about a little more coffee and some boob tube? *(He pours more coffee and switches the TV on.)*

TV ANNOUNCER: This just in. A student at Central High shot two teachers earlier this afternoon. Both men are in serious condition at Mercy Hospital. The motive for the attack is not yet known; it is known, however, that the student, a junior at Central High, was unhappy with the grades the two teachers had recently given him. More on this story at six o'clock—

BRUCE: *(As they look at each other, then at the hallway, then back at each other, Bruce suddenly looks relieved.)* There! You see honey! Things could be a lot worse! *(The music increases, as the lights fade to a blackout.)*

END OF PLAY

How to Survive in Corporate America (A Manual in Eight Steps)

IAN AUGUST

Originally produced by the Rapscallion Theatre Collective, at Kraine Theatre, New York City, August 8–11, 2008, as part of the 1st Annual Salute UR Shorts Festival. Directed by Christopher Speziale. Cast: You—Jon Erdman; Narrator— Katie Hilliard; Cecil, Cecile, Mr. Sessle—Aaron Tredwell

Special thanks go to Rachel Greco, Marlee Tobie, Gina Abello, Liz Greenberg, Jack Halpin, and Art House Productions, the Kens, Eb and K, and my Emcee.

CHARACTERS

NARRATOR, mid- to late thirties.

YOU, mid- to late twenties, a man.

CECIL (pronounced SEE-sul), another man.

CECILE, the same man playing a woman.

MR. SESSLE, midthirties to midforties, also the same man playing another man with a similar name but not exactly.

SETTING

There.

TIME

Then.

• • •

Lights up on an office interior. There is a desk. There is a chair. On the desk is a mug with pencils.

NARRATOR: This is you. You enter.

YOU: Good morning.

NARRATOR: No no no—you are asleep.

YOU: OK.

(You lies down on the stage.)

NARRATOR: It is early. You are sleeping. There are dreams about money. There are dreams about women. There is one particular dream about a woman with money.

YOU: *(Sleepily.)* Lillian . . .

NARRATOR: *(Softly.)* All is quiet. *(Beat. Loudly.)* Your alarm clock goes off at 5:30 in the morning. You smack the snooze button.

YOU: Just another minute.

NARRATOR: Your alarm clock goes off at 5:37 in the morning. You smack the snooze button.

YOU: Shut up.

NARRATOR: Your alarm clock goes off at 5:43 in the morning. You smack the—.

YOU: All right, all right. I'm up, I'm up.

NARRATOR: You are tired, possibly hung over. You move to the bathroom. You

YOU: Wash face.

NARRATOR: You

YOU: Brush teeth

NARRATOR: You

YOU: pluck one nose hair. Shower, shampoo, condition, repeat. Towel off, pluck second nose hair, floss, pee, yawn. Get dressed, in order: boxers, socks, shirt, tie, product in the hair, pants, shiny black shoes, cologne.

NARRATOR: And now you are ready for your day in Corporate America.

YOU: Money money money! Team planning! Confidence building! Spirits high. Pencils sharpened, pens sharpened, wit sharpened, phone charged. I am ready for Corporate America. Where's my coffee?

NARRATOR: Lesson Number One: To function in the corporate environment, set realistic goals for yourself. One such goal is—

YOU: Work hard.

NARRATOR: Another such goal is—

YOU: Be positive.

NARRATOR: This particular morning, you arrive at your desk feeling pert, at ease, eager to put your best pencil forward. Lesson Number Two: At the head of each workday, take a moment to write down the realistic goals for that day. Then decide which of these goals you will first pursue. Today you will, A.

YOU: Adjust the financials spreadsheet to meet the sales force requirements.

NARRATOR: B.

YOU: Discuss the feasibility of adapting the PowerPoint presentation for the management committee.

NARRATOR: Or C.

YOU: Attempt to kill a man with my mind.

NARRATOR: You choose C: Attempt to Kill a Man with Your Mind.

YOU: Perfect.

NARRATOR: Coffee in hand, tie straightened, you are ready to go. Once the objective is determined, you must—Lesson Number Three—clarify the demands of said objective.

YOU: I certainly could use some clarification. Hmm . . . it seems as though the choice I made is the right choice. Although I guess, before I can continue, I need to determine which particular man I will attempt to kill. With my mind.

NARRATOR: There are few people with whom you work that you wish to see dead. There are several people with whom you work that you would not mind seeing dead. And then there is Lillian.

YOU: Lillian is beautiful, blond, single—a real catch. We do lunches at the taco place down the street. Nachos with extra guac. She hardly eats any of it, but when she does, it's pretty sexy. She works out a lot and she's got a tight little ass, even though I'm not allowed to mention that. Sexual harassment laws, you know. But that's OK, because I think she's aware of how tight her little ass is.

NARRATOR: Lesson Number Four: Do not sexually harass women in the workplace. Only men.

YOU: Whatever. So I guess Lillian is out. There is, however, my coworker, Cecil—

(Enter Man as Cecil.)

NARRATOR: Selection A: Cecil.

CECIL: Hey! Buddy! I was thinking, maybe we should pop over to Luna's after work, you know—grab a couple of Mike's Hard Limeades, check out some babes, huh? Those chicks down there are *rockin'*, lemme tell ya. But *you* know, Buddy, *you* know. Hey—did you catch that game last night? Ohmigod—the Pistons versus the Mets? Crazy! I was sure that someone was gonna make a touch down and then he missed that corner kick? Lost a five spot on that game, no shit, no freakin' shit. Oh, by the way, I did-n't do my half of the promotions project. That's cool, though, ain't it? Yeah, I knew you'd back me up. You're an OK guy, buddy, an OK guy. *(Man exits.)*

YOU: No—no. That's too predictable. Besides, half the fun is watching him pass out in the bathroom after one Zima.

NARRATOR: Quite.

YOU: Then, of course, there's my administrative assistant, Cecile—

(Enter Man as Cecile, eating donut.)

NARRATOR: Selection B: Cecile.

CECILE: I'm not exactly sure how to do this. I'm supposed to type the name *and* talk on the phone at the same time? Can you show me how to use the intercom again? Never mind, just look at pictures of my children. This one has the flu and was throwing up pop tarts and gelt all over my living-room floor, and this one forgot her diaper and made a poopy in the kitchen. Poopy poopy poop. I didn't get the message because I never had my voice mail set up. Did you see Lorraine in accounting? She got so big after her wedding. I'm lucky I have good genes. I'd never let myself get so *fat. (She takes a huge bite of donut.)*

NARRATOR: Like nails on glass.

YOU: But she's useful—I just taught her how my filing system works. It took a few weeks, but the concept of alphabetical has almost sunk in.

CECILE: *(Singing the alphabet song.)* A B D E, F G H . . .

(Cecile exits.)

YOU: No, I don't think it's going to be her.

NARRATOR: Then who?

YOU: Well, the last option is, I guess the obvious one—my boss, Mr. Sessle.

(Enter Mr. Sessle.)

NARRATOR: Selection C: Mr. Sessle.

MR. SESSLE: You there. You finished that spreadsheet yet?

YOU: *(Obedient.)* It's on my list of things to do, Mr. Sessle.

MR. SESSLE: Good. I want it first thing tomorrow morning. No no, make that this morning. Wait—I've got a meeting at three. Reschedule that for tonight around 9:30. You'll still be here, right? No urgent plans, no? Because I have to be here. It's Mrs. Sessle's night to have her affair, and I told her she could use the master bedroom as long as she changes the sheets and doesn't touch my things.

YOU: *(Uncomfortable.)* Uh . . . I don't think . . .

MR. SESSLE: *(Laughing.)* It's a joke, son, just a joke! She can touch my things, she can touch my things.

(Mr. Sessle exits.)

YOU: Bingo!

NARRATOR: Excellent! Once the decision is made, you are ready to begin. Lesson Number Five: Locate the most time-efficient and cost-effective way to achieve your goal. Method One: Murder via Meditation.

YOU: OK, I'll—

NARRATOR: Sit on the floor.

YOU: Then—

NARRATOR: Cross your legs.

YOU: And finally—

NARRATOR: Concentrate. Picture death as a floating lotus blossom in your mind. Chant with me: Lo-tus. Lo-tus. Lo-tus.

YOU: Lo-tus. Lo-tus.

MR. SESSLE: *(Entering.)* OK son, I'm off to my eleven o'clock. I'll be back for lunch where I can regale you with incoherent stories and attempt to convince you that I'm the dominant male in this department. I didn't become Mr. Sessle, senior director of Directions and Management Seniority, for nothing. I became Mr. Sessle, directing senior of Managing Senior Directors, for a hundred and forty thousand dollars a year! That's a helluva lot more than you pull in, isn't it kiddo? By the way—your Buick looks terrible next to my Beemer. Park somewhere else tomorrow. Happy workers need happy visual stimuli!

(Mr. Sessle exits.)

YOU: Lo-TUS. Lo-TUS. Lo-TUS.

(Mr. Sessle enters.)

MR. SESSLE: I was thinking—and you know I do that a lot. And when I think, I dance. I cha-cha. I merengue. But more often than not, I tango. Ah, the tango. And what was I thinking when I was tangoing about the office? I was thinking—about learning—the polka.

(Mr. Sessle exits.)

YOU: LO-TUS. LO-TUS. LO-TUS.

(Mr. Sessle enters.)

MR. SESSLE: Quick question: How would you improve your performance if you had no arms and no legs and all you could say was FISH?

(Mr. Sessle exits.)

YOU: LO-TUS! LO-TUS! LO-TUS! AAAAARRRRGH!

(You collapses on the floor.)

NARRATOR: When faced with adversity, keep a stiff upper lip. Remember that difficulties are an asset. Lesson Number Six: Failure is another word for Opportunity to Improve.

YOU: That's right. I can do this.

NARRATOR: That's the spirit. You stand up. You shake out. You breathe deep. You vocalize.

YOU: *(Vocalizing.)* Me me me me me me me me meeeeee.

NARRATOR: You try again. Method Two: Subliminal Interference.

MR. SESSLE: *(Entering harried, and gripping several loose pages.)* Listen up! Just got a call from the executive veep of corporate omnibuses, and we don't have a moment to pick our corporate nose! Those documents we faxed to the home office yesterday ended up in a men's room in a strip club in Guam. We need to work together to learn how to accurately use the fax machine! Stat!

YOU: I'm on it, Mr. Sessle! First you have to place the pages face down on the DIE machine and then enter in the DIE number we would like to send them DIE NOW to. Once you have the DEATH TO YOU number handy, type in nine for an outside DIE BASTARD line and then one, the area DIE code, and the phone DIE number. Once you've GOD-DAMMIT DIE YOU STUPID MORON typed in the number, simply press the blinking DROP DEAD green button over here and DIE DIE DIE DIE DIE DIE DIE there it goes!

MR. SESSLE: *(Thoughtful.)* Hmm. Hmm. Makes sense. Makes sense. But I don't get it. *(Suddenly perky again.)* Well, we'll be staying late tonight until we can learn this new technique. Why don't we order in pizza? Your treat.

(Mr. Sessle exits.)

YOU: *(Watching him exit.)* DIE?

NARRATOR: There may come a time when you begin to feel disappointed. Possibly, suicidal.

YOU: Suicidal?

NARRATOR: You are tired once more. Your efforts seem in vain. You become unmotivated, detached. You sigh. You cut yourself with a letter opener. Maybe you poke at your hand with a sharpened pencil.

YOU: Ouch.

NARRATOR: There is nowhere to turn. You look to drugs and or alcohol. You may decide to ingest A.

YOU: Tequila.

NARRATOR: B.

YOU: Arsenic.

NARRATOR: Or C.

YOU: Patio furniture.

NARRATOR: But you remember to maintain hope in the face of adversity. Delay in achievement does not determine whether or not your objective will eventually be achieved.

(Enter Mr. Sessle.)

MR. SESSLE: Good! You're still here! I need to make water. But first, I need to tell you that the corporate bigwigs up top have determined that our department is one position too full. Apparently, my managerial style is too specific for me to delegate to more than three people. Therefore, I need to discuss a downsizing proposal.

YOU: You're firing me?

MR. SESSLE: You? No, of course not. Would I come to you and tell you that I was firing you? No, I'm having you fire someone else! I'm delegating. That's what good bosses do!

YOU: I don't fully understand.

MR. SESSLE: Why, I'm having you fire Lillian, of course! Good-looking, yes, but I think we can do without her! You'll just have to take on all of her responsibilities without any of the compensation. I'm too busy. I'm taking a watercolor class on Tuesday nights. Which reminds me . . . gotta go to the little director's room!

(Mr. Sessle exits.)

NARRATOR: You are angry.

YOU: I am angry.

NARRATOR: You are livid.

YOU: I am livid.

NARRATOR: You are renewed! Lesson Number Seven: Let anger be your kick in the ass. Frustration and agitation can often serve as motivation!

YOU: I wanna try again!

NARRATOR: Method Three: Rupturing Rage! Plant your feet!

YOU: Planted!

NARRATOR: Clench your fists!

YOU: Clenched!

NARRATOR: Tighten your muscles! And . . . *(Mr. Sessle enters.)* GO!

(You shoots his gaze over to Mr. Sessle; he is seething. There is nothing but raw hatred emanating from his body. His blood is pumping. Mr. Sessle is oblivious . . . at first.)

MR. SESSLE: I was thinking, we should have one stapler for the entire company, and every time someone wants to use it, they must supply their own stap—*(Looks at You.)* What are you doing?

YOU: *(With concentrated fury.)* Must . . . not . . . Lillian . . .

MR. SESSLE: *(Clutching his arm, getting nervous.)* What's . . . going on? Am I . . . getting heavier? *(Feeling pain in his chest.)* Having . . . difficulty . . . breathing—shouldn't . . . have had . . . seven . . . donuts . . . breakfast—damn . . . Cecile . . .

YOU: Lillian . . . must . . . save . . .

MR. SESSLE: Delegate . . . must delegate . . .

(Mr. Sessle collapses. You stops, breathing heavily.)

YOU: I did it.

NARRATOR: Hard work and effort can often result in triumph. Feel free to pat yourself on the back.

YOU: I can't believe I did it!

NARRATOR: You smile. You shake your own hand. Victory is a delicious sensation. Like tiramisu.

YOU: Oh my God! He's dead! He's really dead!

(Suddenly, Mr. Sessle sits straight up.)

MR. SESSLE: Who's dead?

(You leaps back, screams in terror.)

MR. SESSLE: *(Shaken by his collapse.)* Not so loud! Not so loud. I can hear you. Now help me up.

YOU: *(Disappointed, but still stunned.)* Mr. Sessle—you're all right!

MR. SESSLE: It would seem. Whoo! That was a bit scary, wasn't it? I think—I think I could use a little vacation. Yes, that's it—too much time in the office. Think I'll spend a week in Bermuda. Sun, sea, and Caribbean prostitutes who charge in chickens. Yes, chickens. That's what I need.

YOU: Yes, sir.

MR. SESSLE: You're a good egg, you know. You really are.

YOU: Thank you, sir.

MR. SESSLE: Maybe I'll take two weeks. Layoffs can wait until after I'm back.

YOU: *(Relieved.)* Yes, sir.

MR. SESSLE: That's right. And then maybe you can teach me how to use that damned fax machine.

(Mr. Sessle exits the stage, exhausted.)

YOU: Yes, sir.

NARRATOR: You are a little disappointed, but all is back to normal in Corporate America. Lesson Number Eight: Sometimes the status quo can be quite appealing. You are content with the outcome of your objective. You may have hit a stumbling block along the way, but you can always return to your list in the morning and begin anew.

YOU: I can.

NARRATOR: You return to your desk and stare into space. And while you stare, you dream. You dream about money. You dream about women. You have one particular dream about a woman with money.

YOU: Lillian . . .

(Lights fade to black.)

END OF PLAY

In the Trap

CARL L. WILLIAMS

Produced by Scriptwriters/Houston at Lambert Hall,
Houston, Texas, August 17–20, 2007, in 17th Annual Ten by
Ten. Directed by Steve Carpentier. Cast: Mike Cabot—Simon
Martinez; Warren Willis—Mat Boudreaux; Phyllis Willis—
Julie Dierschke. Also produced by Stormy Weather Players in
the Chad One-Act Play Festival, Cornwall,
New York, August 24–25, 2007.

CHARACTERS

    MIKE CABOT, thirties, wry humor.

    WARREN WILLIS, thirties, rich, arrogant.

    PHYLLIS WILLIS, thirties, attractive, pleasant.

SETTING

    Sand trap on a golf course. No set decoration necessary.

TIME

    The present.

•   •   •

At rise: Mike, scruffily dressed, is sitting on the ground.

MIKE: *(Anguished, looking up.)* Oh, the terrible sun! Relentless! Merciless! *(Looks around.)* And all around me . . . nothing but this horrible sand, stretching endlessly away! Sand and sand and nothing more. I will surely perish here!

    (Warren, dressed very smartly in a golfing outfit, enters with a golf club, stops and glares at Mike.)

WARREN: Excuse me. *(No response from Mike.)* I said, excuse me.

MIKE: *(Irritated.)* I might. First you have to tell me what you've done.

WARREN: What do you think you're doing here?

MIKE: I'm in the middle of a great adventure. I'm lost in the far reaches of the desert, slowing wasting away.

WARREN: You're sitting in a sand trap . . . on the golf course at St. Martin's Country Club. A private club, I might add. And more than that, you're sitting on my golf ball.

MIKE: What?

WARREN: I saw it land there, just before you sat down.

MIKE: *(Looks down.)* So that's what it is. *(Reaches under him and pulls out a golf ball.)* What a relief. I thought I had developed hemorrhoids. *(Tosses the ball to Warren.)*

WARREN: *(Angrily.)* Do you know what you've done?

MIKE: That's what I asked *you.*

WARREN: This constitutes an improved lie, and now I have to do a drop, costing me a stroke!

MIKE: Sounds complicated. Why not just throw the ball over there somewhere? Toward that little flag.

WARREN: That would be cheating!

MIKE: Oh. Cheating's not good, is it?

WARREN: Of course not.

MIKE: That's common knowledge, isn't it?

WARREN: Then you should know it, being as common as you are.

MIKE: Common? How many other guys do you find sitting in sand traps? But I see plenty of decked-out dudes like you, strolling around the course. So which of us is common?

WARREN: If you don't leave, I'll call security. How would you like that? Huh? I'll have you hauled off to jail!

(Phyllis, in a golfing outfit, enters carrying a golf bag.)

PHYLLIS: *(Calling.)* Warren? *(Approaches.)* Warren, what's the problem?

WARREN: I found this—this—*person* lounging in the sand, interfering with my ball.

MIKE: It's not as perverse as it sounds. *(Stands up, brushes himself off.)*

PHYLLIS: *(Looks at him closely.)* I know you!

WARREN: What? You know this—

MIKE: Person.

WARREN: You know him, Phyllis?

PHYLLIS: We went to high school together! You're Mike Cabot.

WARREN: And you're Phyllis Murdock.

PHYLLIS: I always wondered what became of you.

MIKE: I wondered, too. About you, I mean. So . . . you're a caddie now?

WARREN: She is not! She's Mrs. Warren Willis.

MIKE: Oh, no . . . no, wait— That would make you Phyllis Willis!

WARREN: There's nothing funny about that!

MIKE: You're right. It's not funny at all, if you're Mr. Willis.

PHYLLIS: Mike, what are you doing here?

WARREN: I already asked him that. He won't give a straight answer.

MIKE: Of course I'll give a straight answer. I'm exploring the Sahara.

WARREN: See?

PHYLLIS: You're exploring the Sahara in a sand trap?

MIKE: It would take forever to explore the real Sahara. And where would I sleep at night? No, it's better this way, exploring a microcosm that represents the larger reality.

WARREN: *(Snide.)* Very philosophical. But some of us prefer making our mark in the *real* world.

PHYLLIS: Warren's the CEO of the Ashbury Holding Company.

MIKE: And what does your holding company hold?

WARREN: I doubt if you would understand. Let's just say I manage investments.

MIKE: Your own or someone else's? Or do they start out as someone else's and end up as your own?

WARREN: What do you mean?

MIKE: How could I mean anything when I'm not bright enough to understand?

PHYLLIS: Don't mind Mike, Warren. He was always a character. *(Laughs.)* One time in Mr. Harwell's class he wrote on the blackboard, "Mr. Harwell is hot for Miss Johnson," another teacher. When Mr. Harwell came in and saw it, he grabbed for an eraser, but Mike had *glued down* all the erasers. So Mr. Harwell is up there frantically wiping the board with his sleeve, and everyone's just dying from trying not to laugh.

WARREN: *(Dryly.)* What a wit.

MIKE: So that's what you remember about me. That I was a character.

PHYLLIS: Why not? I think you enjoyed being the class character.

MIKE: Probably not as much as you enjoyed being the society girl . . . a swirl of frills and curls and eager optimism. Your face was always full of smiles. Has life gone well for you?

WARREN: She married me, didn't she?

PHYLLIS: *(Sounding not altogether sure.)* Yes, I'd say my life has gone well. I'd say that. And you . . . what do you do when you're not . . . exploring?

MIKE: A little of this, a little of that.

WARREN: And a lot of nothing.

MIKE: We can't all be captains of finance. Or lieutenants. Or even corporals. I'm just a foot soldier in the proletariat.

WARREN: Sounds communistic.

PHYLLIS: Mike's too much of an individualist to be a communist.

MIKE: I can't get over the fact you actually do remember me.

PHYLLIS: Why shouldn't I? You remembered me.

MIKE: Yes, but you were always queen or princess or sweetheart of whatever big event was going on, with your picture in the school paper.

PHYLLIS: Only because you put it there, since you were the one taking the photos. Did you go on with journalism?

MIKE: No, but I still take a fair number of pictures.

WARREN: A reporter. There's an occupation for you.

MIKE: Don't like reporters much, huh?

WARREN: They're parasites.

PHYLLIS: Warren has had some business difficulties lately, and the press has been so unfair, making all sorts of allegations.

MIKE: Making them, or reporting them?

WARREN: What's the difference? It's slander. It's libel. It's—it's—

MIKE: Communistic?

WARREN: All right, I've had enough out of you. I'm going on with my game. You can stay here and wallow in the sand, for all I care.

PHYLLIS: Calm down, Warren. Here—take your bag. *(Hands him the golf bag.)* I'll go get the cart. Nice seeing you again, Mike. Really.

MIKE: Same here, Phyllis.

(Phyllis exits.)

WARREN: *(To himself.)* All I wanted was a peaceful round of golf.

MIKE: Looks like you've been left holding the bag.

WARREN: Is that supposed to be a joke?

MIKE: Not according to your business partners.

WARREN: What do you know about that?

MIKE: Only what I read in the paper. And maybe a little more. Suddenly you're the company leper, and everyone's backing away.

WARREN: Would you care to explain that remark?

MIKE: The lawsuit against you and your holding company by Rhineheart Investments. I guess they didn't like the way they were being held . . . or maybe taken.

WARREN: You don't know anything about it.

MIKE: Maybe not. But *you* do, and that's why they really, really want to see you in court. *(Pulls out a document, hands it to him.)*

WARREN: What is this? A summons!?

MIKE: You're a hard man to get through to at your office . . . all that security. And your home would've been impossible. So . . . here we are.

WARREN: You're a process server?!

MIKE: I do a little of that. Oh, and I do a little of this, too. *(Pulls a photo from his pocket, hands it to him.)* I took this photo of you and Diane. You know Diane, don't you? Certainly *looks* like you know her.

WARREN: How did you get this? Now I understand. You're a blackmailer!

MIKE: A blackmailing, process-serving communist? No, I'm a private investigator.

WARREN: A private—Did Phyllis hire you?

MIKE: Phyllis? Of course not, or she'd have left you by now and that summons would be for divorce court. No, I was hired by the folks at Rhineheart, who are pretty darn sure they've been swindled. It's funny all the things you can turn up once you start digging.

WARREN: You had no right.

MIKE: Oh, but you had a right to cheat on your wife and cheat on your clients and even cheat on your business partners. Let me think back . . . didn't we decide that cheating's not good? Golly, you may even be "hauled off to jail."

WARREN: Sitting in this sand trap, waiting for me . . . you knew everything. You even knew Phyllis was my wife.

MIKE: It's a shame about Phyllis. I used to have a crush on her, as you might've guessed. Which doesn't mean anything, because everyone had a crush on her.

WARREN: She'll hate you for this. *(Crumples the photo, flings it at him.)*

MIKE: Hate's a strong emotion. It has to grow out of some other strong emotion, like love when it's gone sour. *(Picks up the photo.)*

WARREN: It's just a cheap payday for you, isn't it? With a little wicked fun besides.

MIKE: If you want to talk about paydays and wicked fun, imagine this. Phyllis finds out you were unfaithful, so she divorces you and takes half your wealth. Then she turns to some old friend for solace . . . just any old friend . . . whoever may be around . . . and she ends up falling in love with him and marrying him, and they live a long, rich life together. Be sure to check the paper for a wedding photo.

WARREN: *(Brandishes the golf club.)* I ought to take your head off.

MIKE: First you better improve your swing. You've got a terrible slice. I could tell just where the ball was going.

PHYLLIS: *(Offstage, calling.)* Warren—come on, honey! I can't drive down there to get you.

WARREN: *(Snappish.)* Coming! *(Glares at Mike, picks up the bag.)*

MIKE: Don't worry, Warren. She'll stick by you, longer than anyone should. As for the money, you won't have much left once the lawsuit is settled and you've paid all your attorney fees. So just be happy then with whatever you've got. And if you've still got Phyllis, that's a lot. More than I'll ever have.

WARREN: I don't need to tell you where you can go.

MIKE: Been there.

(Warren exits. Mike sits down on the ground.)

MIKE: *(Dramatically.)* Oh, the terrible sun! The thirst! The hunger! The heat and the hopelessness! *(Drops the act, dejected.)* Yeah, that about boils it down and sums it up. It's never easy, out here in the desert.
(Blackout.)

END OF PLAY

Moon Man

JAMI BRANDLI

Originally performed in the Boston Theater Marathon at
the Stanford Calderwood Pavilion, the Boston Center for the
Arts, May 20, 2007. Produced by Alarm Clock Theatre.
Directed by John J. King. Cast: Lilith—Mikki Lipsey;
Frankie—Peter Brown; Moon Man—Andrew Dufresne.

LILITH, seventies, feisty but having trouble dealing with her reality.

MOON MAN, thirties to seventies and from the moon.

FRANKIE, late forties to early fifties, Lilith's son who is dealing with his mother as best as he can.

SETTING

An older lady's small bedroom.

TIME

The present.

•   •   •

Lights up on the bedroom, which is not messy but not clean either—a sign of a person who's lost interest in the everyday habits of cleaning up after themselves. There's a bed next to a nightstand with a telephone. A small TV is on, but barely audible. Wearing her fancy nightgown, Lilith stands next to her window, which shows a full moon. It appears on the verge of swallowing the Earth. Lilith is anxious.

MALE VOICE: *(Offstage.)* Lilith . . .

LILITH: Who's that?

MALE VOICE: *(Offstage.)* Lilith . . .

LILITH: Who said that? Answer me! *(To herself, pleased.)* It's him.

MALE VOICE: *(Offstage.)* You know who it is . . .

LILITH: No, I don't. *(To herself, trying not to be pleased.)* Yes, I do.

MALE VOICE: *(Offstage.)* Yes, you do.

LILITH: NO, I DON'T. *(To herself.)* I've got to call Frankie. *(Lilith goes to her bed, spreads out her nightgown in a half pose, and dials her phone. To phone.)* Frankie? Frankie! Pick up the phone, it's your mother. I, ah, I need help with something. The toaster! The toaster is broke again and . . .
   (Moon Man enters stage left, like a vision. He's dressed in a white suit holding a bouquet of white flowers behind his back. He turns off the TV.)

MOON MAN: Lilith, it's me.

LILITH: *(To phone.)* Frankie, the toaster is on fire! The curtains . . . The house, it's going to burn down! Come over now!
   (She hangs up the phone.)

MOON MAN: Lilith, honey. Baby. Now why did you do that?

LILITH: You know that big house across the street? That mansion? That's where my son lives. Frankie's a corporate lawyer. He worked his way to the top, so you better watch out when he gets here.

MOON MAN: What? Is he going to sue me?

LILITH: Frankie's going to pummel you, with his big hands, just like his father's. He's going to rip your head right off.

MOON MAN: We've been over this many, many times before. He isn't doing anything to me. He can't. And besides . . . you want me here, Lilith.

LILITH: Don't tell me what I want.

MOON MAN: Then why did you leave your door unlocked like I asked?

LILITH: That's a lie.

MOON MAN: Is it? *(Beat.)* You're wearing your fancy nightgown again.

LILITH: My husband gave it to me.

MOON MAN: When he was alive. You're wearing it for me.

LILITH: All of my pajamas are in the wash.

MOON MAN: Your pajamas are always in the wash when I come here.

LILITH: That's because I'm clean.

(They eye each other. Moon Man smiles.)

MOON MAN: You know, on the Moon there isn't much to do. A lot of waiting around until the Moon is full again, or at least half full. So I wind up thinking a lot. I think about you, Lilith. I think about catching a Moon beam and riding it straight here. So we can be together. So we can talk . . . and touch. That's all I think about until I'm in your room. I brought you something.

(Moon Man reveals the bouquet of white flowers. Lilith looks at them for a moment. She's touched, then realizes she shouldn't be.)

LILITH: Look at this place. Do you see a vase that I can put them in? You might as well throw them into the trash because they'll be all wilted by the morning. DEAD. I hate flowers.

(Moon Man kneels next to her bed.)

MOON MAN: But these flowers are tough. They're Moon flowers. Now let me in.

LILITH: I hate the Moon.

MOON MAN: We're playing this game again? You love the Moon.

LILITH: Where's my son?

MOON MAN: Lilith, let me in your bed . . .

LILITH: I got to call Frankie again.

(She dials the phone. The Moon Man continues to kneel next to her.)

MOON MAN: You love me, Lilith. Say it. I love you, Moon Man . . .

LILITH: *(To phone.)* Frankie? Frankie! Wake up and pick up your phone! Something terrible has happened . . . ah . . . now what was it?

MOON MAN: The toaster is an arsonist. Your tiny house is on fire.

LILITH: That's right! The house is on fire!

MOON MAN: Your curtains are ablaze!

LILITH: My curtains!

MOON MAN: Your rug!

LILITH: My rug!

| MOON MAN: Your sheets! And | LILITH: My sheets! And |
| Your hair! | my hair! |

MOON MAN: Come quick, Frankie. She's burning up!

LILITH: Come quick, Frankie. I'm burning up!

| MOON MAN: And she means it | LILITH: And I mean it |
| this time! | this time! |

(She hangs up the phone.)

MOON MAN: Now give your Moon Man a kiss.

(Moon Man leans in. Lilith slaps him before he can kiss her. The flowers fall and scatter on the floor. A moment. Moon Man stands up and rubs his jaw. Lilith looks at her hand.)

LILITH: I—

MOON MAN: Your son's here. You better cover up.

(Lilith quickly covers her nightgown with the blanket.)

LILITH: Go away. I don't want you here.

MOON MAN: So we're playing that game now . . .

(Frankie enters wearing his robe, a little out of breath and aggravated. He's been through this before. He doesn't see Moon Man.)

LILITH: *(Concerned.)* Frankie, you're out of breath.

FRANKIE: I ran across the street . . . Some fire, Ma.

LILITH: Oh. I, ah . . . I fixed the toaster.

FRANKIE: You fixed the toaster? Just now?

LILITH: Yes.

FRANKIE: I thought it was on fire.

LILITH: It was.

FRANKIE: So what about the curtains and the rug and your hair?

LILITH: I put out the fire, goddamnit.

(Moon Man laughs. Lilith shoots him a look. Frankie notices she's looking at something. He steps toward his mother; Moon Man steps toward the window.)

FRANKIE: You left the front door unlocked. Again.

MOON MAN: That's because she left it open for me.

LILITH: That's a lie.

FRANKIE: No, it isn't. The door was unlocked. You have to lock it. *(Beat.)* Look, I know it's been a hard couple of years since Dad's passed on . . . that's why I bought you this house, so we can be close. But Ma, I can't watch after you every second of the night. I have to sleep. And Barbara gets upset every time you pull me out of bed with one of your phone calls.

LILITH: Barbara. She's always hated me. Wants to put me in a home with the rest of the droolers.

FRANKIE: Ma.

LILITH: This way she can have you all to herself. That's why you never visit me, because Barbara forbids you to.

FRANKIE: Never visit you? I'm here two times a day, sometimes three.

LILITH: Four times would be nice.

FRANKIE: I'm not having one of these arguments tonight. Just make sure you lock the door. I'll lock it on my way out now. I've got to get some sleep, all right? Big day tomorrow.

(Frankie turns to leave. Moon Man takes a step closer to Lilith.)

LILITH: *(Quickly.)* Someone told me to unlock it.

FRANKIE: What?

LILITH: Someone told me to unlock the door. A man.

FRANKIE: A man?

MOON MAN: He's not going to buy it, Lilith.

FRANKIE: Who? And why would he tell you to unlock your door?

LILITH: You won't believe me if I tell you.

FRANKIE: Are you telling me the truth?

MOON MAN: *(Sarcastic.)* Of course she is. She's your mother.

LILITH: Of course I am. I'm your mother. I'm not lying to my own son.

MOON MAN: Ha!

LILITH: *(To Moon Man.)* Don't you laugh at me . . .

FRANKIE: I'm not going to laugh at you. Just tell me.

LILITH: You promise?

FRANKIE: Yes.

(Frankie walks over to her bed. Moon Man walks over to the window. Lilith looks at both men, then her eyes settle on her son.)

LILITH: Give your mother a kiss and a hug first.

FRANKIE: Do we have to do this right now?

LILITH: Please?

(Lilith gets out of bed for the kiss, and Frankie notices her fancy gown.)

FRANKIE: You're wearing a fancy nightgown.

LILITH: I can't look nice every once and a while? Your father gave this to me for our thirty-fifth wedding anniversary.

(Moon Man snorts. Lilith gives Frankie a kiss on his cheek. Her hug lingers out of her desperation for his company. She's trying not to be desperate, but she doesn't want to let go either. Frankie finally pulls away.)

LILITH: Another one.

FRANKIE: Ma.

LILITH: Did I ever tell you the time I made you a business suit when you were five? Pin striped. You looked exactly like your father. Boy was he surprised! It was the dearest thing—

FRANKIE: MA.

MOON MAN: You're pushing him. He's tired.

FRANKIE: I'm tired. Now. Who is this guy?

MOON MAN: He wears a suit, all white.

LILITH: He wears a suit, all white.

FRANKIE: Is it Mr. Mignosi from down the street?

MOON MAN: No.   LILITH: No.

FRANKIE: What about Mr. Stephanos? I've seen him wear a lot of white, like those linen shirts.

MOON MAN: No.   LILITH: No.

FRANKIE: Well, who is it? *(Beat.)* Ma. If you're telling me the truth, I'm not going to laugh. God knows there are weirdos anywhere you go. But if you're lying to me . . . If you're lying, I won't get mad. Just tell me now, so we can get this over with. I have a big case tomorrow and I NEED TO SLEEP.

LILITH: But I'm not lying.

FRANKIE: Who is it, Ma?

MOON MAN: Moon Man.   LILITH: Moon Man.

("Moon Man" sounds like a song.)

FRANKIE: What was that?

MOON MAN: Moon Man.   LILITH: Moon Man.

FRANKIE: Moon Man. As in the Man in the Moon?

LILITH: I don't know if there's another Moon Man walking around, but that's his name . . .

MOON MAN: Moon Man.   LILITH: Moon Man.

FRANKIE: Moon Man?

LILITH: Moon Man.

FRANKIE: *(Restraining anger.)* OK. Let's say, I believe you. Let's say there's a guy named Moon Man who wears a white suit, and he's told you to keep your front door unlocked. Now, why would he do that?

LILITH: I don't know.

FRANKIE: Why would you listen to him?

LILITH: I don't know.

FRANKIE: You don't know. Is Moon Man from the Moon?

LILITH: Of course!

FRANKIE: So how did he get to Earth? Fly his own private rocket ship?

LILITH: How should I know! He says he travels on Moon beams but that doesn't make sense to me. I think he's lying about that.

FRANKIE: NO. I think you're lying, Ma. I think you're lying right to my face. You'll do anything to keep me here with you.

LILITH: But I'm not lying, Frankie!

FRANKIE: I'm going back to bed now.

LILITH: Go then! Go! You don't care about me. All you care about is Barbara and your job and your big house and your golf. And what do I do all day? Huh? I sit. I sit and I sit and I sit! *(Slight beat.)* But then, when the Moon starts to show its face, he comes to me, at night. Moon Man. He does. He talks to me and he wants me to do things . . . Don't you want to know what kind of things?

FRANKIE: No.

LILITH: He wants to get in bed with me.

FRANKIE: And why would he want to get into bed with you?

LILITH: Because. Because . . . He's . . .

MOON MAN: She's . . .

MOON MAN: LONELY.   LILITH: LONELY.

FRANKIE: Lonely?

MOON MAN: *(Softly.)* Lonely . . .   LILITH: *(Softly.)* Lonely . . .

(Lilith and Moon Man look at each other for a moment. Frankie notices she's staring at something. He becomes concerned and softens.)

FRANKIE: Ma. You can't keep doing this.

LILITH: Doing what?

FRANKIE: This. I can't keep doing this. I tried for six months, and I thought maybe this arrangement would work, that maybe—

LILITH: But I'm telling you the truth. He's right there! At the window! Can't you see him? And the Moon flowers he brought me? They're on the floor because I slapped him! He's looking at the Moon, at his home! You see him, Frankie . . . Don't you?

FRANKIE: Ma . . . Listen. I'm going to have Barbara make an appointment with Dr. Babson tomorrow.

LILITH: But I don't need to see Dr. Babson.

FRANKIE: And after work, I'll take you to Dr. Babson, and we'll see what we can do about this. Maybe get you some sleeping pills, or some kind of pill . . . or maybe Dr. Babson will recommend something else.

LILITH: Something else? You mean the home . . . don't you? *(Extremely desperate.)* Barbara's going to make you send me to the home. Please, Frankie, not the home. Please. I'll be good. I promise! *(Lilith gets into bed and pulls the covers up to her neck.)* See? I'm going to sleep. Right now. I'll keep quiet all day and I'll sleep all night.
(Lilith shuts her eyes.)

FRANKIE: Ma, we'll talk about this tomorrow, OK?

LILITH: I can't hear you. I'm sleeping. *(Beat.)*

FRANKIE: OK. Now listen. I'm turning off my ringer and the answering machine for the rest of the night. I'll come by in the morning to check in. You'll be fine. You will. I'll turn on the TV for you.
(He turns on the TV. He kisses her gently on the cheek and leaves. Lilith opens her eyes. Moon Man picks up the flowers. Long beat.)

MOON MAN: I guess I'll be going, too, Lilith.

LILITH: Wait. I . . . I want to thank you for the flowers. So. Thank you.

MOON MAN: But you hate flowers.

LILITH: I do. They make me sad. They rot. But they can't help it . . . ` *(Beat.)* Stay with me? Please.
(Lilith lifts up the blankets for Moon Man. He places the flowers at the foot of the bed and then joins her under the blankets. As the lights fade, a spotlight focuses on them—a Moon beam. They hold each other. Blackout.)

END OF PLAY

October People

MARK LAMBECK

Produced by the Stratford Arts Guild in association with
SquareWrights Playwright Group at Stratford Theater,
Stratford, Connecticut, September 14–15, 2007, as part of
Comic Timing, a one-act festival. Directed by Jack Rushen.
Cast: Sam—Rodney T. Moore; Holly—Genai Corban;
Guy—Joseph Mallon.

CHARACTERS

SAM, early thirties, in the movie industry.
HOLLY, early thirties, Sam's close friend, a lawyer.
GUY, late fifties, divorced, slightly intoxicated.

SETTING

In a restaurant.

TIME

The present.

PROPS

SAM, an oversized menu.
HOLLY, an oversized menu.
GUY, a cocktail glass.

•   •   •

At rise, Sam and Holly are seated at a table with three chairs in a restaurant. There are two place settings, two glasses of water, and a basket of bread sticks on the table. Sam's oversized menu lies unopened in front of him, but Holly has her nose deep into hers. Sam sips some water.

SAM: *(Putting down glass.)* My point is that lately you only HALF hear me. There's things I wanna share with you. Isn't that what friends do? Talk about things.

HOLLY: *(Still intently buried in the menu.)* Uh-huh.

SAM: Ya know, I might be saying something REALLY important. I could be warning you a scorpion is crawling across the table toward you.

HOLLY: Uh-huh. The scallops look good. I haven't had those in a long time.

SAM: This is not what our friendship used to be. You used to want to know what was happening with me. But now . . . now I feel like I can talk and talk and you're not even listening to me.

HOLLY: *(Around menu.)* Why don't you shut up. I'm not even listening to you.

SAM: *(Shouting.)* For Chrissakes Holly, that's my point!

HOLLY: Why are you yelling?

SAM: *(Yelling.)* I'm not . . . *(Lowers his voice.)* . . . yelling. *(Gulps some water.)*

HOLLY: Yes, you are. Although, considering the waiter's disappeared, it's not a bad idea. I'm starving. *(Calling and waving.)* WAITER!

SAM: I know. Your crankiness quotient goes up when you're hungry.

HOLLY: *(Face back in menu.)* Are you having an appetizer? I think I want the stuffed mushrooms. Or maybe the fried mozzarella sticks.

SAM: *(Annoyed.)* Can you just . . . put the menu down . . . and listen to me?

HOLLY: *(Irritated.)* What? What is SO important?

SAM: I'm trying to tell you that I got a movie.

HOLLY: Uh-huh.

SAM: Uh-huh? That's it?

HOLLY: So you got another movie. You've done, what, fifteen . . . twenty movies.

SAM: This will be twelve.

HOLLY: Right. So I've heard news like this before. I'm happy for you.

SAM: Ya know, some people would be thrilled to be such close friends with a movie star.

HOLLY: You're not a movie star, Sam. You're a stand-in.

SAM: For Dermott Mulroney, Edward Norton . . . Mark Wahlberg!

HOLLY: So the back of your head resembles some second-string actors who get tired waiting for setups, and YOU have the privilege of standing in while the real star is off to the craft table for croissants.

SAM: At two hundred dollars an hour plus meal and overtime benefits—not a bad gig. I meet stars, producers, directors—all kinds of important people. I get a behind-the-scenes view. Not everybody has that kind of opportunity. It takes . . .

HOLLY: Talent? You don't even get to speak.

SAM: I was going to say, it takes patience, cooperation, and the extraordinary ability to stay engaged for hours on end. Not everyone can do that. So yes, talent. Absolutely.

HOLLY: OK. So you play a critical role in today's movie-making industry.

SAM: There's no need to be condescending.

HOLLY: I wasn't being—

SAM: Especially coming from you—heh, a lawyer. In some circles, you're the lowest of the bottom feeders.

HOLLY: I was being sincere. I'm sure standing still for an hour is a challenging, demanding job.

SAM: It's not just standing. I have to keep in shape. These people have an image to maintain. I've been Norton three times now, and this is the second for Wahlberg. I've worked hard. Not that you've noticed.

HOLLY: *(Dismissive.)* I know you work out.

SAM: Four to five days a week. I never know when I'm gonna get the call. It's not easy keeping this body. But you haven't even . . .

HOLLY: *(Sarcastic.)* You're buff, Sam. You're the hottest thing since Wahlberg did those Marky Mark underwear ads in the nineties. He should be counting his blessings to have you.

SAM: Damn right. He's really let himself go.

HOLLY: Speaking of porking out, where the hell's our waiter? I want mozzarella sticks, salad, mashed potatoes, wine, and scallops.

SAM: You just don't care. You think what I do is a BIG joke.

HOLLY: I never said that.

(Guy, a chunky man in his fifties with thinning hair and a tweed jacket, suddenly appears with drink in hand. He sits in the middle chair, uninvited.)

GUY: I used to have lots of hair.

HOLLY: *(Taken aback by Guy's sudden appearance there.)* What?

GUY: I had a head of hair like John Travolta in his Barbarino days. Thick.

HOLLY: Excuse me, who ARE you?

SAM: We're kinda in the middle of something here.

GUY: I used to have SUCH hair. And a prostate.

HOLLY: *(Calling and waving.)* Waiter?

SAM: Hey, buddy. You can't just come over here and sit down uninvited. Who the hell ARE you?

GUY: It's not buddy, it's Guy. I mean, that's my name—Guy.

SAM: What the hell do you think you're doing, Guy?

GUY: Who would have thought it would be THIS crowded on a Tuesday? They sat me at the bar. Three drinks ago. They won't let me order there. They said I have to wait for a table.

SAM: So go wait for a table . . . somewhere else.

GUY: I'm alone—divorced. She wanted someone who could stay awake till the end of a movie. Eh, you don't wanna know. They keep seating couples first. Couples with perfect full heads of hair.

SAM: Look . . . Guy.

GUY: And I'm getting soused on a barstool. You two look like a nice couple. Ya had this extra chair here, so I thought . . .

SAM: You thought wrong.

HOLLY: That's not fair. If he was here first, they should've seated him.

GUY: *(To Sam but indicating Holly.)* See? You have a smart wife here.

SAM: She's not my wife.

GUY: Girlfriend?

HOLLY: We're just friends. *(Reaches for Sam.)* Very good, longtime friends.

GUY: Uh-huh. *(Really looks at Sam.)* Yeah. I see that now.

SAM: What does THAT mean? Never mind. I don't wanna know. You can't stay here.

HOLLY: Why? Why can't he stay here?

SAM: Because we're in the middle of a conversation, Holly.

GUY: Holly? Nice name. Very, uh . . . festive.

HOLLY: But he's starving.

SAM: So are we. Having a table hasn't gotten us food.

GUY: *(Pointing to basket.)* You have bread sticks!

SAM: You can get mixed nuts at the bar.

HOLLY: Why are you being such a jerk about this, Sam?

SAM: ME?!!! This looney plops himself down outta nowhere and starts complaining about hair loss and prostate problems.

GUY: Not a problem anymore. Lately, it's my eyes. Glasses to see far . . . glasses to see up close. Once you pass fifty! Don't ask.

SAM: He's crazy! We don't even know this guy.

GUY: That's my name. *(Indicating the bread sticks.)* May I?

HOLLY: Please. Help yourself.

SAM: But we were having a private celebration.

GUY: *(Eating a bread stick.)* Yeah? Whatya celebrating?

HOLLY: It's our birthday.

GUY: Today?

SAM: Mine's the fifteenth, Holly's the sixteenth. Not that it's any of your business.

GUY: Yeah? Mine's today. How do ya like that? We're all October people.

HOLLY: Wow. What a coincidence.

GUY: Right. Coincidence.

SAM: What's that supposed to mean?

GUY: I think it was lucky that I just happened to sit down with the two people in this restaurant who have so much in common with me.

SAM: It's just our birthday month. I bet if you took a show of hands right now, a third of the people in this restaurant could be born in October.

GUY: There's more to it than that.

HOLLY: Yeah? I'm intrigued.

GUY: *(Turns to Sam.)* You like things in their place. You have inner strength you didn't know you had. When there's something you want, you throw yourself completely into it. You're intelligent, dependable, and compassionate . . . usually. But you can be needy.

SAM: What are you, psychic?

GUY: I'm like you. An October person. We're not so different. *(To Holly.)* And you—you're sharp. A good negotiator. Like a lawyer. You make friends easily, but you're impatient. And sometimes ya forget how important your friends are to you.

HOLLY: *(To Sam.)* Wow . . . he's good.

VOICE-OVER: Would the guy in the tweed jacket please return to the bar. Your table is ready.

GUY: *(Gets up.)* That's me. *(Lifts glass.)* So . . . *(Singing.)* "Happy birthday to us, happy birthday to us . . ." *(Gives Holly a peck on the cheek and extends his hand to Sam.)* Happy Birthday!

SAM: *(Stands. Shakes Guy's hand.)* Happy Birthday, Guy.
(Guy starts to leave.)

HOLLY: Wait. *(Gives Sam a look to support her. Under her breath to Sam.)* Sam! *(To Guy.)* Please. Stay. *(Hands Guy her menu.)*

SAM: *(Gets up, indicates chair.)* Uh, yeah. Why don't you stay and let us celebrate your birthday with you. You can tell us more about yourself.

HOLLY: Or more to the point, you can tell us about *us!*

GUY: OK. *(Sits. Takes out his glasses.)* How's the Cornish hen here?

HOLLY: *(Raises her water glass.)* A toast to October people. We need wine!

SAM: Right. *(Calling out.)* Waiter? Can we get a waiter over here, please?

END OF PLAY

The Other Shoe

LISA SOLAND

Originally produced at Sundog Theatre, Staten Island, New York, March 29, 2008, after winning the Sundog Theatre Playwriting Competition. Directed by Catherine Lamm. Cast: Man—Eric Petillo; Woman—Erin Callahan; The Dropper—Nathan Ullrich.

WOMAN (MERCI), a woman in her twenties or thereabouts.
MAN (JOHNNY), a man, about the same age.
THE DROPPER, either sex, any age.

SETTING

A single street lamp stands on an otherwise empty stage. This is the place where lovers say good night.

TIME

The present: evening.

•   •   •

At rise: Man and Woman come to stand beneath the lamp, exposing themselves to pleasant warmth.

MAN: I've had such a wonderful time tonight. Really, I have.

WOMAN: Oh, me too. Me too, Johnny.

MAN: What a fluke it was meeting you. I could have walked right by.

WOMAN: You almost did.

MAN: I almost walked right by. That would have been so foolish of me.

WOMAN: Well, it can happen.

MAN: You are . . . beautiful, merci. I have never met anyone quite like you.

WOMAN: It's really something.

MAN: It seems too good to be true.

WOMAN: Yes, doesn't it?

MAN: You are everything I've always wanted in a woman. Everything. And not just the way you look—your soft hair, your eyes, but everything. Inside too.

WOMAN: Inside?

MAN: Oh, that's the most important part.

WOMAN: It is, isn't it? I always thought so, but it seems I could never get anyone else to agree with me.

MAN: Well, you're lucky you're beautiful. Some women aren't. Some women aren't so lucky.

WOMAN: Yes, but that shouldn't matter. They, too, should find a man who loves them for what they are on the inside.

MAN: Yes, you're right but it doesn't always work out that way.

WOMAN: Yes, I suppose. But it should. I believe there's someone for everyone.

MAN: Well, there's certainly someone for me. I know that now. I had almost lost hope.

WOMAN: Oh, me too. I had entirely lost hope. Sitting home alone, each and every night, waiting . . . waiting for my husband to come home and he never does.

MAN: What?

(The Dropper enters carrying a ladder and one shoe.)

WOMAN: He never comes home. I wait for him. Don't get me wrong, I wait for him, but he just never comes. A woman gets awfully tired of waiting. *(The Dropper sets the ladder up just above Man and Woman. He perches himself on top and waits.)*

MAN: Excuse me?

WOMAN: A man should never let a woman wait too long.

MAN: Wait. I mean, uhh . . .

WOMAN: Yes, Johnny?

MAN: Merci, I'm a bit confused. You're married?

WOMAN: Why, yes. I thought I'd mentioned that.

MAN: Uh, no. No, you did not mention that.

(The Dropper from up on top of the ladder drops a single shoe that falls to the ground between Man and Woman. Woman freezes. Man looks down, then up.)

MAN: *(To The Dropper.)* Who are you?

THE DROPPER: Never you mind. You just go about doing whatever it is you're doing. Being stupid, that's it. You just go on being stupid.

MAN: *(Insisting.)* Who are you? And what is this?

THE DROPPER: You can see me?

MAN: Yes, of course I can see you.

THE DROPPER: Well, you're unique in that way, but you're still as dumb as a doornail. You're all alike, you men. Well . . . women too. Dumb.

MAN: Here. *(Trying to hand him back the shoe.)* You dropped this.

THE DROPPER: Leave it there. It's my job.

MAN: You're job is to drop things?

THE DROPPER: Yes. Leave it.

MAN: What does it mean?

THE DROPPER: It means you fucked up again, buddy. How many times have I had to visit you? Ten? Fifteen? Something like that. When are you going to get it, huh?! When is it going to occur to you that you can't pick 'em? *(Beat.)* Ah! Go home. Go to sleep. Just pretend it never happened. And then you can start all over again tomorrow.

MAN: Pretend what didn't happen?

THE DROPPER: This . . . date. This woman – Merci. Merci means "thank you" in French but in American it means "you fucked up again." Shake her hand and thank her for being the next in a long line of women who have screwed you over. The shoe's dropped, buddy. Call it a day.

MAN: Wait, wait, wait. You are the shoe dropper and this is the other shoe, is that it? Is that it?

THE DROPPER: That's it. Good job! I should screw a lightbulb onto the top of your brilliant head.

MAN: How come I've never seen you before?

THE DROPPER: How am I supposed to know? What do I look like to you, a search engine? I got a job to do, and I do it.

MAN: No, how come I see you now? *(Looking at Merci.)* She doesn't.

THE DROPPER: Nope. But then again, she doesn't see much of anything. They don't, these instigators—the ones that *cause* the dropping. They don't see much at all except for their own selfish needs and desires.

MAN: *(Waving his hand in front of Woman's eyes.)* She frozen or something?

THE DROPPER: Yes, time has seemed to stop, hasn't it? Well, sure. What do you expect?! Nothing good can happen when time keeps running everyone down.

MAN: So you've been here before with me . . . ?

THE DROPPER: Sure . . . .

MAN: But I've never seen you until now.

THE DROPPER: Nope.

MAN: Why?

THE DROPPER: Oh, hell. I don't know. Maybe it's because this is your last time to call on me. Sometimes when it's the last time, guys actually *get it,* or girls. I shouldn't make this job of mine gender-specific. It's not, you know. They all do it. They all lie.

MAN: "My last time." What do you mean?

THE DROPPER: I remember a couple of years ago, there was this fellow. Nice chap but always calling on my services. Always calling on me to . . .

MAN: Drop.

THE DROPPER: That's right. I got so tired of seeing his sad, confused face. Always surprised. It's like, get a clue, man. Always surprised?! Why is that? How can you *always* be surprised?! *(Imitating his clients.)* "I'm married." "You're what?" "Married." "Oh, I didn't know that." "You didn't? I told you." "You did?" "Yes. Weren't you listening?" Women always use that—"Weren't you listening?" And men say, "Oh, my ring? I don't wear it due to my work." Same ol' crap. Then one day, this fellow sees me walking up with the ladder, and he turns and looks at me and says, "Who are you?" And I thought that was mighty strange. No one sees me. No one ever sees me. But he does. He does this time. *(Beat.)*

I go about my business. I climb up the ladder with shoe in hand and wait. I wait for the right moment, and it always comes. The words might change. It's usually, "I'm not available," but sometimes it's like this forty-year-old guy said once, "We can't go to my place 'cause we'll wake up my mother." Regardless, it's always something unexpected. Well, unexpected to the victim but not to me. I always see it coming a mile away. I got the sight. That's why I got the job. I got the sight, and everyone else is so . . . fucking blind.

MAN: OK, so let's say I want this to be my last time . . . ?

THE DROPPER: Do you?

MAN: What?

THE DROPPER: Don't say it unless you really mean it.

MAN: Mean what?

THE DROPPER: *(To self.)* How quickly they forget. *(Beat.)* Do you want this pattern to end or don't you!?

MAN: Yes. I do. I think. How do I do it? How do I make this my last time?

THE DROPPER: Tell her to go fuck herself. When she comes to, tell her to fuck herself.

MAN: Is that the right approach, though?

THE DROPPER: It works. I've seen guys do it. They don't stalk you after you say that.

MAN: There must be a nicer way.

THE DROPPER: Well, do it nice if you must, but whatever you do, don't ask her why—why she did it to you. That never works and you end up being sucked in again and you never get out. Next thing you know the broad is getting a divorce and you're stuck with her, then another guy comes along and she really does it to you . . . again. Don't try to understand it. Don't ask any questions. The victims will never understand it. That's why you don't see it coming. If you could understand it, you would see it coming. DON'T ASK HER WHY. Just get the hell out.

MAN: OK. OK. *(Getting ready.)* Bring her to.

THE DROPPER: Bring her to?

MAN: Yeah, wake her up.

THE DROPPER: I'm The Dropper, not God.

MAN: *(Referring to God.)* He's in on this too?

THE DROPPER: Hell, yes. Who do you think's given you all these chances . . . chances to figure it out? Wake up, buddy. I just drop the shoes. But He's the one in charge.

MAN: Oh, man. I feel like an idiot. God must think I'm an idiot.

THE DROPPER: Just get it right. When she comes to, just get it right.

MAN: OK, OK. I'm ready.

THE DROPPER: Tell Him. Not me.

MAN: *(Looking up to the Almighty.)* I'm ready. *(Nothing. Looking to The Dropper.)* Nothing.

THE DROPPER: You must not be ready.

MAN: *(Losing patience.)* Ah, screw it. I just thought she was pretty. That's all. She didn't tell me. What was I supposed to do?

THE DROPPER: Maybe she told you, but you didn't hear her. Maybe you unconsciously, purposefully blinded yourself from the truth. That's usually the case.

MAN: *(Nodding his head, trying to understand.)* Yeah, yeah.

THE DROPPER: Maybe you *like* unavailable women.

MAN: Maybe you're right. But why would I do that? I'm lonely. It sounds so sappy, but I'm really lonely. I would really enjoy the company of someone . . . Not like this, but the company of a good woman.
(Man's true sincerity is heard by Him and Woman awakens.)

MAN: Oh, oh. Hello, there.

WOMAN: Johnny?

MAN: Yes.

WOMAN: I think I'm falling in love with you.

THE DROPPER: *(Comes down a couple of rungs of the ladder so he can whisper to Man.)* They always say that when they've been found out. Don't fall for it, man.

MAN: *(Confused.)* Falling in love . . . ?

WOMAN: Yes. You're everything I've always wanted in a man. Devoted, attentive, appreciative . . .

THE DROPPER: Hey man, don't give in. Pretend she looks like the lobster she really is—red all over, with two big claws trying hard to grab hold of you in such a way that you will never get loose again.

MAN: *(Confused.)* How could you fall in love with me? So quick?

THE DROPPER: Oh, my God. He did it. *(Looking up.)* He did it! He asked a question. He's trying to figure it out. He's trying to understand. Oh,

God. Forget it now. It's over. *(The Dropper folds up the ladder and begins to leave.)*

WOMAN: *(To Man.)* How could you even ask that question? Of all the men I've ever met, you are like . . . you are like a real, live knight in shining armor and you make me feel like the real woman I've always wanted to be.

MAN: Really? *(Noticing that The Dropper has packed up and is leaving.)* Wait. Hey, where are you going?

THE DROPPER: You're on your own, buddy.

MAN: No, don't leave me, now when I really need you.

WOMAN: Who are you talking to?

MAN: *(To Woman.)* Please, wait. Wait right here. *(To Dropper.)* Hey, shoe guy. Come back. Please, don't go now. Please!

(Man drops to the floor and grabs hold of The Dropper who drags Man out with him, grasping onto his leg.)

THE DROPPER: Well, that's one way out.

WOMAN: *(Calling out after him.)* Hey! I don't wait. I just want you to know. If you leave now, I won't be here when you get back.

(Blackout.)

END OF PLAY

The Perfect Red

PAOLA SOTO HORNBUCKLE

The Perfect Red (originally titled *Adam's Apple*) was produced by GB Productions at the Fifth Annual North Park Playwright Festival at North Park Vaudeville and Candy Shoppe, San Diego, November 2–3, 2007. Directed by Chris Willemin. Cast: Jessica—Lynda Bell; Dan—Gerald Cirrincione; Adam—Eric Peterson.

CHARACTERS

 DAN EDWARDS, forty-five, generous and idealistic owner of an art gallery.

 JESSICA HOWELL, forty, Dan's girlfriend, a painter in search of meaning and inspiration.

 ADAM VITERI, thirty, Dan's long-lost friend, a brilliant but eccentric painter on a spiritual search for meaning.

SETTING

 The living room of a small bungalow near downtown San Diego. There are many paintings, books, arts and crafts, and painting materials strewed about. It is the home of an artist and an art aficionado. There is a designated painting area, a couch, and a small desk to the side.

TIME

 2007.

•   •   •

SCENE 1

A light is focused on a painting on a stand. It is dark with dried-up leaves pasted on top. There are a few chairs and a table. Jessica enters visibly upset. She goes and looks at the painting. Dan enters also upset.

DAN: What happened, Jessica? What's gotten into you?

JESSICA: Dan . . . .

DAN: Would you mind answering the question?

JESSICA: Dan, I'm sorry.

DAN: Sorry? You insult an influential art professor, scream at your own painting, and walk out of your first one-woman art show sponsored by my art gallery . . . Is this how you repay me? I believed in you!

JESSICA: He insulted my work!

DAN: Who?

JESSICA: The art professor.

DAN: What did he say?

JESSICA: He said he's seen more talent looking at his five-year-old's crayon doodles, and that at least he knew it was alive.

DAN: He said that?

JESSICA: Maybe he's right!

DAN: Now come on. Don't let one criticism get you down.

JESSICA: My art is dead. It's dark, dull, and dreary.

DAN: So you like earth tones. Nothing wrong with that.

JESSICA: Is this the message I give out to the world? Muddy dullness? Depressing earthiness? The color of the planet after it dies? A few dead leaves pasted on a wasted landscape? Great! That's just great! Some poor person searching for meaning will walk into your gallery and find . . . what? Dried-up nothingness . . . from a nobody.

DAN: What if that poor person is not looking for meaning, just a painting to match his Berber carpet?

JESSICA: Dan, be serious. This is important to me. It's my life's work.

DAN: I am being serious. And I seriously think you should stop being so serious. I have to sell paintings to make money. If people want to buy muddy, earthy, or any natural paintings, I'll be happy to sell it to them. I am not a painter, but I love art. I can spot talent a mile away. You've got talent. So stop beating yourself up about what some drunk, midlife-crisis, probably-going-through-a-divorce art professor had to say and trust yourself and your talent!

JESSICA: I do . . . trust myself; and I think the art professor was right. *(Pause.)* I am going for a walk to clear my head.

DAN: You are going to have to walk all the way to LA and back for that. Don't be long. I have a very early day tomorrow and I am exhausted.

(Jessica gives him a look and exits. There is a knock on the door.)

DAN: What? Back so soon? Did you forget your key?

(Enter Adam.)

ADAM: The door was left open. You should be more careful, Dan. A stranger might just walk on in.

DAN: Adam? *(Complete shock.)* My God . . . it's really you.

ADAM: What's left of me that is.

DAN: I thought you were dead. Where have you been?

ADAM: On a search. *(Dan looks at him puzzled.)*

DAN: For what?

ADAM: The *perfect red.*

DAN: For the past ten years?

ADAM: Yes.

DAN: You've been on a search for the perfect red for the past ten years. My girlfriend is in a fury because her art is dead. Sometimes I think I should have stayed in real estate. When did you get into town?

ADAM: A few hours ago.

DAN: Do you have a place to stay?

ADAM: Well, not really.

DAN: Fine. You can stay here.

ADAM: It would only be for a few days.

DAN: We have a sofa bed in the study; make your self comfortable. We have a lot of catching up to do.

ADAM: Yes, we do.

DAN: *(Flustered.)* And we will start first thing tomorrow morning. Right now I am going to bed. I don't think I can take much more excitement in one day. *(Starts to leave, stops, turns to Adam.)* I still can't believe you are here. It's so good seeing you, Adam.

ADAM: Good seeing you too.

(Dan exits. Adam stares at the painting and then sits on a chair. Enter Jessica. She sees Adam and is startled.)

JESSICA: Oh! I'm sorry; I didn't realize Dan was expecting company. Hi, I'm Jessica, Dan's girlfriend.

ADAM: I'm Adam, an old friend. I just got into town. Dan wasn't expecting me . . . but he was nice enough to put me up for the night. Is that your painting?

JESSICA: Yes. It is.

ADAM: You don't believe in God, do you?

JESSICA: I'm not sure what I believe.

ADAM: I know.

JESSICA: How could you know?

ADAM: Your painting whispered the thought inside my mind.

(Jessica sits, startled.)

SCENE 2

Two weeks later. Dan is doing paperwork on the chair and table with a calculator, and Jessica is standing, painting a colorful piece.

DAN: Jessica, I'm not sure what to do about Adam.

JESSICA: Maybe he has no where else to go. Did he tell you where he's been the last ten years?

DAN: No. Adam is driven by different forces than the rest of us. He hardly talks to me. He seems preoccupied, obsessed almost. Every time I try to engage him in conversation his eyes go blank, and he starts staring off into the distance.

JESSICA: He talks to me. Mostly about art.

DAN: Or else he sits and stares at . . . apples! Big apples, small apples. He buys bags and bags of apples.

JESSICA: What's with the apples? I've made three apple pies this week alone.

DAN: I don't know. Doesn't it bother you? I let him into our lives, our home? I've dealt with him before . . . but you . . . I worry about exposing you to someone who is . . . so eccentric.

JESSICA: Well, he is a little eccentric. But he is also very interesting and inspirational when he does talk. I like him. I like the fact that he is also a painter. He's helped me with my work.

DAN: I've noticed you started painting more colorful pieces. *(Pause.)* I've never told you the story about him. He's not your average guy. He grew up out in the desert, out in Arizona. His parents belonged to some type of ultra-religious commune, some type of cult. Bizarre teachings. He escaped from the commune, hitched to California, then escaped again into a fantasy world of his art. Painted day and night.

I found him by chance. He was sleeping on the beach, trying to sell his art on the street. Barely getting by. I remember the first day I met him. I was walking on Pacific Beach. I saw a half-dollar in the sand and knelt down to pick it up. His shadow fell on my hand. I looked up and there he was. Blocking my light. His face in darkness, a halo of gold bursting forth from his sun-bleached hair. He was a vision. I felt instinctively that I was meant to help him. I finally understood why people give up their jobs, their families, their homes to follow a guru into the wilderness. He has that power. After I saw his art, my life changed forever.

JESSICA: You never told me. Why didn't you ever mention him to me before?

DAN: Too painful. *(Pause.)* His art blew me away. It was abstract. Brilliant. Transcendent. I was given a peek at the multilayered, electric mind of the infinite. I was hooked. Anything to be a part of it, to be near it. *(Pause.)* I basically adopted him. I converted my garage into his studio, gave him a room in my house, became his manager. I knocked on doors, promoted his work, got him shows. He was successful. I got him a show up in LA. It got great reviews, but he never showed.

JESSICA: He didn't show to his own exhibition?

DAN: No.

JESSICA: Why?

DAN: Who knows? Suddenly he was gone. When I got back from LA, I found the studio had caught fire. He must have left a cigarette burning. He had left without a trace. Luckily, a neighbor called the fire department and they put it out before it reached the rest of the house.

JESSICA: This is the first time you have seen him since the day he left? *(Dan nods.)* And you never asked him what happened?

DAN: I tried to. He won't answer.

JESSICA: Can I ask him?

DAN: Sure. Maybe you will have better luck. Well, I better get to work. I need to make some calls from the office. See you for lunch at the deli across the street. One o'clock?

JESSICA: I'll be there. *(They kiss good-bye. Exit Dan. Jessica continues to paint. Enter Adam with a bag of apples that he sets on the table and sits.)*

ADAM: Is that a new painting? *(Picking up an apple and staring at it, later putting it down.)*

JESSICA: Yes. All thanks to you. You inspire me. You really do. *(Pause.)* Adam?

ADAM: Yes?

JESSICA: Why did you leave San Diego ten years ago?

ADAM: *(Hesitates.)* Well . . . I had a vision. It haunted me.

JESSICA: What kind of vision?

ADAM: It was red. The perfect red.

JESSICA: The perfect red? What do you mean?

ADAM: Many years ago I arrived here. I was poor, but I was happy. I was painting and selling my paintings when I could. Then I met Dan. He really helped me out. He promoted my art. People loved my work. I was a success. It kept up for a few years. One night I was in my studio finishing up a painting due in Los Angeles that night. I felt . . . lost. I worked with colors day in and day out, but suddenly, it didn't mean anything. My art was so abstract even I couldn't figure it out. People kept saying "It's wonderful" but it meant nothing to me.

I didn't know who I was or why I was painting. Suddenly a huge butterfly drifted through the window and placed herself in the middle of my painting. Her wings were a shade of red unknown to me. So beautiful . . . I just fell in love. I was hypnotized.

For what seemed an eternity I stared at her . . . just stared at her. But then a feeling of uncontrollable rage overwhelmed me. She was laughing at me. Laughing! Daring me to imitate her beauty and laughing that I couldn't. Each detail of her silky wings seemed to flicker at me in contempt, framed by the background of my ridiculous art.

So I crushed her. My hand rammed itself into the painting, crushing her.

JESSICA: Why?

ADAM: Because she was alive and my art wasn't.

JESSICA: You wanted to kill her?

ADAM: No. I loved her. I just wanted to trap her inside my painting forever so she could never escape. I had caught a glimpse of God for the first time in my life. I wanted to seal it for eternity.

JESSICA: What happened afterwards?

ADAM: I lifted my hand and saw myself: a dead bug stuck in a world of ugly make-believe. So I left. To try and find what I lacked.

JESSICA: Did you find it?

ADAM: No. But now I have a notion of what it is. Years of solitude left me emptier than before. I started drinking. I hit rock bottom. One day, I was glancing at a book of medieval art, when a painting caught my eye. It was Adam and Eve in the Garden of Eden. Eve was offering the apple from the Tree of Knowledge of Good and Evil to Adam. It suddenly hit me. (*He picks up the apple and looks at it again.*) The perfect red was the color of the apple just before Adam bit into it. Afterwards, it turned to brown!

(*Jessica walks up to him, holds his face with both her hands, and places a slow, gentle kiss on his forehead, like one would a child. She takes the apple and hands him a paintbrush.*)

JESSICA: Adam, paint for me.

ADAM: No.

JESSICA: Paint for me. Finish my painting.

ADAM: I can't . . . I can't . . . I haven't captured the perfect red!

JESSICA: You are closer than you think. Please . . . try . . .

ADAM: No.

JESSICA: Try. For me.

(*Adam picks up paintbrush and shyly starts to paint. Energy surges though his body. He seems in a trance. Enter Dan running. He motions for Jessica aside.*)

DAN: Jessica. I've made some phone calls . . . I found his Amtrak train stub. He came from Phoenix. It seems there was a fire there at a church. A church he frequented. The authorities are looking for someone that fits his description. To question him. I think he had something to do with the fire. He might have been involved.

JESSICA: A fire? In the church? Did it have painting of Adam and Eve in it?

DAN: I don't know. Why do you ask?

JESSICA: I bet it did.

DAN: What should we do?

JESSICA: Nothing. Nothing is what we are going to do.

DAN: What?

JESSICA: Dan, you lost him once before. Do you want to lose him again? What do you prefer? Brown nothingness or the perfect red?

DAN: The *perfect red*? What do you mean?

JESSICA: Dan . . . .CHOOSE! BROWN NOTHINGNESS or the PERFECT RED? What do you prefer? MEDIOCRITY or MAGIC?

DAN: *(Taking it all in. He looks at Adam.)* Well, he's here for now.

JESSICA: He's ours. For now.

> *(They look at each other in complicity. They move to the table where they sit and watch Adam in his painting trance. Jessica picks up an apple and offers it to Dan, who takes it. She takes one too, and they both bite into it.)*

END OF PLAY

Squalor

GINA GIONFRIDDO

Originally commissioned and produced by the stageFARM,
at Cherry Lane Theatre, New York City, October 4–
December 1, 2007, as part of Vengeance, a series of short
plays. Directed by Alex Kilgore. Cast: Pete—David Wilson
Barnes; Mike—David Ross; Marnie—Carrie Shaltz (Oct.
4–Nov. 10) and Rebecca Henderson (Nov. 13–Dec. 1).

CHARACTERS
>PETE, thirty.
>MARNIE, twenty-five to thirty.
>MIKE, thirty.

SETTING
>Marnie's living room in a tiny, spartan house in Ohio.

TIME
>The present.

•　•　•

On the couch, Pete types on a laptop, his feet up on a coffee table. Uninspired by his present circumstances, he appears half awake and out of sorts, hitting a few keys now and then just to pass the time. Marnie enters with a sheaf of papers. At a distance, she's often mistaken for a boy: thin, wiry, no femininity in her clothing or physicality. She's a loud, supercharged, boy-woman—the kind of person who can't touch caffeine because she's naturally revved up to a degree that resembles 'roid rage. She kicks Pete's feet off her table.

MARNIE: I've been reading your chat logs. Your chat logs are shit.

PETE: *(After a beat.)* Meaning . . .

MARNIE: They're shit!

PETE: I'm gonna need more specific feedback if I'm gonna—

MARNIE: *(Overlapping.)* I do not for one minute believe you're a twelve-year-old girl.

PETE: Well. I'm not.

MARNIE: I'm not a fifteen-year-old boy, am I? Your mother is sixty-one years old. When she does this job, child sex predators beg to meet her.

PETE: Yeah . . . I didn't need to know that. Look: Three more days, my mom will be back from her surgery, I'm outta here. I'm sorry if my performance has been—

MARNIE: *(Overlapping.)* Don't apologize to me, man. Apologize to the children.

PETE: Can I make a suggestion? I know when you and my mom do this, she plays the little girls and you play the little boys, but—

MARNIE: Oh—You think we're playing?

PETE: No—

MARNIE: You think we enjoy our work? This work disgusts me. I keep a bucket next to my desk because this work makes me vomit.

PETE: Whatever. I know I'm replacing my mom, but since I actually am a boy, and you actually are a girl, I don't see why—

MARNIE: You make all the excuses you want. What I see is a lack of commitment. If this was the war on Iraq instead of the war on American perverts, I would go to my chief and request a new partner.

PETE: OK. A—Not even George Bush refers to this war as a war "on Iraq." B—Soldiers don't have partners or chiefs; you're thinking of cops. C— You in Iraq is an impossibility. You wouldn't pass the psych exam. I can't do this; I quit.

(Pete starts to get up; Marnie bars him from leaving.)

MARNIE: Quit? You think this is hamburgers and hair appointments? You can't quit a war.

PETE: Yes, you can.

(She's not moving.)

PETE: I've been here eight hours and I want to go home.

MARNIE: Fuck eight hours. Does a soldier clock out? Does a cop?

PETE: Yes, they do. Please move.

MARNIE: Oh, you have somewhere to be?

PETE: Yes. Home.

MARNIE: Fine, but when you leave here, you're still on the job. I want you reading *Teen People*, watching *Zoey 101*. I want you hangin' at the mall . . . at Limited Too, Claire's, Build-a-Bear . . .

PETE: You're not well.

MARNIE: *(Re: chat logs.)* You asked one of these pervs to bring you Pabst. Twelve-year-old girls don't want Pabst! They want Mike's Hard Lemonade and a My Pretty Pony.

PETE: I'm not sure that's true.

MARNIE: *(Re: his chat logs.)* You can't even keep the Duff sisters straight! Your research is shit!

(A pinging sound from Pete's laptop indicates he's received an instant message. Marnie bolts for the laptop.)

MARNIE: That's an IM. You just got an IM.

PETE: No, you did. I'm going.

MARNIE: *(Overlapping.)* Get the fuck over here; let me show you how it's done.

(Pete, a little curious and having nowhere to go, considers it.)

MARNIE: You be the perv; I'll be the prey. Read!

(He joins her. For now, italics indicate typed chat that the character reads aloud as he or she types. Marnie alters her voice slightly, trying to sound younger and more feminine. Nothing too cartoonish. It's a very serious role-play for her, and it would piss her off to be laughed at. Pete reads the perv's side of the chat straight.)

PETE: *How R U?*

MARNIE: *Sooo bored. How r u?*

PETE: *Having a bad day. Sad face.*

MARNIE: *Awwwww. Being sad sux. When I'm sad, I comb my ponys hair. (To Pete.)* Girls love horses. When you run outta things to say, just talk about horses.

PETE: *Do you live on a farm?*

MARNIE: *LOL. My pony is a toy. Do U like horses?*

PETE: *They're OK. How old R u?*

MARNIE: *13 next week. What about U?* Now. If he continues chatting after this point, he is babyfucker scum who deserves to be raped in prison until he dies.

PETE: What if he's just . . . bored and goofing around?

MARNIE: I'm in a chatroom for teenage girls, and my user name is Rainbowbrite. Any man who IM's me has a broken brain that cannot be fixed. *RU Still there? RU OK?*

PETE: He's gone. I don't think there are as many pervs out there as you think there are.

MARNIE: *(Re: computer.)* Yes! He's back!

PETE: *Maybe don't want to chat. But Thx u seem nice.*

MARNIE: *Awwww. I'm 2 wurried for you!!*

PETE: He just said he doesn't want to chat with you.

MARNIE: *When I'm sad helps 2 talk.*

PETE: Now you're baiting him. You know you're not supposed to do that.

MARNIE: *Sad is the opositt of rainbows. Sadface.*

PETE: Jesus! Nobody talks like that. And I don't think kids spell as badly as you think they do.

MARNIE: *RU there sad frend? (To the computer.)* Come on, man! *(Her cell phone rings or vibrates in her pocket. She pulls it out and checks the number before answering.)* Finally he calls. I've been chatting with this scumbag for a month. *(Re: computer.)* Keep chatting. Do not log out.

(On her phone now, Marnie seems to assume the persona of a young black boy.)

MARNIE: Yo. *(Pause.)* Man, I thought you were dissing me! I been all hurt n' shit. *(Listening.)* Arrested? That's what you're worried about? Damn. I won't tell. *(Pause.)* Nah, I'm all virgin and shit, makes me embarrassed. You could be my first. Yo! *(Hand over mouthpiece, to Pete, in her natural voice.)* I am this close to vomiting. God, I hate this! *(Back on the phone.)* I'm playin' with my thing, man. My thing feels good when I pull on it. *(Hand over mouthpiece, to Pete, in her natural voice.)* When I think I'm gonna vomit . . . I think of the children. *(Back on the phone.)* You're where? *(Pause.)* Then come on over. My parents so neglectful, they ain't even home . . .

PETE: He's back. He says . . . *might help 2 talk.*

MARNIE: *(To Pete.)* Then fucking talk to him! *(Into phone.)* No, no. That's the TV next door. I'm all alone . . .

(Marnie exits to the kitchen. Mike enters from upstage and stands behind the sofa. He's the "perv" Pete is chatting with. There is nothing physically off-putting or odd about Mike, but he's got a heavy, humorless energy that sucks the air out of a room. The characters aren't conscious of each other's presence on the stage.)

MIKE: You seem so nice. Usually when I say I'm sad, the girl stops chatting.

PETE: *How old r u?*

MIKE: Not a teenager.

PETE: *Y r u in a teen chatroom?*

MIKE: Cuz I am a loser. LOL. *(Pause; ruefully.)* Lots of laughs.

PETE: *Y R U a loser?*

MIKE: Can't get a girl.

PETE: *Why?*

MIKE: Not hot and told I'm creepy.

PETE: *What makes you creepy?*

MIKE: Don't know. It's just what they say. Girls. I drank too much last night. When I drink I get really sad.

PETE: *Maybe u shouldn't drink.*

MIKE: Have to. Girls like to party.

PETE: *Not all girls.*

MIKE: The girls I want. They party. They drink a lot and it makes them dance. I drink to be like them and I get all weird.

PETE: *Weird how?*

MIKE: Obsess on bad stuff. I think about bad stuff all the time, but when I drink it gets very intense and I feel like my thoughts are strangling me.

PETE: *What kind of bad things?*

MIKE: Whatever's current. The bridge collapse in Minnesota. The family in Connecticut that was set on fire by burglars. People who put babies in microwaves. The meth epidemic.

PETE: *Wow.*

MIKE: I'm really jealous of them. Girls. Must be nice to get happy when you drink.

PETE: *Not all girls get happy when they drink. Trust me.*

MIKE: Does your mom drink?

PETE: My mom? Oh, right. *No. But I've . . . known women who turn mean when they drink. They don't all get nicer.*

MIKE: *(Annoyed.)* I didn't say they get nicer; I said they get happy. And happy to them is laughing and calling me a creep and a freak.

PETE: *(After a beat.) Maybe you should see a doctor.*

MIKE: I don't need a doctor. I need a girlfriend.

PETE: *You think a girlfriend can change what's inside your head?*

MIKE: The right one, yes. But I don't think I need to change.

PETE: *Thought you were feeling strangled.*

MIKE: Don't mind that. Just mind girls calling me freaky.

PETE: *Maybe U should date a Goth chick.*

MIKE: *(Offended.)* No! I like cute girls who laugh and dance!

(From here on, Pete gives up typing and just talks.)

PETE: Can I be honest, dude?

MIKE: Sure.

PETE: I think you're setting yourself up for disappointment. You're this deep guy who thinks deep thoughts, and you're out chasing fuckin' Girls-Gone-Wild bimbos who don't care about shit but themselves and landing a rich husband. You're a smart, thoughtful dude wasting his time with daiquiri swilling, Juicy wearing . . . bitches. Pardon my language. You've convinced yourself that you suck, so a desirable woman has to be the total opposite of you. And that's not right.

MIKE: YOU ARE AMAZING! This is why I came to this chatroom! Girls under fifteen have such incredible no-bullshit purity and insight!

PETE: *(Unnerved.)* Let's keep this about you.

MIKE: J. D. Salinger understood . . . that there are very special young girls who cultivate mature wisdom while preserving the innocence of their child selves.

PETE: Wait—

MIKE: Did you ever read J. D. Salinger's story, "To Esme, with Love and Squalor"?

PETE: No.

MIKE: Esme is a little girl who meets a soldier shipping off to war. She asks him to write her letters filled with squalor. Esme wants to share his squalor! She's my favorite character in literature next to Phoebe in *Catcher in the Rye.*

PETE: *(A stab at redirecting.)* LOL. Laugh out loud.

MIKE: Right around sixteen, girls change. They become, like you said, bitches.

PETE: I shouldn't have said that. I got burned in my last relationship, so I'm still—

MIKE: How old was he?

PETE: He? Right. He . . . He wasn't that great a catch, I guess. He lives with his mom. No job. In his defense, his mom is, like, morbidly obese and is right now having her stomach stapled and making her son fill in for her at her shitty job.

MIKE: How old is this guy?

PETE: Too old to be living with his mom. But, again, in his defense, he had a great job and his own place until two years ago. He was a waiter, yeah, but at the top steakhouse in the state of New Mexico. He made very good cash.

MIKE: You like older men. I knew it.

PETE: No! I don't. I just . . . I know where you're coming from. With women. I gave up—I mean—my ex-boyfriend gave up a decent life to move home and take care of his mom. This girl he fell for . . . Me, I guess . . . She didn't give him shit credit for that. All she saw was no job, no money.

MIKE: I have enough money. I own my own business.

PETE: How old are you? You never said.

MIKE: *(After a beat.)* Thirty.

PETE: Me, too. I mean . . . OK, look. I'm gonna be straight with you. Total honesty here.

MIKE: I love honesty. We share that.

PETE: I've been lying this whole time. I'm a thirty-year-old guy. My name is Pete. The stuff I told you about getting dumped . . . That was all true. But I'm the guy in the story. I'm in this chatroom because I'm getting paid to lure child predators to a house where the police arrest them. Are you still listening?

MIKE: Yes.

PETE: Let's forget this ever happened. We're in the same boat; you seem cool . . . Let's go to a bar. I'm not gay, I just feel like a loser going out alone.

There's this bartender I think you'd like. Her name's Ruth. She told me my chance with girls would be better if I had a wingman. Never heard that word before Ruth said it. I think it means, like, an airplane needs two wings to fly. One guy, one wing . . . Can't get off the ground. Shit, I typed a fucking book here. I'm not gay. I just need a friend—er—wing-man. What do you say?

(Long pause.)

MIKE: LOL. Lots of laughs.

PETE: No, not LOL. That's the truth. My name is Pete.

MIKE: You're Esme. You are brilliant and mischievous. It amuses you to mimic adult voices.

PETE: Read what I just wrote, man. Game over. Let's drink till we forget this ever happened. What do you say?

MIKE: Sadface. Not funny anymore. Say you are kidding.

PETE: I'm thirty and I have a dick.

MIKE: Sadface! Sadface sadface sadface . . .

PETE: *(Resumes typing.)* You really are a pervert, aren't you? I just tried to be a friend to you, you fucking shot me down.

MIKE: Be who you were at the beginning. Say "awwwwww" and tell me don't be sad.

(Marnie returns.)

MARNIE: Nailed him! Busted! Dragged off to jail crying for his mommy! Paulie slammed him to the ground and cuffed his ass. I yelled, "Hey, babyfucker! Who's a rape doll now?" My thirty-seventh arrest. How's your perv? He still sad? *(Marnie makes a crude "boo-hoo, I'm crying" gesture.)*

PETE: I know what you mean now.

MARNIE: Yeah? How's that?

PETE: He's making me want to throw up.

(Juiced, ecstatic, Marnie seizes the laptop and sits beside Pete.)

MARNIE: God, I hate perverts! Fuck! Gimme the 411; what's he into?

PETE: He liked it better when you were chatting. When you said "awwwww" and pretended you cared.

MARNIE: Sick Fuck. *Y R you sad, u r 2 nice!!!* *(To Pete.)* Don't feel bad. I've been doing this a lot longer than you. I'm a pro.

MIKE: *(Enormous relief.)* Thank you! I knew you were joking. U R an imp. Can we meet?

MARNIE: Pervert scum! *That would be 2 fun!!! What would we do?*

(Handing Pete her cell phone.)

MARNIE: Speed dial six on my phone, ask for Paulie Junior. He's the cop I bust with.

MIKE: I will call you Esme while you stroke my head.

MARNIE: He said stroke my head!!! That's an explicit proposition. Tell Paulie he said "stroke my head."

PETE: He means this head. *(Indicating.)* The one on your shoulders.

MARNIE: *(Taking phone.)* I was like you once. Fucking naïve. *(On her phone.)* Paulie! Get back to the house; I'm reeling in another one.

MIKE: Are you still there, Esme?

MARNIE: What the fuck is an Esme? *Strokeing sounds kewl. (Into the phone:)* Yeah, yeah. He asked for sex. He asked to meet. I didn't push. It'll hold up in court, just get back here. *(She disconnects the call.)*

MIKE: Esme? Esme?

MARNIE: *Had to say by to my folks. They went out & left me alone. Sadface.*

PETE: I think that's pushing.

MARNIE: Please. Is there any amount of pushing that could get you to drive to a twelve-year-old girl's house?

PETE: If the twelve-year-old had the mind of a thirty-year-old because she was, in fact, a thirty-year-old pretending to be twelve just to fuck with me . . . Yeah, I might just drive on over.

MARNIE: Listen to me! I don't care if the kid exhibits Shakespeare's eloquence, Jesus's compassion, Oprah's wisdom, and Robyn Byrd's filthy mouth. If she says she's twelve and you go to her house, you are a pervert who deserves to be raped in jail until you suicide.

MIKE: What do you smell like, Esme?

PETE: I think despair can push a man to some questionable choices.

MARNIE: *Vanilla body butter and cherry coke.*

PETE: I'm assuming some guy molested you when you were a kid. I'm gonna assume that's why we don't see eye to eye on this.

MARNIE: Never been a victim myself. But that's a common misconception about me.

MIKE: If I get sad will you think I'm not fun?

MARNIE: *Sad guys are 2 kewl!!!* Freak. I'm not a victim; I'm just a woman with a gift.

PETE: A gift?

MIKE: I'm going to bring you a book by J. D. Salinger.

MARNIE: *Kewl. Also Bring Skittles and Mike's Lemonade.* My gift is my guts. I have the guts to dive into the pit, into the blackest, foulest squalor and not pass out from the stench. Did I ask for this gift? No. Do I wish I could give it back? Some days, yes. Doesn't make me stop.

MIKE: Give me your address.

MARNIE: Oh, you creep. You creepy fucking freak. *Can U come now?*

MIKE: Yes.

MARNIE: *29 Madsen Lane. Come soon. Can't wait!!! (To Pete.)* Want to watch me and Paulie bust a babyfucker? Or you got someplace better to be? *(A silent beat. He doesn't have anyplace better to be. None of these people do. And he's pissed at Mike for refusing to be his wingman. If Mike had said yes, Pete could go to the bar now. Pervert or not, the guy is uncharitable.)*

PETE: Nah. I want to watch you nail him.

END OF PLAY

Three Turkeys Waiting for Corncobs

DON NIGRO

    BOB.
    GEORGE.
    PENNY.

Bob, George, and Penny are three wild turkeys.

SETTING
    Somebody's backyard by the woods.

TIME
    The present.

•   •   •

Lights up on Bob, George. and Penny, three wild turkeys who live in the woods and show up every day in the backyard of people who throw out corncobs for them.

BOB: Have they thrown out the corncobs yet, George?

GEORGE: Not yet, Bob.

BOB: I want some corncobs, George. I love corncobs.

GEORGE: We all love corncobs, Bob. We're turkeys.

BOB: I like corn better than anything.

PENNY: Yesterday you liked bugs better than anything.

BOB: I like bugs, but I like corn more. Except sometimes when I get really good bugs. But mostly I like corn. I mean, sometimes bugs can get away. But corn almost never gets away. Corn doesn't move like bugs. You can trust corn.

PENNY: Bob, did you ever think maybe there's more to life than corn?

BOB: Sure.

GEORGE: Like what?

BOB: There's bugs. There's corn. And then there's bugs.

PENNY: But don't you ever think maybe life is more than just corn and bugs?

BOB: I'm confused, Penny. You mean like trees?

PENNY: No, I don't mean trees, Bob.

GEORGE: We're turkeys, Penny. We love corn and bugs. What else is there?

PENNY: I've always wanted to play the saxophone.

GEORGE: The saxophone?

PENNY: Yes.

GEORGE: You've always wanted to play the saxophone?

PENNY: Yes.

GEORGE: Penny, turkeys can't play the saxophone.

PENNY: Why not? Because I think that's just an example of prejudice. Give me one good reason why a turkey can't play the saxophone.

GEORGE: We don't have any fingers. You need fingers to play the saxophone.

PENNY: We have feet. Maybe we can play the saxophone with our feet.

GEORGE: I don't think so.

PENNY: Have you ever tried?

GEORGE: No, Penny. I've never tried to play the saxophone with my feet.

PENNY: Then how do you know you can't?

BOB: This is getting too deep for me.

GEORGE: But we don't have any lips.

PENNY: I've got lips.

GEORGE: You don't have any lips, Penny. You're a turkey. Turkeys don't have lips.

PENNY: Then what's this thing on my face?

GEORGE: That's your beak, Penny. You can't blow into a saxophone with a beak. To blow into a saxophone, you need lips.

PENNY: I don't care what you say. I'm going to play the saxophone. I don't know exactly how yet, but I am. And some day, when I'm a world famous turkey saxophone player, you're going to look through somebody's back window at their television and see me playing the saxophone, and you'll say, look, Bob, there's Penny, and she's playing the saxophone.

BOB: Have they put the corncobs out yet, George?

GEORGE: Not yet, Bob.

PENNY: I feel the same way about the saxophone that Bob feels about corncobs.

GEORGE: No you don't.

PENNY: Yes I do.

GEORGE: You can't compare saxophones with corncobs.

PENNY: Why not?

GEORGE: Because a corncob is an entirely different thing from a saxophone. You can't eat a saxophone. And you can't blow on a corncob. Well, I suppose you can blow on a corncob if you want to, but it doesn't make any sound.

PENNY: How do you know that, George? Have you ever tried to blow on a corncob? Have you ever tried to play a saxophone? Have you ever tried to do anything but eat corn and bugs? You're such a negative turkey.

GEORGE: Penny, where are you going to find a saxophone? We live in the woods.

PENNY: There might be a saxophone tree.

GEORGE: I've been in this woods my whole life and I've never once seen a saxophone tree.

PENNY: Just because you've never seen a saxophone tree doesn't mean there isn't one somewhere in the woods.

BOB: Do they have waffle trees? Because I had some waffles once, and they were really good.

GEORGE: Waffles don't grow on trees, Bob. You've got to make waffles.

BOB: I never made any waffles. I found them under a tree. I think it was that tree over there.

GEORGE: Somebody threw them out there with the corncobs, Bob.

PENNY: I'm going off to look for a saxophone tree.

GEORGE: Penny, that's stupid.

PENNY: Don't call me stupid. I'm a turkey with a dream, and my dream is to find a saxophone tree and pick myself a saxophone and learn to play it with my feet. Call me crazy, but that's my dream.

GEORGE: Penny, you're never going to find a saxophone tree.

PENNY: If Bob can find waffles, I can find a saxophone tree.

GEORGE: You're just going to get lost. You're going to get separated from the flock. And do you know what happens when you get separated from the flock? You become flockless. You have nobody to gobble with. You just walk and walk and you're alone forever and slowly you start to go mad. Remember what happened to Nelly. She set off one day looking for something and we never saw her again.

PENNY: That's not going to happen to me.

GEORGE: How do you know, Penny? How do you know anything?

PENNY: I don't think Nelly's lost. I think she found a saxophone tree. She's probably playing the saxophone under that tree right now. And that's where I'm going. And you can't stop me. Good-bye, George. Good-bye, Bob. I hope you find more waffles.

(Penny goes.)

BOB: Good-bye, Penny. *(Pause.)* Penny went away.

GEORGE: Yes.

(Pause.)

BOB: Nelly went away. And then Penny went away. And I think some other turkeys went away before that, but I don't remember too good. What's the matter, George? You look sad. Are you thinking about waffles? Do you miss Nelly? Do you miss Penny? Is that why you look so sad? Maybe we should have been more supportive about the saxophone tree, do you think, George? George? Do you think I could learn to play the saxophone?

GEORGE: I don't know, Bob. Maybe.

BOB: Hey, George?

GEORGE: What is it, Bob?

BOB: George, what's a saxophone?

(Pause.)

GEORGE: Here come the corncobs, Bob.

(Bob looks toward the corncobs. George looks back to where Penny has gone. The light fades on them and goes out.)

END OF PLAY

To Darfur

ERIK CHRISTIAN HANSON

Originally performed at Quo Vadimus Arts ID America
Festival, the Clemente Soto Velez Cultural Center, New York
City, November 9–21, 2007. Directed by Deena Selenow.
Cast: Ryan—Michael Mergo; Alice—Elizabeth Romanski;
Bob—Phillip W. Weiss.

RYAN, late twenties to early thirties, businessman.

BOB, fifties, blue-collar worker, short, stocky, clean-shaven, staunch Republican.

ALICE, forty-two, a bartender, average body and average looks.

SETTING

A bar.

TIME

January 2007.

• • •

Lights up. Alice scrubs the countertop with a white washcloth. Already at the bar is Bob, dressed in denim and working on his second bottle of Budweiser. A moment later Ryan enters in a suit and already loosened tie. He's had a whirlwind of a day and it shows. He walks up and has an immediate seat on a particular stool. Being a regular, Alice has a glass of B&B prepared for him and puts it down within his reach. Pause. Ryan lets out a sigh that travels around the bar.

ALICE: Whatsit today, Ry??

RYAN: Today . . . today . . . it's, um . . . *(Picking up his glass.)* it's . . . *(Has a sip.)* today *(Has another sip.)* . . . it is . . . Darfur. *(Ryan has another sip.)*

ALICE: Who's that?

RYAN: Who?

ALICE: Yes. Who.

RYAN: WHO???

ALICE: *(Missing Ryan's sarcastic line of questioning.)* That's what I said, who. *(Brief pause.)*

RYAN: Darfur isn't a who.

BOB: *(Chiming in.)* That an over-the-counter med? Prescription thingamajig for, um, uh . . . back pain?

(Ryan puts his head down because he knows Bob isn't joking.)

RYAN: Darfur . . . is . . . a . . . region . . . in western Sudan.

BOB: Woulda bet my money on it bein' a drug for back pain . . . ya know . . . one a those like ointments?

ALICE: Sounds like a coat store.

RYAN: COAT?

ALICE: Darfur . . . sure . . . like a place you can buy mink coats.

(Bob starts laughing, and Ryan shoots both of them a look.)

RYAN: C'mon, you guys . . . you know . . . please tell me you're pulling my leg and you know what's going down over there?

BOB: Over there? As in where?

ALICE: Yeah, over there *where*?

RYAN: In Sudan. *(Pause.)* In Africa . . . ???

(Bob and Alice nod in unison.)

RYAN: People . . . kids . . . kids and families are dying by the goddamn minute over there . . . wait . . . wait . . . *(Ryan allows a pause to hammer home a point.)* There went a mother. *(Pause.)* WAIT! *(Pause.)* There went a daughter . . . wait . . . a brother . . . wait. *(Pause.)* Somebody's father . . . *(Pause.)* And here we are . . . sipping our booze . . . in an overly heated bar . . . TV's galore . . . and what are we doing? NOTHING. Not only are WE doing nothing about it, but WE know nothing about it . . . at least the two of you don't . . . Hell, *(Directed at Bob.)* you thought it was a goddamn ointment and you . . . *(Directed at Alice.)* thought it was a what . . . a what again?

ALICE: A mink coat store.

(Brief pause.)

BOB: Educate me then.

RYAN: Edge-a-what?

BOB: On this Darfur place . . . educate me . . . educate *us.*

RYAN: All right, yeah, well, what I know of it . . . which is limited and perhaps not one hundred percent accurate because I tend to confuse things and facts when I get passionate about something, and well, once I include booze into that equation, well, there's no telling whether I'll be entirely accurate, but since you know absolutely NOTHING about Darfur . . . everything I say will sound like facts . . . in which they are, they are *facts* and I do promise to get like ninety percent of the situation correct, it's just that it's been a long, long day and given that I am pounding this liquor, there's no . . .

BOB: Tell me what you know about Darfur, man!

RYAN: OK, OK, will do . . . *(Pause.)* Basically, it's a place consumed by ethnic cleansing . . . genocide . . . we're talking . . . a new . . . and I don't say this for effect . . . but . . . a new . . . Holocaust . . . and while there isn't *just* one face of evil in all of this chaos like Hitler, basically the situation is awful . . . I mean, last time I checked . . . we were up to over five hundred thousand deaths . . . and the number isn't exactly slowing down.

ALICE: Who's fighting?

RYAN: The, um . . . this militia that calls itself the um, Janjaweed . . .

ALICE: JANJA-WHA?

BOB: JENGA-WHEAT?

RYAN: *(Sounds it out slowly.)* Janja-weed. They're also known as the, um, "devils on horseback," and they go around . . . 'cause they're pissed at the rebels . . . these guys go around taking out noncombatants like it's no big thing . . . and babies . . . BABIES! *(Pause.)* Oh, and yeah, these guys are big fans . . . huge fans of rape and dismemberment . . .

BOB: But how'd the fight start? I don't know why these rebels and the Janja-people are fighting.

ALICE: *(To Bob.)*: 'Nother Bud?

(Bob nods quietly.)

RYAN: How'd the fight start, how'd the fight start? *(Thinking it over.)* How did the fight—Oh! In 2003, in 2003 . . . rebel groups accused the Sudanese government of oppressing non-Arabs, and they, I think, granted there's more to it than I am gonna mention, but in 2003, the um, Darfur Liberation Front took credit, credit, for um, attacking this police station located in a place called Golo.

BOB: Where the hell is Golo?

RYAN: I can't say for sure . . . don't worry . . . next time I come in, I'll have more and more info for you guys, so, well, after, after a series of attacks by the rebels, the Sudanese government, while they *(Forms quotations with his fingers.)* "publicly denied" that they've provided money and other forms of assistance to the Janjaweed . . .

BOB: *(On "Janjaweed.")* Devils on the horseback.

RYAN: Correct.

ALICE: The horseback or just . . . horseback?

RYAN: The latter . . . you really don't need to say "the."

BOB: Honest mistake.

RYAN: Honest yes, but still . . . a mistake.

(Pause.)

BOB: OK, so this whole thing is going on . . . still . . . since 2003 . . . with the people . . . the families and the kids dying . . . the rape and the dis— *(Bob pauses because he forgot the actual word.)*

RYAN: *(Finishes for him.)* Dismemberment.

BOB: And it's now, what . . . four years after the whole conflict began cuz a this Golo attack thing . . . and it bothers you tonight . . . tonight of all nights . . . because *why*?

RYAN: Because, because . . . time-out . . . drink pause.

(Ryan has a long sip and Bob follows suit on his beer.)

RYAN: Because . . . the UN . . . the UN wants to deploy thousands . . . say around . . . approximately . . . um . . . twenty-thousand-plus soldiers . . . peacekeeping forces that would attempt to resolve the whole freaking conflict, but Sudan . . . the Sudanese government has stated that they will treat these peacekeeping troops as enemies . . . and . . . and . . . and . . .

(Ryan gets lost in thought. Alice attempts to contain his disoriented state by offering him another round.)

ALICE: 'Nother?

RYAN: Yes. Please.

BOB: And . . . *(No reply to this remark.)* And . . . ?

(Ryan turns toward Bob.)

RYAN: And what?

BOB: *And* was the last word you said.

RYAN: It was?

BOB: It was . . . that's the part you left off at.

RYAN: And, huh . . . and . . .

BOB: *(Trying to find the place he left off.)* Peacekeeping troops will be treated as enemies and such, so then what, THEN WHAT?

RYAN: Oh, yeah . . . the aid agencies . . . there are a couple've 'em . . . Action Against Hunger . . . Save the Children . . . and like, four or five that I can't recall the names of, well, these agencies . . . *(Liquor taking effect.)* . . . these aid agencies . . .

BOB: Aid agencies?

RYAN: Yes. These aid agencies . . . they all claim . . . not sure who's doing the talking for 'em, but they all claim that all of their humanitarian efforts are on the verge . . . nearing a total collapse because there has been violence . . . loads of it apparently . . . made on the aid workers! *(Pause.)* And since the African leaders and global . . . global leaders too . . . since they all can't seem to resolve a goddamn THING, well, all of the aid . . . all of the lives risked to save all a these people in these entirely remote areas may end up being for nothing . . . imagine that? All of the aid . . . all of the innocent people who perished trying to help alleviate the chaos over there will all be for nothing . . . because nobody . . . no higher-up is gonna step in and take care of business . . . 's a shame . . . 's a goddamn tragedy is what it actually is . . . *(Long pause.)* And I want it to end . . . I want it ALL to end. *(Pause.)* And this second . . . a mother was probably raped . . . and a kid's arms were probably lopped off, but that's OK . . . because why? Can someone tell me? Why?

(Long pause.)

BOB: 'S not my problem.

RYAN: Not your problem?

BOB: Nope. Not.

RYAN: 'S not?

BOB: Heck no.

RYAN: That's a wonderful thing to say . . . truly is.

BOB: *(Dismissive yet attempting to do his point justice.)* I don't know where'n the hell Sudan *(Says it like Sue-dan.)* is, and as a matter a fact, I don't even care . . .

RYAN: You don't?

BOB: No.

RYAN: That's just . . .

BOB: They're in their country . . . I'm in mine . . . and in case you've forgotten, pal, we got our own war to worry about . . . our own troops fighting daily, so forgive me if I don't start caring about some *(Struggles with the word "atrocities," but gets it.)* atrocities . . . in somebody else's country . . . hell, maybe if this, uh, conflict was 'a happening outside . . . out in the say, parking lot, well, then maybe I'd get offa my stool and get out there . . . or if it was at that mall down the way . . . sure, I might be enraged enough to get down there and take out summa those Janga-guys, but we are talkin' another country man . . . another country . . . 's hard enough to give two craps about the next person, let alone another country.

RYAN: *(Under his breath, but still heard.)* How American of you.

BOB: How American of me? THAT whatcha said? Why does an American hafta care about what's happening in countries I couldn't find on a map . . . WITH directions?! *(Pause.)* I am an American . . . dang prouda it too . . . and I'm sorry kids and mommas are dying . . . I really am . . . God's honest truth . . . cross the ole heart and hope to die, but that don't make me less of an American for sayin' I don't care what's happening . . . that doesn't decrease my love for this country . . . I'll tell 'a ya that much . . . rip my heart out pal and it'll be covered in stripes and stars . . . just like the American flag . . . so, I am sorry it bothers you . . . 's very kind of you to actually CARE about THAT situation and THEIR problem over there, but what are you actually doin' about it, huh, what are *you* doing to HELP their situation?

RYAN: That's the thing . . . I do . . . NOTHING . . . I read and read and read . . . and I talk . . .

BOB: And complain . . .

RYAN: And complain, yes, I do . . . I do complain, I just . . . I wish I knew what to do . . . I tell you what I wish . . . *(Long pause.)* I wish I had the GALL to fly down there . . . hop on a red eye and go'n do something . . . help somebody . . . anybody down in Darfur and see if I can make one hell's a difference . . .

BOB: And die doin' as much.

RYAN: I know . . . but, so what? Wouldn't it be for a *cause?* Wouldn't it be for the . . .

BOB: In a perfect world.

RYAN: I just, I wanna . . . AAAAAAAAGHHH!! I want something done . . . some degree of improvement . . . I don't wanna hear the death toll is RISING over there. *(Pause.)* I guess what I'm saying is that I can't . . . eat, sleep, drink, work, or do ANYTHING in peace knowing that there's another Holocaust going on in this world and for whatever reason . . . unbeknownst to me . . . we . . . we are doing NOTHING . . . NADA . . . about it . . . I just wish wish wish that you cared about it too and everyone else in this world, fuck it, everyone else in this *bar* . . . I just wish everyone could take a break from their lavish lifestyles and do something . . . this country . . . people in it . . . it seems like we hate bad news so much that we don't even acknowledge it . . . like a buncha diabetics who eat thousands a candy bars a day and zoom to a quicker death because a world of pain and actual suffering is too much to even ponder . . . I just wish more people would write, um . . . letters . . . raise money . . . speak out . . . hell, I just want everyone to know about this and since it seems that nobody here knows what the heck's happening outside of their own bodies, I figured I'd *vent*.

(Pause.)

BOB: Why don't ya speak up? Make an announcement?

RYAN: *Here?*

BOB: Yes, here.

RYAN: In the bar?

BOB: Nobody's in the bar . . . I'm talking about over there . . . in the restaurant part a this place.

RYAN: I can't make a . . . what would that accomplish?

BOB: Lotta people eating here tonight . . . chances are . . . you'd get *sum*body that might go home and do a little Darfur homework after a certain individual made them aware of the place.

RYAN: That would . . .

(Ryan takes a large sip of his drink. Bob speaks for him.)

BOB: Be American . . . hell . . . I don't care about what you're moaning about . . . not in the least, but *sum*body might . . . and since I am such a die-hard American . . . I don't discourage you from offering your opinion . . . freedom of the ole speech, pal . . . but don't come into this bar, like you do every single night, and raise a stink about some political crisis that we should all just stop breathing and care about . . . don't you dare suggest I am un-American for not givin' two rats' asses about those people.

RYAN: I should make an announcement.

BOB: Go for it.

RYAN: Just get on up . . . and say what's on my mind.

BOB: Spread a lil' bit of information.

RYAN: I should . . .

BOB: All you gotta do is swivel yerself offa that stool, stand up, and speak, "Ladies and gents, I have something I want to say."

RYAN: They wouldn't listen . . . they wouldn't care.

BOB: One person might . . . that's one person that knows more . . . isn't that what you essentially want, *more* people to know?

RYAN: I do.

BOB: Then share it.

(Alice emerges to offer her opinion.)

ALICE: If you make an announcement and my boss comes over to kick you outta here, don't you dare say that I allowed it.

BOB: He wouldn't incriminate ya, Alice . . . now would he?

RYAN: No, I . . . would just, um, speak . . . for a . . .

BOB: A brief amounta time.

RYAN: Right.

BOB: Then do it. *(Pause.)* Like ya said, pal, a woman was just raped and a kid was just dismembered, so I'd make that speech quick.

(Ryan spins off his stool, determined, inspired, and full of confidence. That feeling evaporates quickly when he can't seem to get the words out. He stands there for a long pause trying to fight the nerves, but he can't do it. He turns and has a seat. While Bob would love to mock his poor attempt, he opts for a different approach; he presents a different solution to Ryan's woes.)

BOB: Tell you what . . . I won't do nothing about this Darfur . . . won't even go online later and see what's what, but tell ya what I'm gonna do . . . and Alice . . . she should join us . . .

(Alice passes by.)

ALICE: I *should* do what?

BOB: Join us on this.

ALICE: On what?

RYAN: *(Confused by what Bob's implying.)* Join ya on what?

BOB: That whole situation you speak of won't affect my life, but from what you've said about it . . . it sure does sound awful and I can sympathize, so I tell ya what I'm gonna offer and it ain't gonna be much, but still . . . it's *sum*thing.

RYAN: What are you going to offer?

BOB: A toast.

RYAN: Toast?

BOB: Yes. That way . . . we can all acknowledge this horror that you speak of and we can move on to a new topic . . .

RYAN: A toast is what you're offering?

BOB: Ain't much I know, but I can assure you I'll be thinking about those people in the ten or twenty seconds it takes to do our toast and that may not be good enough for a young man like you, but to me . . . to think of anybody else but me and my family for more than one second . . . that's a major achievement. *(Pause.)* So, do you accept?

RYAN: *(Skeptical.)* Accept a toast . . . that's going to improve the situation over there?

BOB: I didn't say that, pal, but it'll be my equivalent to prayer.

ALICE: I'll toast.

BOB: Fix yourself a beer, Alice.

(Alice does so from the tap. Pause.)

RYAN: Fine, fine, I'll take the toast . . . given your aversion to the whole tragedy over there, I can tell you're trying if you've gotten to the point of offering me a toast, so . . . let's do it . . . I'm down . . . *(To Alice.)* just hit up my glass, please?

(Alice takes his glass and fills it with B&B. Pause.)

BOB: Everybody ready?

ALICE: Ready.

RYAN: Yeah, yeah, yeah, I guess . . . um, sure.

(Pause.)

BOB: To . . .

(Alice puts her glass of beer out. Bob reaches his out toward hers. Ryan hesitates, but joins in after a long beat.)

BOB: To all a the terror and mayhem or whatever you wanna call it . . . down in Darfur . . . may it end as quickly as humanly possible.

(They all tap their glasses.)

RYAN: *(In a trance of hopelessness.)* To Darfur . . .

(Bob and Alice drink from their glasses, while Ryan remains in a daze.)
(Long silence. Lights dim. Blackout.)

END OF PLAY

Whatever Happened to Finger Painting, Animal Crackers, and Afternoon Naps?

NORA CHAU

Originally produced by Ma-Yi Theatre Company as part of the
Ma-Yi/Youngbloods Mashup Theater at Ensemble Studio
Theatre, New York City, March 2007. Directed by Mike Lew.
Cast: Mark March—Teddy Bergman; Jane March—Audrey
Lynn Weston; Mr. Reade—Ed Lin. Also produced by
Momentum Productions as part of the Fresh Reading Theater
at Roy Arias Theatre, New York City, April 16–18, 2007.
Cast: Mark March—Nick Bosco; Jane March—Chiasiu Chen;
Mr. Reade—Matte Chi.

MR. READE, admissions officer to an elite New York City nursery school.

JANE MARCH, young affluent trendy mother.

MARK MARCH, young affluent father.

SETTING

An elite New York City private nursery school.

TIME

The present.

• • •

Among the urban in-the-know parent set, this school is the "Harvard" of all nursery schools. However, some say admission into this school is tougher than Harvard, Yale, and Fort Knox combined. Mr. Reade, an admissions officer, sits before the Marches. The Marches are a young couple interviewing—hoping to get a slot in the fall for their young son, Thomas.

MR. READE: Well, howdy there, folks.

JANE MARCH: Hello.

MARK MARCH: Thanks for meeting with us today.

MR. READE: But of course—my pleasure. I don't want you both to be nervous. There's nothing to worry about. This is just the first step of many steps in a long process to see if your child a is good match for our school—and vice versa. But of course if I don't like you—you won't get past this first step.

MARK MARCH: Right. Well, then we will just have to make sure you like us.

JANE MARCH: We're very likable people.

MARK MARCH: Jane was voted most popular in high school.

MR. READE: I was kidding!

JANE MARCH: Oh.

MARK MARCH: *(Laughing loudly.)* That WAS funny!

(Jane joins in the laughter. The two practically laugh until they are crying. They wipe tears away from their eyes. Mr. Reade just watches and waits until they are done with their too-eager-to-please bit.)

MR. READE: Yep. *(Beat.)* Shall we move along now. You're Jane. And you're Mark. Jane and Mark March. And your son is—

JANE MARCH: Tommy.

MARK MARCH: *(Correcting her.)* Thomas.

JANE MARCH: Right. Thomas.

MARK MARCH: I mean, we called him Tommy when he was just a baby. But now that he's two—we think it's more appropriate to call him Thomas.

JANE MARCH: Tommy is such a baby's name. Thomas is much more fitting for a toddler, don't you think?

MARK MARCH: *(Looking at his wife.)* Yeah, I think it's the right call.

JANE MARCH: I mean, I don't want you to think that we didn't put thought into it. We did.

MARK MARCH: We did.

JANE MARCH: We're very thoughtful parents.

MR. READE: I can see that.

MARK MARCH: We don't understand parents that just name their kids any which old names that just pop into their heads. I mean a name is either a blessing or a curse. People expect certain things from certain names.

JANE MARCH: Names have connotations to them.

MR. READE: I see.

MARK MARCH: I mean Thomas—the name Thomas—what do you think of when I say the name Thomas?

(There is silence as Mr. Reade looks expectantly at them for an answer as the Marches look expectantly at Mr. Reade to take a stab at this.)

MR. READE: Oh? Me? I see, we're being interactive here—well, when I think of Thomas—I think of—*(Beat.)* Thomas English Muffins.

JANE MARCH: *(Disappointed.)* Oh.

MARK MARCH: *(Trying to keep the ball rolling.)* Or Thomas Jefferson, right? Yeah?

MR. READE: Yeah, I guess so.

MARK MARCH: Or how about Clarence THOMAS? Huh? That too?

MR. READE: Sure, why not?!

MARK MARCH: Well, just to wrap it all up. Names are very important. Thomas is a leader. Tommy is a boy band member. Thomas is well read. Tommy is hip.

MR. READE: Right.

JANE MARCH: Not that we have anything against hip people—

MARK MARCH: Or boy bands for that matter. But it's just not the right name for our son. Or a future student at this school.

MR. READE: Hopefully.

MARK MARCH: *(Chugging along.)* Hopefully!

MR. READE: Well, then . . . can you tell me a little bit about Thomas?

JANE MARCH: Oh he is just the sweetest most unique boy.

MARK MARCH: Hungry for knowledge!

JANE MARCH: He likes the things most normal two-year-olds do—the playground, his blankie, the *New York Times* . . . sushi.

MARK MARCH: We want him to be normal and yet at the same time—we want him to develop a unique sense of self—different hobbies and interests—a real voice—his own opinions.

MR. READE: That is important.

MARK MARCH: I mean—he loves Charlie Chaplin.

MR. READE: Charlie Chaplin, you say?

JANE MARCH: Oh yes. He loves Charlie.

MR. READE: We put on the tramp's movies, and Thomas is just glued to the screen.

JANE MARCH: Not that we let him watch too much TV Just every now and then.

MARK MARCH: And Charlie Chaplin movies are so much better than the junk that is out there today.

JANE MARCH: He is just the cutest little pantomimer already.

MARK MARCH: And he LOVES film noir.

JANE MARCH: *(Nodding at Mark.)* Oh yes—he does.

MR. READE: Film noir.

MARK MARCH: Yes, indeed. Especially that from the early 1940s.

MR. READE: Wow. I don't even know what film noir is.

JANE MARCH: That's funny! You are such a joker, Mr. Reade.

MARK MARCH: Honey, I think he is being serious.

JANE MARCH: Oh.

MR. READE: I don't get out much. I clock a lot of time here at work.

JANE MARCH: I bet. Educating the minds of our youth!

MR. READE: Well, I don't actually—

MARK MARCH: And that's the thing. I mean, how many people really know or understand film noir, much less two-year-olds? That's what makes our Thomas special.

MR. READE: He does sound special.

JANE MARCH: Oh he is.

MARK MARCH: He also likes listening to NPR.

MR. READE: You don't say?

MARK MARCH: I don't think he understands everything that is being discussed.

MR. READE: He is only two.

MARK MARCH: But I think he gets the gist of most of it.

JANE MARCH: Definitely. The other day he was just asking me about trade issues with China.

MR. READE: Really?

JANE MARCH: Yes.

MARK MARCH: He is a very bright boy.

MR. READE: *(Nodding his head.)* Special.

MARK MARCH: He has a Mandarin nanny.

MR. READE: Oh?

MARK MARCH: We want him to be able to mingle effortlessly with the Chinese. China is the next big superpower.

MR. READE: So, I've heard. *(Beat.)* And does he get along with other kids? His siblings perhaps?

JANE MARCH: Oh, we don't have any other children.

MARK MARCH: We don't want to take any focus away from Thomas. We want to give him our undivided attention.

MR. READE: Sometimes it helps to have other kids around to interact with— a social setting.

JANE MARCH: Do you recommend having another child then?

MR. READE: Well, that's not for me to say. I mean—do you want to have more children?

MARK MARCH: Would it help Thomas with his admissions here?

JANE MARCH: I mean, we want to do what's best for Thomas, of course. And if it means nine more months of pregnancy—and another—

MR. READE: That's not what I was suggesting. Is he involved in any play groups? Does he have any friends?

JANE MARCH: Well, he does try to play with the kids at the park.

MARK MARCH: But we try to not encourage it too much.

JANE MARCH: They are very germ-y.

MARK MARCH: And they watch things like *Sponge Bob* and *Teletubbies*! It's not really the right kind of connections or friendships we want him to have.

MR. READE: I see.

MARK MARCH: We're not snobs.

JANE MARCH: Not at all.

MARK MARCH: We're just picky.

MR. READE: Right.

JANE MARCH: We don't let him have soda either. So, it's not personal, you know. Or racist. Or elitist.

MARK MARCH: It's for his own good. *(Beat.)* He plays an instrument.

MR. READE: He does?

MARK MARCH: Well, not very well. But with more practice—we're hoping he'll get the hang of it.

MR. READE: He's two?!

JANE MARCH: Two and three months.

MR. READE: And he plays an instrument already?

MARK MARCH: Just the violin.

MR. READE: They make violins for two-year-olds?

JANE MARCH: It's a little big for him.

MARK MARCH: Is there a music program here?

MR. READE: Yes. You can call it that. It's more of a playtime for the children. Where they can get used to instruments. Test 'em out. Bang 'em around.

MARK MARCH: Playtime?

MR. READE: Yes, playtime. Is there a problem?

MARK MARCH: Oh no—nothing. It's just that—while we believe in playtime—we also don't want him to be wasting hours here doing that.

MR. READE: Playing is an important part of a child's growth and learning experience, Mr. March.

MARK MARCH: I understand that. It's just—it's a lot of money for us to be paying for our son to be playing all day. Or to just bang things around!

MR. READE: I see.

MARK MARCH: I don't think you do.

MR. READE: Pardon me?

MARK MARCH: Nothing.

MR. READE: If you have something to say—please feel free to say it.

JANE MARCH: *(Warningly.)* Honey . . .

MARK MARCH: I just think that—maybe the children here would benefit from a real music program—a real fucking music program—not some fucking Holly Hobby shit. Are there at least computer classes they can enroll in?

MR. READE: Computer classes?! They're still in diapers! They can't even control when they potty—you think they can control a mouse?

MARK MARCH: That's ageism, Bob. Ageism.

MR. READE: That is not ageism.

MARK MARCH: OK, well, you're setting up a self-defeating prophecy here. By not having computer classes made available to them—you're telling them they can't do it. They're just too stupid. Incompetent. And they will buy into that. What kind of attitude is that to pass onto them?

JANE MARCH: Honey. You don't mean that. He doesn't mean that.

MARK MARCH: I do mean that! And don't tell me what I mean or don't mean.

JANE MARCH: No, you don't mean that. You meant to say self-fulfilling prophecy. A self-defeating prophecy is the complementary opposite of a self-fulfilling prophecy: a prediction that prevents what it predicts from happening. And I think even if you were to use the correct term of what you really meant—you'd still be using it incorrectly!

MARK MARCH: Is now really the time to show how smart you are?! Is it, Jane?! Don't correct me in front of—him!

MR. READE: You can correct him all you want in front of me, Jane! I don't mind! Not at all.

MARK MARCH: You know what? Frankly, I'm not sure this is the kind of place we want Thomas at.

MR. READE: Frankly, I don't think this place wants your kind here either!

(Mark March gets up and knocks his chair down in the process.)

MR. READE: Whoa, whoa—easy now—that's my favorite chair!

MARK MARCH: What's that supposed to mean?

MR. READE: That I like that chair the best.

MARK MARCH: Don't fuck with me!

MR. READE: What do you think it means? I was throwing your words right back at you!

MARK MARCH: You think our son isn't good enough for your school?

MR. READE: No, I didn't say that. I just don't think you as parents would be a good match for the school.

JANE MARCH: Please don't base your decision off Mark's behavior. He's a dick sometimes.

MARK MARCH: Hey, we're supposed to be a team here!

JANE MARCH: You're ruining Thomas's chances here!

MR. READE: Yes, you are!

JANE MARCH: Apologize to Mr. Reade.

MARK MARCH: No!

JANE MARCH: Apologize.

MR. READE: Yeah, apologize. *(Fakes cough.)* Think of Thomas. *(Fakes cough.)*

MARK MARCH: Fine. I'm sorry. Please accept my apology.

MR. READE: OK.

(Mark picks up Mr. Reade's favorite chair and sets it back into what he thinks is a lovely and refreshing position.)

MARK MARCH: Here you go, favorite chair.

JANE MARCH: *(Nudging him.)* And . . . *(Beat. Then warningly.)* And . . .

MARK MARCH: And I didn't mean what I said about this not being the kind of place we want Thomas at. So, please reconsider.

MR. READE: I'm sorry, I can't do that. I feel strongly that this is just not the right fit.

MARK MARCH: Is that your final answer?

MR. READE: Yes, I'm afraid it is.

JANE MARCH: It would just mean so much to us if our son was in an educational environment like this.

MR. READE: I will make note of that in the records. *(Beat.)* I'm sorry, Mrs. March—I just really don't think it will work out. I thank you for your interest in our school at this time.

MARK MARCH: You cocksucker.

MR. READE: What did you just say?

MARK MARCH: Cock. Sucker. Cocksucker. You're a cocksucker.

MR. READE: Oh, you know what—I'm so scared of you—you're so—*(Fumbling for the right words.)* bad ass. I change my mind—Thomas can start next week.

JANE MARCH: *(With joy.)* Really?

MR. READE: *(Disgusted.)* No, not really. I'm afraid I'm going to have to ask you both to get the fuck out of my school.

MARK MARCH: I don't think so. We settle this right here and now. Or we'll settle it after school by the flag pole. One way or other this gets settled.

JANE MARCH: I'm really sorry—he's just stressed—he took off from work today so he could be here.

MARK MARCH: Shut up, Jane.

MR. READE: Fine. I'll get security to throw you the fuck out. And I'll make sure no other nursery school that's worth going to will even see you in this town again!

MARK MARCH: And I'll be waiting outside for you by the flag pole. *(Punches into his left hand.)* Three o'clock!

(Mr. Reade exits with his eyes trained on them until he gets to the door where he runs like a scared administrator. He trips as he is running and looks back at them in a panic before getting up again.)

JANE MARCH: Great. Good job there, Mark.

MARK MARCH: The guy is a dick. He had it out for us from the start.

JANE MARCH: He's going to blacklist us—blacklist us, Mark!

MARK MARCH: So what? We'll just wait two more years and then apply for preschool.

JANE MARCH: You've ruined Thomas's chances of getting into a good college.

MARK MARCH: We could always home-school him. Or move to Long Island.

JANE MARCH: The Harvard of nursery schools!

MR. READE: *(Offstage.)* They're in here.

END OF PLAY

PLAYS FOR
ONE MAN
AND
TWO WOMEN

The Answer

VANESSA DAVID

Originally produced by Eastbound Theatre, in association with
SquareWrights, at the Milford Center for the Arts, Milford,
Connecticut, July 7–8, 2008. Directed by Richard Mancini.
Cast: Mike—David Victor; Denise—Lynn Mosher;
Becky—Candice Sisbarro.

CHARACTERS

MIKE, forties or fifties. Recently divorced, his wife got the business, and he's stepping out on his own—with a little help, he hopes.

DENISE, thirties or forties. Not just a job jumper, a career jumper: she hasn't found the right fit yet. Good with people and computers, she wants to prove her self-worth.

BECKY, twenties or thirties. While searching for herself, she found "The Answer" in a musical. But, seeing the show every night has taken its toll, and she's late for work today.

SETTING

A sparse but stylish and sparingly chic office. There is a recliner and a straight-back or dining-type chair. Upstage there is a very small table with a cordless phone and a calendar, maybe some papers. There is also a rolling office chair.

TIME

The present.

•   •   •

At rise: Mike and Denise are seated at opposite sides of the stage. Mike sits in a recliner or some other comfy chair with his feet up. He is sketching in his pad. Denise sits in a dining-type chair, with a laptop perched in its proper place. She's also working away. The rolling office chair is unoccupied.

DENISE: Mike, may I please show you what I'm working on?

MIKE: I prefer we work separately.

DENISE: It's just—I'm right out of school . . .

MIKE: And already you know more than me. They didn't have them when I
. was in school.

DENISE: Computers?

MIKE: We had them at my old firm, but I never had to learn. We hired guys for that.

DENISE: Well, let me show you what I'm working on, and I'll show you how it works. It's easy.

MIKE: I'm sure it's wonderful, what you're working on.

DENISE: Is this how you worked at your old firm?

MIKE: Things didn't work out at the old firm. When you want a better result . . .

DENISE: Do something different. Words to live by.

(The phone rings; neither one moves. It rings again.)

MIKE: She's not here to answer that.

DENISE: So it's my job?

MIKE: I can't afford voice mail. Let's sell this design first.

DENISE: *(Getting up to answer phone.)* The design we're working on separately . . . Mike's Architectural Designs. This is Denise, how may I help you? . . . Oh, hey, Becky. Where are you? I didn't know pay phones still existed. Oh . . . oh . . . oh, that stinks. Oh, OK. I'll tell him. See you soon.

MIKE: Now what?

DENISE: She overslept after going to see that show again and she couldn't find her cell phone and she doesn't have a land line so she had to go find a pay phone—did you know they still existed?

MIKE: Is she coming in?

DENISE: Yes, she'll be here in a second. She found a pay phone a block away.

MIKE: So why didn't she just come in? Why'd she have to call?

DENISE: I don't know, ask her.

MIKE: I'm not good at talking to people.

DENISE: You've been talking to me just fine.

MIKE: I mean, as a boss.

DENISE: You are my boss.

MIKE: Well, technically, yes, but you haven't been late once in the two-week history of the business.

DENISE: So, you have a problem reprimanding people?

MIKE: She needs to stop going to that musical *The Answer*. It sounds a little pretentious.

DENISE: It got great reviews, except the *Times*. She hasn't missed one yet.

(Becky enters, singing from the show.)

BECKY: THE ANSWER IS THINK POSITIVE THOUGHTS AND YOU WILL EXPERIENCE AN ABUNDANCE OF LUCK!!!

MIKE: Good morning, Becky. *(Struggling.)* Please try to keep the singing to a minimum today.

BECKY: No problem, boss. Good morning, Denise. That's a lovely outfit you're wearing.

DENISE: Thank you, I got it on eBay!

BECKY: You're kidding! Oh, I'd never buy clothes off the Internet. I need to try things on. You're brave!

DENISE: Nah, I guess my body's just true to size.

BECKY: Oh, I wish my body was true to size. But it will be! I'm going to *(Sings.)* THINK POSITIVE THOUGHTS AND I WILL—

MIKE: Becky!

BECKY: Sorry!

MIKE: *(To Denise.)* Don't encourage her.
(Mike and Denise return to their work as best they can while Becky hums the remainder of the stanza at her teeny desk.)

DENISE: Oh, Becky. There were a bunch of menus in the fax machine. We may want to get off those lists, save paper.

MIKE: How did we get on fax lists already?

BECKY: I signed us up yesterday on my lunch hour. I went to every restaurant in the area.

DENISE: Oh, about that. We only get a half hour for lunch.

MIKE: Yes, I've been meaning to tell you.

BECKY: Then why is it called lunch hour?

MIKE: I don't know the answer to that.

BECKY: *(Sings.)* THE ANSWER IS—

DENISE: *(Quickly, to prevent Becky from singing.)* Let's call it a lunch break.

BECKY: That's good. That'll help me remember it's not an hour. I'll go get those faxes.
(Becky exits.)

MIKE: You didn't peek, did you?

DENISE: What?

MIKE: At my designs? When you went over to the fax machine?

DENISE: No. I don't need to peek at your designs. I've got a pretty good idea of your style from how you decorated this place.

MIKE: You can foresee my architectural designs from my interior decoration? You've been watching too much reality television.

DENISE: I like to think I understand people. I've been a lot of things, worked with lots of people.

MIKE: When I saw "farmhand" and "emergency room nurse" on your résumé, I knew I had to hire you.

DENISE: You have a thing for nurses with vegetables?

MIKE: Who doesn't? No, I love plants—but I'm a klutz. I'm constantly cutting myself.

DENISE: That's an addiction, you know.

MIKE: Nah, just bad luck. I kill all my plants. I actually put fake flowers in my flower bed this year so I'd have something to look at and a communications satellite landed in it.

DENISE: You do have bad luck.

MIKE: Bad luck, dumb luck . . . all but good.

(Becky enters with menus.)

BECKY: Anybody like Indian food? I figure if we only get a half hour for lunch, we can order in and bond over some curry.

MIKE: Denise and I have a lunch meeting today.

BECKY: Oh, is that what you're working on?

MIKE: Yes.

(The phone rings.)

MIKE: Oh! The phone is ringing.

BECKY: Oh, let me get that. "Mike's Architectural Designs. We know the answer!"

(Denise shrugs to Mike, wondering what lunch meeting he's referring to. He puts his fingers to his lips to shush her.)

BECKY: Hold on one moment please, he'll be right with you. *(To Mike.)* It's your ex-wife.

MIKE: I don't want to talk to her; tell her I'm not here.

BECKY: But I just told her that you'd be right with her.

MIKE: Well, tell her I just left.

BECKY: I can't lie. Lying is not the answer! *(She quietly sings and dances the phone over to Mike.)* THE ANSWER IS THINK POSITIVE THOUGHTS AND YOU WILL—

MIKE: —take it in the other room.

(Mike exits with phone.)

BECKY: I think I've mastered the choreography. *(She sings and does the choreography complete with big Broadway finish.)* THE ANSWER IS THINK POSITIVE THOUGHTS AND YOU WILL EXPERIENCE AN ABUNDANCE OF LUCK!!!

DENISE: *(Beat.)* That's amazing.

BECKY: Isn't it? You've gotta see it!

DENISE: And you learned that just from seeing the show every night?

BECKY: And both weekend matinees! I've seen every show since it went into previews. There's only one other guy who can say that. And he's a jerk.

DENISE: Well, that's not very positive.

BECKY: You got me there. I definitely want to beat him though. He's so smug because he saw every performance by the original cast of *Rent*. I missed opening night, emergency appendectomy.

DENISE: Competitive theater going. Learn something new every day.

BECKY: So how come you two work on your own? Shouldn't you be working on the same thing together?

DENISE: Mike wants us both to "create without censors." He'll pick which one he likes better, and we'll go with it.

BECKY: Won't he just pick his own?

DENISE: If he had that kind of confidence, he wouldn't have hired me.

BECKY: Are you confident?

DENISE: In myself? Yes. In my career choices? Not always. But I think I'm on the right track.

BECKY: *(Singing and dancing.)* THINK POSITIVE THOUGHTS AND YOU WILL—

MIKE: *(Entering.)* Becky, please. We appreciate the floor show, but we really need to get some work done.

(She sits at her desk, he goes to his chair. She does some silent choreography.)

MIKE: She wanted to outsource some work to me.

DENISE: Hmm?

MIKE: My ex-wife. I used to work for her—with her. She got the business in the divorce.

DENISE: I'm sorry.

MIKE: Nah, it's good. Clean start. I told her no. *(Beat.)* She liked to claim my work as her own.

DENISE: Is that why you don't want me to see your work?

MIKE: No, no.

DENISE: You're afraid I'll steal your ideas?

MIKE: Well, maybe.

DENISE: I can't prove myself by stealing, can I? That'll just prove me a fool.

(Phone rings.)

BECKY: "Mike's Architectural Designs. We know the answer."

MIKE: I need to tell her not to say that.

BECKY: This is she. How'd you get this number? Oh! I knew I left my phone at the theater. Oh . . . Oh . . . Hold on. I'm going to take this in the other room.

MIKE: Great! Another one of her marathon phone calls.

DENISE: At least she went in the other room this time.

MIKE: Maybe I need to think about replacing her.

DENISE: Have a talk with her. She's a nice girl; she just needs to rein it in a little.

MIKE: Maybe *The Answer* will go on tour, and she'll follow it around like the Grateful Dead.

DENISE: Apparently people do that.

MIKE: Just a few days, a minitour, so we can get some work done. Then we can sing and dance. Ding-dong the job is done.

DENISE: I'm getting plenty of work done over here in the twenty-first century.

MIKE: I'm old school. Yo.

BECKY: *(Entering.)* Um, uh, I have to go. I left my phone at the theater, and one of the ushers was holding it for me, and the hospital called and they had blood from the appendectomy in a registry, and it turns out a seven-year-old girl needs a piece of my liver, so I have to go.

(Mike and Denise jump up to stop her.)

DENISE: Wait!

MIKE: Uh, yeah. Shouldn't you think about this?

BECKY: Boss, this is a no-brainer.

DENISE: What about *The Answer*? Beating Mr. Smug?

BECKY: He can have the distinction of being the only one to see every performance of the original cast of *The Answer*. *(Beat.)* This is *my* moment in time.

DENISE: Whitney Houston.

BECKY: Why didn't they make a musical out of *The Bodyguard*?

DENISE: I don't know.

BECKY: Me neither. *(Beat, then to Mike.)* I'll call you later and give you the specifics. This is it for me! I'm gonna lose some weight with the surgery. A part of me will forever be doing a positive thing for another human being. I've got a great job to come back to with great people. I feel like singing!

MIKE: You'd better get going!

DENISE: Yeah, that seven-year-old girl . . .

BECKY: Group hug!

(They hug. Becky hums as she exits.)

MIKE: Wouldn't it be kinda funny if that were true? If the answer really was to think good things and good things would happen?

DENISE: It kinda is true.

MIKE: This from a former emergency room nurse?

(Beat.)

DENISE: C'mon, you show me yours and I'll show you mine.

MIKE: Pardon?

DENISE: Your design.

MIKE: Oh, uh. Sorry. For a minute there I thought it was *my* moment in time.

DENISE: No, Mike. I'm a lesbian.

MIKE: Oh. Good. Well then. *(Beat.)* You first.

(She shows him.)

MIKE: Of all the—Look!

(He shows his.)

DENISE: Not bad!

MIKE: Well, they're almost identical!

DENISE: Oh, I like how you did that!

MIKE: And I like how you did that!

DENISE: I did these too.

MIKE: Oh my goodness, you do understand my style. And you've executed it perfectly!

DENISE: Thanks.

MIKE: Amazing.

DENISE: See? *(She sings.)* THE ANSWER IS

(He joins her.)

BOTH: THINK POSITIVE THOUGHTS AND YOU WILL EXPERI-ENCE AN ABUNDANCE OF LUCK!!!

END OF PLAY

Do-Overs

LARRY HAMM

Originally produced by Theatre Odyssey at the Sarasota
Reading Festival, Cultural Pavilion, Sarasota, Florida,
November 3, 2007. Directed by Jack Eddleman.
Cast: Woman—Cael Barkman; Man—Tommy Carpenter;
Young Soul—Mary Burns.

WOMAN, thirties.

MAN, approximately the same age as Woman.

YOUNG SOUL, a younger woman, fourteen to eighteen, she carries a pager.

SETTING

A waiting room in that place where souls gather.

TIME

Present day, sort of.

•   •   •

Lights up on Young Soul, anywhere onstage. Woman and Man enter from opposite ends of the stage, meeting in the middle, arms waving and fingers pointing.

WOMAN: You sunuvabitch! What were you doing suddenly popping up in my life?

MAN: Why was I popping up in your life? So typical! It's always about you. What about my life?

WOMAN: But, I'm here again. Dearly departed. Passed away. Dead.

MAN: Hey! I'm in the same boat you are. It's not like I survived the accident.

WOMAN: Yeah, but it wasn't MY fault. I wasn't the one who drove left of center.

MAN: I made a mistake. It happens. Sure, it was gruesome and tragic, but you'll get over it. You always do.

WOMAN: Not this time. This lifetime was special. I had everything—a great job as a magazine editor, men begging to take me to expensive places, a beautiful condo overlooking the ocean. And then, SMACK, you come out of nowhere and it's over.

MAN: It's not like I did it on purpose.

WOMAN: You were drunk, weren't you? *(To Young Soul.)* He has such a problem with alcohol. Even when we were cattle, he would seek out fermented fruit.

MAN: Well, I wasn't drunk. I had a couple of drinks, that's all. I was just sleepy. I put in long days at the office. I wasn't some fancy schmanzy magazine editor spending my evenings boffing the upper class. I worked for a living.

WOMAN: How dare you!

MAN: What a shock. You're defending your promiscuity with violence.

WOMAN: Listen, buddy, I wasn't promiscuous. In spite of what people say, it doesn't get you what you want. If it's one thing I've learned after several lifetimes, *(To Young Soul.)* on the way up the mountain men will leap across dangerous chasms for you, but once they've planted the flag, they can't wait to rappel down the quickest route.

MAN: So you're telling me YOU were chaste?

WOMAN: Not exactly chaste. After all, a girl needs recreation, and sometimes I was too busy to make it to the gym. What I'm saying is that I was selective. For instance, there was this one guy, Arthur, oh my gawd. He gave new meaning to a "work of art."

MAN: You're disgusting.

WOMAN: Look who's talking—the one who's the male every lifetime. *(To Young Soul.)* If you ever get a choice of genders, don't be the female. Making the nest, digging the burrow, giving birth, laying eggs, caring for the young, while the male follows you around with an empty expression hoping to have a chance to fertilize something. Be male if you can. You never have to think. Females always get the short end of the stick. *(To Man.)* Even when that stick is already short.

YOUNG SOUL: I was a worm once. I had both sexes.

WOMAN: Now, that would solve a lot of problems.

MAN: And double your potential dates.

YOUNG SOUL: If you want to date a worm.

WOMAN: Believe me, honey, there are lower forms of life asking for your number at every bar in this universe.

YOUNG SOUL: But I was a worm!

MAN: You're making it sound like it's the end of the world. Sometimes, you gotta pay your dues, kid. Build up a little good karma.

WOMAN: When you're in one of those lifetimes, you've got to look at the positive side. A worm can be a marvelous creature. You live as a part of the earth.

YOUNG SOUL: I had no eyes, arms, or legs. I ate dirt, secreted slime, and a month after I crawled from the egg, a child yanked me from the ground, stuck me with a hook, and fed me to a fish.

WOMAN: Not all these things work out.

YOUNG SOUL: And in my second life, I was an ant, working my ass off as soon as I was hatched only to have a size-ten loafer mush me when I was crossing the sidewalk.

WOMAN: Your third life had to be better.

YOUNG SOUL: I'm still waiting for my third life. I'm hoping to be a human so I can speak and tell everyone off.

WOMAN: Be careful what you wish for. Sometimes it's better to be an animal: no self-consciousness, no knowledge of death . . .

MAN: No underwear to change. No boss micromanaging you.

WOMAN: No need for makeup.

MAN: No anniversaries or birthdays to remember. No one nags you.

WOMAN: *(To Man.)* No "my boy is perfect" mother-in-law. *(To Young Soul.)* Besides, there are all kinds of tremendous things to be. We've had some really good lives as animals.

MAN: Yeah. I really liked it when we were rabbits.

WOMAN: Of course you did. Eating and fornicating. Add a remote control and a big screen TV, and it would have been paradise for you. It wasn't a picnic for me, I'll tell ya. Popping out litter after litter while you hopped around from hole to hole acting like God's gift to Beatrix Potter.

MAN: But I thought you liked bunny love?

WOMAN: OK. Maybe it wasn't my worst time as an animal, but the lifetime I really enjoyed was when I was a praying mantis.

MAN: Oh my God!

WOMAN: The look on your face when I bit your head off.

MAN: *(To Young Soul.)* You see what eternity's brought me?

WOMAN: Oh, you didn't exactly try to get away. I was worth it.

MAN: You're sick.

WOMAN: No, you're sick. I wasn't the one spreading his wings and begging for the encounter.

YOUNG SOUL: You're both sick, and you're making me ill as well. I'm standing here waiting to become the spirit to what, without my radiant being, would be no more than an animated corpse, and all I can see is a life as pathetic as what you two have led.

WOMAN: *(To Man.)* See what your attitude has caused. You're such a bad example.

MAN: I am? What about you, Miss Art for Art's Sake? What kind of an example have you set, putting down half of every species?

WOMAN: *(To Young Soul in monotone.)* I'm sorry. Not all males are worthless and dull.

MAN: Right. And you might add that men have accomplished most of the greatest achievements in the history of the world.

WOMAN: Here we go again.

MAN: What about unifying the world like Alexander the Great?

WOMAN: A wonderful male role model. He was gay.

MAN: Creating beauty like Michaelangelo.

WOMAN: Also gay.

MAN: Literary masterpieces like William Shakespeare.

WOMAN: Part-time gay.

MAN: A new world of light and sound like Thomas Edison.

WOMAN: *(A bit flustered.)* Closeted gay.

MAN: Men have engineered bridges and buildings and rockets that have propelled them to the moon. Men explored the world. Men moved civilization from holes in the ground to penthouse apartments. Men developed efficient tools that allow for everyone, women included, to have free time to spend with more pleasurable activities. Men created technology: inventing computers and designing the software that runs them.

WOMAN: Which explains why Windows crashes just when you need it most.

MAN: You make fun, but it's not a one-gender world for a reason. Women need men. Remember when we were Neanderthals.

WOMAN: I knew he was going to bring this up.

MAN: Well, we were great together as Neanderthals. You needed me.

WOMAN: But you needed me, too. You would hunt and I would gather and we'd have both families over every weekend.

MAN: We had some wild nights together. You called me your savage.

WOMAN: You were such a brute. And sweet. You used to bring me flowers.

MAN: And we'd eat them. Those were wonderful times.

WOMAN: We were young and in love.

MAN: And we had the bite marks to prove it.

WOMAN: And then you had the hunting accident.

MAN: Hunting accident? I was eaten by some kind of large cat. And in less than two days, you moved in with that baboon-faced Unk three caves down. Why did you do that? Huh? Tell the young soul the truth.

WOMAN: I had to have a protector and provider. Those were difficult times. I had to procreate. It was all about survival of the species.

MAN: She needed a man!

WOMAN: All right, I'll admit men can be convenient. I've never denied that. It's just they're everywhere and want to own all they see. It's a male world, and they hold on to it by being aggressive and uncouth. All that chest pounding and crotch grabbing. For centuries, I've had to listen to this one tell me how he has all the answers and how he's going to solve all the world's problems. The next thing you know, everyone's fighting another war.

MAN: I suppose wars are my personal fault.

WOMAN: What about when you were the emperor of Austria?

MAN: Well, we were provoked. Bavaria threatened us.

WOMAN: With what? Pretzels?

MAN: I had my reasons to declare war. I was emperor!

WOMAN: Right. And I suppose you also had your reasons for sleeping with that slut of yours, whatshername.

MAN: Genevieve.

WOMAN: See, he remembers her name.

MAN: She was my wife!

WOMAN: You always have an excuse.

MAN: Listen, we've been through this a thousand times. It was an arranged marriage. I never loved her.

WOMAN: You had six kids.

MAN: For the sake of the monarchy. I kept trying until we had a son.

WOMAN: I'll bet you did.

MAN: You know I didn't want to marry her. My parents made me, and then my advisors told me that divorce was impossible and murdering her "inappropriate." And the church . . . My God can the pope be a pain in the ass!

WOMAN: Blame it on religion.

MAN: I'm not. But I tried my best. I would dress in peasant's clothes and sneak out of the castle every chance I had to get free of those advisors and those rules. I didn't want all that responsibility. I only wanted to be with the woman I loved, a little milkmaid who lived in the village.

WOMAN: *(Blushing. To Young Soul.)* I was the milkmaid.

MAN: And I was your prince.

WOMAN: And then you stopped showing up.

MAN: I was assassinated.

WOMAN: Poisoned by his wonderful Genevieve and her lover, Duke Somebody.

MAN: And I died with my beautiful milkmaid's name on my lips.

WOMAN: You are such a liar. You died with a mouthful of arsenic-laced paté.

MAN: But my final thoughts were of you.

YOUNG SOUL: Do you always end up with each other?

MAN: Not always. There are those lifetimes when the two of us passed several times without meeting, and I missed her completely. But, even then, we were somehow connected, and I've never lived without wanting her, even when I didn't know her.

WOMAN: And I've never stopped loving him, even when he failed to appear in my life.

MAN: The most important thing is we're still together and will be until the end of time.

YOUNG SOUL: And that doesn't horrify you?

WOMAN: It can be a bit unnerving, but I wouldn't have it any other way. The way I see it, we've been given lifetime after lifetime to learn all we can about love and sex and the beauty of intimacy and bonding.

MAN: I've been a conquistador, a camel herder, and an accountant, but none of it mattered until the two of us found each other.

WOMAN: Like when we were on the prairie.

MAN: Those were long, cold, isolated nights.

WOMAN: With a sky full of beautiful stars.

MAN: Just you and me and the universe.

YOUNG SOUL: *(Removes pager from pocket with a flashing red light.)* I guess it's my turn again.

WOMAN: Do you think you're ready?

YOUNG SOUL: I hope so.

WOMAN: You'll do just fine.

MAN: Good luck, kid.

YOUNG SOUL: I'll try not to be too negative.

WOMAN: Remember to give it your best shot, even if you're a worm.

MAN: Or a cockroach.

WOMAN: Or a politician.

WOMAN AND MAN: Live it for all it's worth.

(Young Soul exits.)

WOMAN: Do you think we helped or hurt her?

MAN: Neither. She'll chart her own course. We all do.

WOMAN: We really must try to make our next lives our best ones yet.

MAN: I'll work to keep up with you.

(They begin to exit.)

MAN: I'm sorry for running my SUV into you.

WOMAN: That's all right. I had a feeling you might be coming.

(They exit to blackout.)

END OF PLAY

Gloom, Doom, and Soul-Crushing Misery

ROBIN RICE LICHTIG

First produced by Groove Mama Ink at the Gene Frankel
Theatre, New York City, July 2007, in the Play in a Day series.
Directed by Stuart Green. Cast: Marushka Venyanko—
Rebecca Hailey; Illya Venyanko—Scott Ross;
Sunshine Beamer—Jessica Luck.

CHARACTERS

MARUSHKA VENYANKO, older than fifteen, no upper age limit. Depressed Russian woman. Wants to be *more* depressed.

ILLYA VENYANKO, same age or somewhat older than his wife, Marushka. A loving husband. Depressed Russian.

SUNSHINE BEAMER, age sixteen on up, male or female. Sticky sweet travel agent with a million-dollar, nonstop, highly annoying smile and a one hundred percent positive attitude. Sings.

SETTING

A spare room in rural Russia.

TIME

The present.

NOTE: A slash (/) indicates that the next character begins to speak his or her line, overlapping the first speaker.

•   •   •

At rise: A room. Dead of winter. Illya and Marushka sit, depressed, in winter coats, hats, boots. Outside, snow falls. Inside, the heat doesn't work. Between them is a rustic table and open bottle of vodka. Silence.

ILLYA: *(Russian accent.)* One.

MARUSHKA: *(Russian accent.)* More.

ILLYA: Time. Repeat.

MARUSHKA: After.

ILLYA: Me.

MARUSHKA: I.

ILLYA: Will.

MARUSHKA: Not.

ILLYA: Laugh gleefully.

MARUSHKA: Ever.

ILLYA: Again.

MARUSHKA: I am trying so hard! *(She bursts into tears.)* I want to be— *(She swigs some vodka. Still sobbing.)* I want to be not so happy!

ILLYA: Today another year older / you should want to slit your wrists.

MARUSHKA: *(Bemoaning the fact.)* But I don't!

ILLYA: Why you are not wallowing in despair is beyond me.

MARUSHKA: *(An encouraging thought.)* Maybe you will have an affair. I will find out and it will send me into a good deep funk.

ILLYA: An affair with who?

MARUSHKA: I don't know. Marsha.

ILLYA: Marsha?

MARUSHKA: Masha / Marsha. It doesn't matter. Olga? Irina? Nikolai Romanovich Petrovich?

ILLYA: I am too depressed to fool around. I have no energy.

MARUSHKA: Me neither.

ILLYA/MARUSHKA: Damn.

> *(Pause.)*

MARUSHKA: Like gas the gleeful laugh rose up.

ILLYA: Why?

MARUSHKA: I don't know. I was asleep.

ILLYA: A dream?

> *(On "dream" a happy operatic trill is heard. Illya covers his ears.)*

MARUSHKA: What was that?

ILLYA: *(Pained.)* Something cheerful. It came when I said "dream."

> *(Operatic trill. When it dies down:)*

MARUSHKA: To make me laugh the D-R-E-A-M must have been happy.

ILLYA: "Happy"? Why, Marushka Sonja Ranevskaya Venyanko? Why? A D-R-E-A-M so happy it caused my wife to laugh gleefully in the middle of the night. We are cursed! What was it about, my love?

MARUSHKA: I can't remember.

ILLYA: It's important.

MARUSHKA: Yes. Wait. I almost have it. It was about . . .

ILLYA: Making babies?

MARUSHKA: No. Now it's gone. Like a disease this happiness.

ILLYA: Like swine flu.

MARUSHKA: Swine flu would be good.

> *(They drink.)*

MARUSHKA: That cheerful D-R-E-A-M is ruining a perfectly good depressing day. I should be laid low under the table.

ILLYA: I am sorry you are not.

MARUSHKA: I am more sorry.

ILLYA: What if you have it again tonight?

MARUSHKA: You must duct-tape my mouth shut.

ILLYA: Then I could not kiss you. God this is depressing.

MARUSHKA: Not depressing enough.

ILLYA: Ay, there's the rub.

(She drinks. He drinks.)

MARUSHKA: All that weight I lost.

ILLYA: You will gain it back. I am hopeful. Or would be if hope was in my vocabulary.

MARUSHKA: Yah. Yah. Next I will shave my legs and wear lipstick.

ILLYA: Oh no.

MARUSHKA: I have tried to be good Russian woman for you.

ILLYA: You put on all that attractive fat.

MARUSHKA: Which melted away.

ILLYA: You eat like a pig.

MARUSHKA: Still it melts.

ILLYA: Maybe you have a tapeworm.

MARUSHKA: If only.

ILLYA: Maybe the goat man has. I can get for you.

MARUSHKA: No! I must get fat for you! And not happy.

ILLYA: The peasants in the village think we are a bad match.

MARUSHKA: I know. "City girl" they whisper. "Moscow lover" they spit.

ILLYA: Let us be silent. Let us drink.

(They drink.)

MARUSHKA: The dream—

(Operatic trill. Illya claps his hands over his ears.)

MARUSHKA: It infects me like a smiley face! I will scour it from my brain! It's still there. Perhaps the villagers are right.

ILLYA: You are my goddess.

MARUSHKA: Yah. Me and my gleeful you-know-what.

ILLYA: Gleeful you-know-what aside.

MARUSHKA: I don't know, Illya Shostakovitch Andreyevna Venyanko. I love caviar. You love boiled cabbage. I listen to Puccini. You write fan letters to Celine Dion. I read Dostoyevski. You read Sponge Bob. Why did I come to Buryat?

ILLYA: Some crazy vacation or something.

MARUSHKA: When you got on the bus, I fell head over heels.

ILLYA: I looked deep into your eyes and thought: I want her to gain one or two thousand zolotnik and come live with me in Buryat.

MARUSHKA: I thought, for him I can bulk up and live in the sticks. One look at that thick neck and I was struck dumb. Yah, dumb. I forgot everything that ever happened before that moment. My brain went to sleep.

It's been sleeping ever since apparently. Today, when you told me that I laughed gleefully in my sleep, my self-satisfied bubble burst. My brain woke up. That damn beam of cheerful light shined in.

(Pause.)

ILLYA: What now?

MARUSHKA: *(Very sad.)* Divorce?

ILLYA: *(Very sad.)* It may be our only option.

MARUSHKA: My darling.

ILLYA: My pumpkin.

MARUSHKA: Don't touch me! I am contagious with happiness! I will return to Moscow with my disease.

ILLYA: Nyet!

MARUSHKA: Da!

ILLYA: I love you!

MARUSHKA: Our life has been ripped to shreds by this dream!

(Operatic trill. Sunshine sweeps in, singing exuberantly. He or she wears a business suit and pulls a small suitcase with a T logo. Sunshine positively radiates happiness.)

SUNSHINE: I am the wish granter. The birthday wish granter. The birthday, mirth day /

ILLYA: Name day.

SUNSHINE: Fame day!

ILLYA: Who are you?

SUNSHINE: *(Singing.)* I am the wish /

MARUSHKA: Illya?

ILLYA: Search me.

MARUSHKA: *(To Sunshine.)* Do you have a car?

SUNSHINE: Whatever vehicle you want.

MARUSHKA: I need a ride to Moscow.

ILLYA: No she doesn't.

MARUSHKA: Shut up, Illya.

ILLYA: That one is pure sugar! I'm getting diabetes just looking in that direction!

SUNSHINE: *(Sweet.)* I'm parched. Got some lemonade?

ILLYA: *(Sour.)* Vodka.

SUNSHINE: I'd adore a lemonade.

ILLYA: If you say "make lemonade with lemons" so help me /

MARUSHKA: *(To Sunshine.)* Are you my / the thing I had when I was sleeping last night that made me laugh?

SUNSHINE: I'm Sunshine. Sunshine Beamer! I've come to grant your name-day wish.

MARUSHKA: I can't get the hang of total depression.

SUNSHINE: That's what you want?

MARUSHKA: With all my heart. My husband says he loves me, but I know he can't one hundred percent because I'm not totally depressed. I would be. I could be. Except for the dr /

(Sunshine emits an operatic trill.)

ILLYA: Knock it off, Beamer!

SUNSHINE: I will help you remember your dream.

MARUSHKA: I don't want to remember it. I want to get rid of it.

(Sunshine pulls the Travelocity gnome from his or her bag.)

SUNSHINE: Tah-dah!

GNOME/SUNSHINE: Travelocity.com! Available for new friends and meaningful relationships!

ILLYA: *(Horrified.)* Get it out of here! It's chipper!

SUNSHINE: *(To Marushka.)* To tell the truth, I didn't have a clue what your dream was. I pulled this out of my ass, excuse the visual, Mr. Gnome. From your husband's reaction, I'd say I hit the nail on the head.

GNOME/SUNSHINE: Are they onboard?

SUNSHINE: He wouldn't be any fun.

GNOME/SUNSHINE: *(To Illya.)* Sourpuss.

SUNSHINE: But her . . . her dream is to travel the world.

MARUSHKA: Travel. That was it.

ILLYA: Travel?

MARUSHKA: A vacation.

SUNSHINE: Fun, fun, fun!

ILLYA: That made you laugh with glee? Marushka! Visa applications. Packing. Passport photos. Unpacking /

SUNSHINE: Fluffy pillows! Andes mints!

GNOME/SUNSHINE: Volleyball in bikinis!

SUNSHINE: All-you-can-eat buffets!

GNOME/SUNSHINE: Showgirls!

SUNSHINE: Mr. Gnome and I will make your dream come true. I can offer a package deal / round-trip, business class from St. Petersburg. Deluxe suite, ten days, first class all the way. Inclusive to Miami.

ILLYA: Miami?

SUNSHINE: Wise choice. I assume you're booking a double. Single supplements are way pricey!

(Sunshine laughs, delighted with him- or herself.)

MARUSHKA: *(Thinking.)* Flying. Hours and hours / breathing the same air as twins with runny noses and an old man with crud in his throat. Food? Forget it. Vodka? Midget bottles. Strapped in. No escape. A six-year-old kicking the back of your seat.

ILLYA: No need to be that miserable.

MARUSHKA: Thank God.

GNOME/SUNSHINE: Look for me reclining in a hammock, sipping a pina colada, peering past picturesque piers at a southern sun slipping softly into a silver sea. A balmy breeze brushes my beard as I chuckle a satisfied, gnome chuckle and /

MARUSHKA: The dream must die!

(Illya holds Sunshine as Marushka grabs the gnome, smothers him with a pillow. The gnome is dead. Illya and Marushka sit exactly as at the beginning. Sunshine is bereft. He or she cradles the gnome. Now Sunshine's depressed too and takes a swig of vodka. Illya and Marushka look at each other, then sigh in unison. He kisses her hand. They sit and gratefully sink into a gloriously darker depression. All is right with the world. Blackout.)

END OF PLAY

The Growth

CHRIS SHAW SWANSON

Originally performed at Theatre Inspirato's 2nd Annual
Toronto Ten-Minute Festival at the Alchemy Theatre, June 14,
2007. Directed by Kevin Shaver. Cast: Sue—Julie Jarrett;
Paul—Tommy Boston; Monica—Janice Peters.

PAUL, twenties to forties, a good guy who wants to comfort his wife; he just doesn't know how.

SUE, twenties to forties, a good wife in a bad mood in anticipation of her upcoming operation.

MONICA, fifty-plus, an older woman whose kind face and manner tend to make strangers regard her as a long lost friend.

SETTING

An airplane cabin. Four chairs can be used to represent one row of seats on an airplane. There should be an aisle/space in the middle.

TIME

The present.

• • •

Paul and Sue enter, looking for their airline seats.

PAUL: Oh, here's our seats, honey. I'm fourteen-B. Right here.
(Paul indicates one of the aisle seats and stands by it.)

SUE: So that makes this one mine.
(Sue sits in aisle seat across from Paul.)

PAUL: *(Surprised.)* Did you book that seat, or did the airline stick you *waaaaaaaaay* over there? *(Paul sits in his aisle seat.)*

SUE: *(Curtly.)* I booked it.

PAUL: *(Playfully.)* I remember when being this far apart would have driven you crazy with lust and desire for me.

SUE: What can I say? I've become a whore for aisle legroom. And bathroom accessibility.

PAUL: As if you'd ever use an airplane toilet.

SUE: In an emergency I would . . . *try* to.

PAUL: You'd pee your pants first.

SUE: Better that than acting like you, ready to whip it out anywhere—shooting at random, hosing down innocent passengers . . .

PAUL: Yeah. Peed pants is better.

SUE: For the general public.

PAUL: Whatever you say, darlin'. Sure you don't want my window seat? If no one shows up?

SUE: *(Snappish.)* If I had wanted it, I would have booked it. *(Pause.)* Look. Right now, I need . . . room. Please try to understand that.

PAUL: So far, it's a pretty empty flight. Maybe we'll luck out and nobody will take either of our window seats.

SUE: Right. Luck for me is in short supply these days. Since this is nonstop, a nonstop talker will probably squeeze herself in here, babbling on and on about the willowy clouds and the teeny-tiny cars below . . .

PAUL: If you move over next to your adoring husband, that won't happen. *(Pause/Heartfelt.)* Have I told you lately that I love you?

SUE: Yep. In fact, about ten times a day since they discovered my tumor.

PAUL: Don't use that word. Tumor.

SUE: But that's what it is—

PAUL: Tumor implies cancer. Your tumor implies . . . *creates* . . . high calcium. There's a difference.

SUE: Both kinds of tumors can eventually kill the tumor owner.

PAUL: *(Gently.)* I know, honey. I know. *(Long pause.)* You're doing the right thing, going to Florida for this operation. *(Hesitantly.)* Your mother would have wanted you to see a—

SUE: Surgeon I found on the Internet?

PAUL: His cure rate is higher than any other parathyroid surgeon in the country—

SUE: So *he* proclaims about *him*self on *his* website—

PAUL: A sweet little one-inch cut on your neck—that's all we'll have to deal with afterward.

SUE: *We'll?* Who's this *we'll?*

PAUL: Right. You've had to bear this burden all by yourself. I forgot.

SUE: I'm just . . . my nerves are shot, OK? Blame it on my high calcium.

PAUL: What will we blame everything on after the *growth* is removed?

SUE: You, of course.

PAUL: I was counting on that. *(Pause.)* Would you mind if I catch a few *zzz*'s? I didn't sleep well last night. You—I mean, your high calcium—kept kicking me.

SUE: Go ahead. *(Pause.)* Really. My chauffeur needs to be well rested tomorrow morning. For some insane reason, I have to be at the hospital by five AM.

PAUL: Are you sure you're OK? Don't need to . . . talk? Flirt a little maybe?

SUE: I'm all talked out. And flirted out. Now, go to bed. *(Pause.)* Sweet dreams, Paul.

PAUL: All right. I'll try to catch a few . . . I'll just . . . just for a few minutes, I'll . . . *(Paul is asleep.)*

SUE: *(Looking at him.)* God, I wish I could do that.

(Monica approaches, holding her ticket and searching for her seat. She stops by Sue's row.)

MONICA: Excuse me. I think that seat by the window is mine. *(Shows ticket.)* Am I reading this right?

SUE: *(Seemingly recognizing Monica.)* You look . . .

MONICA: Yes?

SUE: *(Flustered.)* Never mind. *(Pause.)* Oh, what's wrong with me? *(She gets up.)* Here. Sit down. Please.

MONICA: Thank you. I bet you wish I hadn't shown up. Guess this isn't your lucky day.

SUE: *(Uncomfortable.)* Oh, I wouldn't say that.

MONICA: You wouldn't? *(Pause.)* Well, I'll do my best not to bother you. Who on a nonstop flight needs a nonstop chatterbox . . .

SUE: *(Apprehensive.)* Right.

MONICA: By the way, the attendant told me our flight is going to be delayed fifteen minutes. They want us to remain in our seats, and they thank us for our patience. *(Shrugging.)* Something like that.

SUE: What next?

(Monica pulls out a novel and begins reading. Try as she might, Sue cannot help but study Monica. Monica responds.)

MONICA: *(Without looking up.)* I look like someone you know, don't I?

SUE: Oh, sorry. I was . . . Yes. Yes, you do. It's wild. I know you're not her, and yet I can't help but . . . I'm really sorry.

MONICA: Don't be. I have one of those faces that resembles a million other faces. Happens to me all of the time.

SUE: That must get annoying . . .

MONICA: No—it makes me feel loved! Almost always I resemble someone cherished by the person I've met. My name is Monica. Monica Bliss.

SUE: Nice to meet you. I'm Sue Bentley. That's my husband Paul over there.

MONICA: The man *waaaaaaaaay* over there?

SUE: *(Uneasy.)* Yes. We like the extra legroom you get with aisle seats.

MONICA: Not to mention your close proximity to the bathroom.

SUE: That, too.

MONICA: Well, I'd trade the bathroom for a view any day. Although it's not always clear, the view from the sky. But after all these years, I still prefer being an optimist, so I go with the window seat. Does that make any sense?

SUE: Some people . . . they just have a *gift* for always looking on the bright side . . .

MONICA: Not you?

SUE: I used to be more that way.

MONICA: What happened? You're still so young—

SUE: Life happened, I guess. It can change a person. *(Pause.)* I'd rather not get into my pathetic life story right now . . . No offense . . .

MONICA: I didn't mean to pry. *(Patting Sue.)* Everything will be fine, Sue. You'll see. *(Pause.)* This delay will fly by. *(Pause.)* Fly by. That's a joke. *(Monica goes back to reading, absently loosening her scarf or collar, exposing a rather startling eight-inch scar across her throat, just above the breastbone. Sue sees it and gasps.)*

MONICA: What's the matter?

SUE: Nothing. *(Pause. Sheepishly.)* Actually, I couldn't help noticing your neck, your scar . . .

MONICA: Darn. The secret's out. I tried to hang myself last week.

SUE: What?!

MONICA: Another joke. But this mark *is* from an operation that almost did me in.

SUE: *(Anxiously.)* What was it for? The operation?

MONICA: You don't want to hear the pathetic details of *my* life, either . . .

SUE: Yes I do! If you don't mind telling me.

MONICA: One of my parathyroids was engulfed in a tumor, so I had surgery to have it removed. My surgeon had a problem finding the tumor at first—I bled quite a bit—

SUE: It can be a rough operation—

MONICA: No rougher than living with those high-calcium levels. Besides giving me kidney stones and osteoporosis, the calcium fogged my brain. It got so bad I was hallucinating. One time, I was convinced I was a secret agent and accused my children of being double agents out to kill me—

SUE: *(Remembering.)* Calcium can mess up your mind pretty bad . . .

MONICA: I said horrid, unforgivable things. Told the kids that I hated them— even swore a few times—and I don't swear.

SUE: Why did the doctors let you get so . . . so *sick* before they did something?

MONICA: My blood—it doesn't clot well. And since the operation involves this massive incision with lots of bleeding, the doctors kept advising all of us against it.

SUE: All of you? So your family helped you decide about the surgery?

MONICA: The kids made the decision by themselves. I was too far gone by then. It was either operate or put their dear *double O* nutcase mother in the loony bin. *(Deliberately.)* They made the right choice, Sue.

SUE: *(Wistfully.)* They were lucky that you lived to tell them that.

MONICA: *(Sighing.)* If only I had.

SUE: You didn't tell them?

MONICA: I didn't . . . live.

SUE: *(Pause.)* Wait a minute. You're sitting right here. We're talking. How can you say that you're—

MONICA: Dead? For one thing, there's that death certificate floating around—not that you should believe everything you read. Death really hasn't changed me much. Certainly not as dramatically as *life* has changed you.

SUE: *(Playing along.)* Obviously. You're still the eternal optimist.

MONICA: *Eternal.* That's a joke. Whether you meant it to be or not.

(Nervous, Sue reaches across aisle and shakes Paul, who can't be awakened.)

MONICA: Let him sleep. It's difficult—perhaps more difficult—to be the caregiver than the care receiver. To stand by, helpless, and watch a loved one fret and suffer. Don't you agree?

SUE: *(Unconvincingly.)* I wouldn't know.

MONICA: Really?

SUE: *(Changing subject, flustered.)* It's amazing, all the clouds . . . all the willowy clouds out there . . .

MONICA: We're still on the ground.

SUE: *(Pointing to window, skyward.)* I mean *up* out there . . . *up* . . .

MONICA: Sue. She's very sorry for what she put you and your brother through. You made the right call. Your mother didn't want to go on like that—so scared and paranoid and hurting the people she loves most. It was essential that she have the operation—

SUE: *(Rising emotion.)* She had the wrong one! Mine's going to be outpatient with a tiny one-inch cut. Considering her lousy blood, this Florida procedure would have been perfect for her—I'm sure she would have survived it. I didn't know about the Florida surgeon when she was sick. I didn't do enough research—hell, I didn't do *any* research until I found out I inherited the tumor. Then it was too late for her. I blindly, stupidly, trusted her Ohio doctors. God, if only I had known . . .

MONICA: God. If only you were God.

SUE: I feel like I'm somehow profiting from her death.

MONICA: Suzie-Q, your mother's grateful something good came out of her or-
deal—the discovery of your *growth* in its early stages and a safer surgical
cure.

SUE: Suzie-Q. My mom's the only one who's ever called me that . . .

MONICA: Now what you need to do, *must* do, is forgive her.

SUE: Forgive her? For what? The disease made her say those awful things—
none of it was her fault.

MONICA: Forgive her anyway. Then you'll finally be able to put those last dark
months—days—behind you, freeing you to remember her in the light .
. . when she was not just your mother, but your trusted confidante—
whole and lucid and positive and . . . rather funny. Her jokes were much
better than mine.

SUE: I'm the one who needs *her* forgiveness . . .

MONICA: Then voilá—I give it to you! Even though your only sin here is
doubting her love. Her mind faltered, but her heart never did. *(Indicating heart.)* Deep in here, you know that.

SUE: It ended so badly.

MONICA: That's only if you believe in endings. Clearly, I don't. *(Pause.)* But it
is time I move on.

SUE: Move on? Where?

MONICA: God only knows. Another joke. I *am* getting better at it. Do take
care of yourself.

(Monica gets up leave.)

SUE: I want . . . I want so much to believe that you're an angel sent from my
mom to get me through this operation and to renew my faith in . . . in
having faith in something.

MONICA: Your angel is sitting right across the aisle—no matter how randomly
he pees. You don't have to be an optimist to see the good there. *(Before
exiting.)* Remember her in the light.

(Monica exits. Paul awakens.)

PAUL: Don't tell me we're still on the ground.

SUE: There's been a delay. *(Doubting herself.)* I think.

PAUL: Lucky us.

SUE: Is that window seat taken yet?

PAUL: Let me look. *(He dramatically looks.)* Nope. It's still available.

(Sue moves next to him.)

PAUL: I knew you couldn't resist my hot body.

SUE: *(With difficulty.)* Paul, I think I've been having . . . hallucinations. More every day. There's usually people in them I know—like my mom . . . except not my mom exactly. I was afraid to tell you. I didn't want you to think I was wacko.

PAUL: It's probably the tumor—

SUE: Growth.

PAUL: Get it through your beautiful head. I'm here for you. I'll always be here for you . . . Suzie-Q.

END OF PLAY

Measuring Matthew

PATRICK GABRIDGE

Originally performed at the Heartlande Theatre,
Oakland University, Rochester, Michigan, June 19, 2004.
Directed by Nick Szczerba. Cast: Jennifer—Kendrah McKay;
Matthew—Jay Pringle; June—Marian Fedewa.
Also produced by the Devanaughn Theatre at the Piano
Factory, Boston, May 10–20, 2007. Directed by Lyralen Kaye.
Cast: Jennifer—Emily Evans; Matthew—John Greiner-Ferris;
June—Michelle Barbera.

CHARACTERS

JENNIFER, twenties to forties, an attractive woman who was once in love with Matthew.

MATTHEW, twenties to forties, man obsessed with numbers (and Jennifer).

JUNE, twenties to forties, Matthew's neighbor.

SETTING

Various locations and the window ledge of an apartment building (all minimally represented).

TIME

The present.

•   •   •

A mostly bare stage that will represent several places (apartments and a store). If possible, a suggestion of two large windows with a ledge running between them. At rise: Matthew, holding a tape measure, stands very close to Jennifer.

JENNIFER: I love you.

MATTHEW: *(To audience.)* Jennifer said this to me three times. April 27, May 4, and June 12.

JENNIFER: I'm leaving you.

MATTHEW: This was said twice. Within seconds of each other. Because of my response. *(To Jennifer.)* What?

JENNIFER: Good-bye, Matthew.

MATTHEW: *(To audience.)* Two words. Very effective, succinct. Combination of the five.

JENNIFER: I'm leaving you. Good-bye, Matthew.

MATTHEW: Extremely definitive. A real sense of finality. Five strong words. She made the strong choice. I hoped that she would hesitate, out of some conflicted sense of . . . well, heartbreak and anguish would have been nice. But her voice revealed no apparent equivocation, stammer, or justification.

JENNIFER: I love you.

MATTHEW: This was not said, but I wished that it was. She took eight steps to the door. From my door to the stairs is twenty-two feet eight and a half inches. There are forty-four steps down to the sidewalk. It took her three minutes forty-three seconds to exit the building.

JENNIFER: Matthew. Hi . . . How have you been?

MATTHEW: *(To audience.)* Since she left me, I have come to the grocery store thirty-seven times with the intention of bumping into her. *(To Jennifer.)* Fine. Fine. I . . .

JENNIFER: I'm glad. I'm sorry that things didn't . . . I'm glad you're doing OK.

MATTHEW: OK? Sure. Never better. Hunky-dory. Tip top. Okey-dokey. Fantastique. Super. Swell. I'm just swell, Jennifer. Swell. Swollen. Fine. I'm fine.

JENNIFER: OK. Great. Well . . .

MATTHEW: You look beautiful.

JENNIFER: Thanks. I should really—

MATTHEW: Maybe we could—

JENNIFER: No. Sorry. I don't think so.

MATTHEW: OK.

JENNIFER: Bye.

MATTHEW: *(To audience.)* In her cart, she had flowers, brownie mix, eggs, feta cheese, spinach, pie crusts, evaporated milk. She was making quiche. Quiche and brownies. For another person. You don't make quiche for yourself. For a man. Not me. How many times has she used this meal to test and impress? I'd estimate seven. She made the same thing for me on the first night she had me over. *(To Jennifer.)* Thanks for a wonderful evening. The quiche was delicious.

JENNIFER: I'm glad you liked it. It's the one thing I can cook with confidence.

MATTHEW: So, I was wondering. In terms of first dates . . . How did I rate? Choose whatever scale works best for you.

JENNIFER: I'm not really good at quantifying things like that.

MATTHEW: It'll help me assess how I did.

JENNIFER: OK. B minus. Eighty-one percent. You have nice table manners. Offered compliments. Very good eye contact. Appealing visage. A little mediocre in the conversation department. Seems like you can get a little fixated on things.

MATTHEW: Numbers. I know.

JENNIFER: I'm not sure that's a good quality in a man.

MATTHEW: I brought flowers.

JENNIFER: Which gives you a very good baseline.

MATTHEW: I tried hard at the conversation.

JENNIFER: I noticed.

MATTHEW: I showed you my watch with the built-in altimeter. Wasn't that cool?

JENNIFER: Sure.

MATTHEW: Your place is eighty-five feet above sea level. The sidewalk is at twenty-seven feet, so we're fifty-eight feet above the reference plane.

JENNIFER: Fascinating.

MATTHEW: That means it'd only take one and a half seconds to hit the ground if I jumped out your window. *(To audience.)* I didn't actually say that. I didn't say it out loud.

JENNIFER: *(Answering the phone.)* Hello, Matthew.

MATTHEW: *(To audience.)* I waited seventeen days after bumping into her at the store before I called on the phone.

JENNIFER: I'm fine.

MATTHEW: I considered calling her one hundred and seventy-three times before I actually did. Waiting seemed like the better choice. I didn't want her to think me too obsessive.

JENNIFER: No. I'm busy that night.

MATTHEW: *(To Jennifer.)* Maybe another night. I called and they said the movie will show for seventeen more days, so that gives us sixty-eight possible times, though some of those times are while we'll be at work, so it's really more like fifty-four. I'm pretty flexible.

JENNIFER: Matthew. You're a sweet man. And we had some good times. You are kind and thoughtful and honest. You mean a lot to me. For a while I thought that we . . . I know maybe I made it seem like it was easy for me to say good-bye. But it wasn't.

MATTHEW: Was it something I did? Something I said? Because if it was, whatever it was, I'm sorry. I miss you, Jennifer. More than you can know. I think about you, a lot.

JENNIFER: How many times a day?

MATTHEW: Sev—

JENNIFER: Sorry. That wasn't fair. I know you have an answer. It's not you, not completely. I have to go. I'm sorry, Matthew.

MATTHEW: *(To audience.)* She didn't specifically ask me not to call her again. Not until the eighth time. (I tried to space them out.)

JENNIFER: Don't make me call the police.

MATTHEW: *(To Jennifer.)* I won't. I'm sorry. Do Steve and José know about each other?

JENNIFER: Stay away from me.

> *(Jennifer exits. Matthew steps out his window onto the ledge. He inches his way between the windows.)*

MATTHEW: *(To audience.)* I'm guessing that they did not. They always seemed to arrive on different days, at different times. I wonder which one liked peanut butter. She never had peanut butter when we were together, but she purchased three jars since then. Steve moved away. He installed cable and received eighty-one complaints over the course of four months and thirteen days. So they fired him. (I can't take credit for more than sixty-two percent of those complaints.) He found a better job in Cincinnati. But Jennifer seemed very happy with José. She laughed more, at least twenty percent more than she did with me. Smiled more. Glowed. And I thought how sad it would be for José to become yet another statistic, one of the far-too-many traffic fatalities on our fair streets. I had this thought more than once . . . And all of a sudden I could see a string of actions, leading to a future that, by all calculations, would be a disaster for Jennifer, José, and me. My desire to reduce the number of tragic victims by sixty-six percent led me out the window, onto the ledge. *(Beat.)* Where I met, June, my neighbor.

(June enters and leans out her window.)

JUNE: That's quite a story . . . How many times did you think about squashing José?

MATTHEW: Twelve.

JUNE: Were you ever behind the wheel?

MATTHEW: Twice.

JUNE: Wow. That's self-control.

MATTHEW: I knew I was in trouble when I actually got behind the wheel. I knew it would be wrong. Because it would hurt her (and him, too). And that's not what I wanted.

JUNE: Are you OK? Do you want me to call someone?

MATTHEW: No. I'm fine. I think I'll be fine.

JUNE: Well, I'll just stay a minute. *(Beat.)* Did you talk to someone? A therapist?

MATTHEW: No. Almost. But I felt . . . ashamed.

JUNE: I know. But everyone has times when they get fixated on another person, and maybe they're not quite . . . It's an awfully long way down.

MATTHEW: Seventy-one feet.

JUNE: From the window sill.

MATTHEW: Sixty-eight feet three inches from the ledge.

JUNE: Not quite a full two seconds to the ground.

MATTHEW: Not quite.

JUNE: Not much time for second thoughts.

MATTHEW: Which is a plus, I think. But it's important to get that out of the way first, obviously.

JUNE: And have you?

MATTHEW: I have. This isn't my first time out here.

JUNE: I know.

MATTHEW: You do?

JUNE: You went out twice before. Not really all the way out. Both hands the first time, both hands and one leg the second.

MATTHEW: I didn't know anyone could—

JUNE: You didn't look completely serious yet, so I didn't want to stick my nose in.

MATTHEW: But this time . . .

JUNE: Was a good time for me to weed my window boxes.

MATTHEW: I'm glad you did, June.

JUNE: Me, too.

MATTHEW: Lucky thing you were home.

JUNE: You seem to be most depressed around six-thirty PM, so I changed my hours at work a little.

MATTHEW: To keep an eye on me?

JUNE: Just in case. People can be unpredictable.

MATTHEW: That doesn't stop us from trying.

JUNE: No, it doesn't. *(Beat.)* Matthew.

MATTHEW: Yes.

JUNE: Would you go to the movies with me?

MATTHEW: Are you serious?

JUNE: Yes.

MATTHEW: Because I'm obviously not a very good prospect. You heard what I'm like. There's probably something wrong with me.

JUNE: Definitely.

MATTHEW: And I would think that would be a negative, in terms of appeal.

JUNE: You've lived next door to me for five hundred and seventy-three days, Matthew. Our doors are approximately fifteen feet seven inches apart, jamb to jamb. I'm glad to know what you told me, and I'm glad for all that I've observed about you. And I'm not sorry you're the way you are. You'll have to make your own observations about me. If you're willing.

MATTHEW: I am.

(He takes her hand and climbs inside. Then he gently uses his tape measure to measure her arm, her shoulders, her waist. She smiles with delight. Lights out.)

END OF PLAY

Night Terrors

WENDY MACLEOD

Originally presented by Playwrights Horizons, New York City, November 19, 2007, in Dreamstates, the 4th annual Stories on 5 Stories. Directed by Josh Hecht. Cast: Playwright 1—Becky Ann Baker; Playwright 2— Carrie Preston; Dentist—Larry Pine.

CHARACTERS
    PLAYWRIGHT 1.
    PLAYWRIGHT 2.
    DENTIST.

SETTING
    In front of a plate-glass window in a front rehearsal studio.

TIME
    The present.

. . .

Two female playwrights (the same person), Playwright 1 and Playwright 2, stand wearing identical pajamas. They are trying to get to sleep but are kept awake by their own circling thoughts.

PLAYWRIGHT 1: The lights of Broadway.
    What are they really?
    A playground, a pizza parlor, a grocery store . . .
PLAYWRIGHT 2: A panel, a jury, a prize committee.
    Destiny, posterity, the deciding vote!
    They're reading the oeuvre.
    They're considering the canon.
    They have reservations.
    They're questioning our scope.
    Have we failed to address the oppressed?
    The unexpressed
    The dispossessed?
    Have we found the dialectic?
    Or just skated the surface?
    Have we merely constructed
    Or managed to deconstruct?
    Have we made a case for theater in the age of cinema?
PLAYWRIGHT 1: *(Worried.)* No! I don't think so! Did we?
PLAYWRIGHT 2: We should have worked harder . . .
PLAYWRIGHT 1: What if we started now?
    What if we wrote every day?
    What if we wrote every day for eight hours minimum?

Parked our seats in that chair

For eight lonely hours!

PLAYWRIGHT 2: We can't

Not tomorrow.

We have that thing tomorrow . . .

PLAYWRIGHT 1: The day after that!

PLAYWRIGHT 2: Maybe not *eight* . . . .

PLAYWRIGHT 1: Six! Four!

Two hours a day, ten hours a week . . .

Fourteen if we work weekends!

PLAYWRIGHT 2: Which we won't . . .

PLAYWRIGHT 1: Two hours a day, ten hours a week.

Six pages a session.

A play every two weeks!

PLAYWRIGHT 2: *(Dubious.)* Twenty-four plays a year?

PLAYWRIGHT 1: If we rented an office

Did nothing but write

Wore gloves without fingers

Lived on four hours sleep!

We sequester ourselves

With the famous at Yaddo.

If not Yaddo, then Ojai.

Or maybe MacDowell.

Bag lunch with the famous

At maybe MacDowell.

PLAYWRIGHT 2: *(Agony.)* Why aren't *we* famous?

More famous?

Famous-er?

PLAYWRIGHT 1: *(Happy thought.)* What if we *are* famous?

Famous enough that it goes without saying.

Do we ask the famous?

If they know that they're famous?

PLAYWRIGHT 2: How would we know if we're famous or not?

PLAYWRIGHT 1: We Google ourselves!

(They huddle around a blue light, which suggests a computer screen, and mime Googling. Their faces fall.)

PLAYWRIGHT 1: Check our Amazon rating!

(They return hopefully to the invisible keyboard. Their script on Amazon is down at 515,653. Their shoulders slump.)

PLAYWRIGHT 2: Wish list!

> Order that book.

> Order another.

> Group them together for economy shipping . . .

PLAYWRIGHT 1: No shopping!

> It's time to acknowledge how far we've come.

PLAYWRIGHT 1/PLAYWRIGHT 2: *(Looking at each other.)* Let's read the résumé!

> *(They huddle again and read their résumé aloud.)*

> Reading.

> Reading.

> Workshop.

> Workshop.

> Finalist.

> Finalist.

> Benefit.

PLAYWRIGHT 2: Why Upstairs?

PLAYWRIGHT 1: Shhh.

PLAYWRIGHT 2: Why not the Main Stage?

PLAYWRIGHT 1: Maybe women are on a slower trajectory. They traject more slowly. They come into their power. They become wise women, warriors, crones . . .

> *(During this reverie, Playwright 2 picks up* Arts and Leisure.*)*

PLAYWRIGHT 2: Who do you have to fuck to get a MacArthur?!

PLAYWRIGHT 1: *(Snatching the paper.)* We're a genius!

> *Flashes* of genius . . .

PLAYWRIGHT 2: Fucking *children* winning MacArthurs!

PLAYWRIGHT 1: Hey girly!

> No jumping the queue!

PLAYWRIGHT 2: *(Brainstorming.)* Greek mythology

> People with wings.

> Machines that talk.

> Flowers that walk.

> African folktales.

> Magical realism.

PLAYWRIGHT 1: Think big.

> Think bigger.

> Go global.

> Iraq.

> Darfur.

Monks in Burma . . .

PLAYWRIGHT 2: Why can't we be Tony Kushner?

Why can't we get outside our own . . . ?

Oh my God, we forgot to pay the dentist!

PLAYWRIGHT 1: What keeps dentists up at night?

PLAYWRIGHT 2: What *does* keep dentists up at night?

(A dentist in a lab coat enters.)

DENTIST: What keeps dentists up at night?

Do we not regret

The hygienist lost?

The lease not signed?

The root canal blown?

Waiting too long to go porcelain?

Don't amalgam fillings pepper our nightmares?

No reviews but the waiting room.

Brought bolt upright

by the empty waiting room.

The receptionist flipping through L.L. Bean

Startled by the sound of the opening door.

Why do our monitors fail to impress?

Why do the field trips pass us by?

Can we blame it on location?

The magazine selection?

A general lack of dental hygiene?

PLAYWRIGHT 2: What about dogs? What about cats?

PLAYWRIGHT 1: What keeps animals up at night?

PLAYWRIGHT 2: Oh to be a creature with no ambition.

Our silky fur baking in the sun.

DENTIST: Do they not regret the mouse missed?

The bird lost to the hasty pounce.

Do they not envy the cat next door?

Her wet food?

Her cat door?

Her comely house sitter?

PLAYWRIGHT 1: Does the Manx envy the tail?

The domestic short hair the long hair?

PLAYWRIGHT 2: Oh to be

An inanimate object . . .

PLAYWRIGHT 1: A tree perhaps . . .

PLAYWRIGHT 2: A tree can't fail.

A tree can't fall short.

DENTIST: A tree has no payroll to meet.

No appointments to fill.

PLAYWRIGHT 1: We don't presume to judge a tree.

Compare that tree to other trees.

PLAYWRIGHT 2: The leaves blow.

Its circles grow.

To survive is to triumph.

PLAYWRIGHT 1: Affirmations!

ALL: We are now enjoying the process.

We are now enjoying the journey . . .

PLAYWRIGHT 2: *(A cry from the heart.)* I hate traveling!

I want to *arrive*!

I want to *be* there!

I want results!

I want fame!

I want feature articles!

PLAYWRIGHT 1: Standing O's!

PLAYWRIGHT 2: Pulitzer Prizes!

PLAYWRIGHT 1: Tonys!

PLAYWRIGHT 2: Obies!

PLAYWRIGHT 1: *New Yorker* profiles!

PLAYWRIGHT 2: Sag Harbor!

PLAYWRIGHT 1: *(Fantasy.)* Why there's Joe Mantello!

PLAYWRIGHT 1/PLAYWRIGHT 2: *(Waving.)* Hey, Joe!

PLAYWRIGHT 2: Invitations to Prague!

PLAYWRIGHT 1: Two new plays a year!

PLAYWRIGHT 1: With movie stars in every role!

PLAYWRIGHT 2: Rave reviews!

PLAYWRIGHT 1: Above the fold!

PLAYWRIGHT 2: Bidding wars!

PLAYWRIGHT 1: Buzz!

PLAYWRIGHT 2: Movie sales!

PLAYWRIGHT 1: Biographers!

PLAYWRIGHT 2: And last but not least

PLAYWRIGHT 1/PLAYWRIGHT 2: We want our name spelled right!

(They've worked themselves into a lather. They look at each other.)

PLAYWRIGHT 1: Melatonin.

PLAYWRIGHT 2: *(Something stronger.)* Sominex.

DENTIST: *(Something strongest.)* Vicodin.

> *(Dentist whips out a prescription pad, writes on it, tears it off. The sheet flutters to the floor. They mime swallowing their pills in unison. Their thoughts get a little floaty.)*

DENTIST: We must try to remember . . .

PLAYWRIGHT 1: Where did I read that . . . ?

DENTIST: We must try to remember . . .

PLAYWRIGHT 2: Where *was* that?

DENTIST: We must try to remember.

That the sun and the moon and the stars . . .

PLAYWRIGHT 1: The waiting room!

PLAYWRIGHT 2: That magazine!

DENTIST: We must try to remember

That the sun and the moon and the stars will not go out when we die.

PLAYWRIGHT 1: We are going to die . . .

PLAYWRIGHT 2: *(Good news.)* We are going to die!

Whatever we do or don't do, we are going to die!

Shakespeare doesn't care if he's on the syllabus

Or that Coriolanus is a big fat mess.

PLAYWRIGHT 1: Shakespeare is with his dead son

And the dark lady of the sonnets

Who may or may not be that guy.

DENTIST: Our teeth will rot away . . .

PLAYWRIGHT 2: Our pages will be recycled . . .

PLAYWRIGHT 1: Our time here is less than the circle on a tree trunk.

PLAYWRIGHT 2: Think of the world without us . . .

ALL: And sleep.

> *(The three, standing in a row, reach for the unseen bedside lamp and turn it off as the lights go sharply out.)*

END OF PLAY

Zachary Zwillinger
Eats People

LAUREN D. YEE

Originally produced by and performed at Bindlestiff Studios,
San Francisco, February 9–24, 2007, as part of their
production, The Love Editions. Directed by Yato Yoshida.
Cast: Zachary Zwillinger—James Lontayao;
Lauren—Shenna Bautista/Anna Borja;
Sugar Plum Fairy—Julie Kuwabara.

Love kills. Love consumes. These two statements are entirely true for poor Zachary Zwillinger, who finds himself unable to control his simultaneous desires to love and to eat his numerous girlfriends. What leads him to such ends and will he ever be able to curb his desires?

CHARACTERS

ZACHARY ZWILLINGER, male, an idealistic young man with an insatiable sweet tooth and a hunger for love. Socially awkward and unable to control his yearnings for sugar.

SUGAR PLUM FAIRY, female, Zachary's current or former girlfriend, the Sugar Plum Fairy of the *Nutcracker*. Nervous, fragile. A modern-day version of the Victorian woman—somewhere in her closet are the smelling salts.

LAUREN, female, Zachary's friend and confidante, who, not being made of sugar, has nothing to worry about. A witness to Zachary's unfortunate attempts at a sustained romance.

SETTING

A bare stage.

TIME

Indeterminate.

NOTES: Although the action occurs at different points in time, the flow should be continuous without too much attention paid to the changes in time. If a slide projector is too difficult to obtain or use, various creative substitutes for the slides are acceptable.

A slash (/) indicates that the next character begins to speak his or her line, overlapping the first speaker.

• • •

Zachary Zwillinger and the Sugar Plum Fairy dance together in a series of movements that is part tango, part make-out session. The Sugar Plum Fairy laughs as Zachary Zwillinger attacks her neck with gentle kisses/bites. The action becomes more violent as Zachary Zwillinger takes a bite, another bite, then devours the Sugar Plum Fairy with almost unconscious desperation. After consuming her, Zachary Zwillinger comes to a moment of realization and falls into operatic despair. The scene is dramatic/ridiculous. Spotlight on Lauren.

LAUREN: My friend Zachary Zwillinger eats people. He falls in love with them, courts them with flowers and balloons, and ultimately consumes them. A gigantic modern-day black widow spider. Only male. And with fewer eyes. His actions are neither intentional nor vindictive. Zachary Zwillinger's taste for his beloved is his one fatal flaw. *(Beat.)* Zachary Zwillinger doesn't actually eat *people,* per se. But that's just because he never falls in love with people, per se. Zachary Zwillinger falls in love with things—*people*—that are kind of like people in the same way that they are kind of like food. Like Strawberry Shortcake. *(Slide of Strawberry Shortcake.)* Or the Green M&M. *(Slide of the Green M&M.) Kind* of like people but kind of like . . . well, *edible.* Sugary edible. Zachary Zwillinger is addicted to sugar. He's in *love.* With things—*people*—made of sugar. And it's a growing problem because A: man cannot live without his beloved, and B: man cannot live without his food. B would deprive him of A, and yet both are equally important and equally necessary for a satisfied and sustained life. It's a constant moral dilemma.

(Lights up on Lauren and Zachary Zwillinger.)

ZACHARY ZWILLINGER: I am the worst person in the world.

LAUREN: Debatable.

ZACHARY ZWILLINGER: Everything I touch!

LAUREN: You fall in love with the wrong people.

ZACHARY ZWILLINGER: But every time . . . ?

LAUREN: Love hurts. *(Beat.)* Love kills.

ZACHARY ZWILLINGER: It's not love. *(Beat.)* I don't *think* it's love. Because then . . . that would be kind of depressing, wouldn't it?

LAUREN: Potentially.

ZACHARY ZWILLINGER: I *wanted* to love her for the rest of my life. *Truly.* But at the same time, I was always thinking, "God, I hope she's not the one." I hope I hope I hope.

LAUREN: Maybe when the one comes, you won't feel like eating her.

ZACHARY ZWILLINGER: But I like a girl because she's so kind and so sweet . . . and so tasty and so filled with delicious disaccharides. And I realize that the characteristics that I find attractive in a girl, I also find attractive in food.

LAUREN: You don't *need* to eat them. Sugar's an extra, you know. It's the cap on the pyramid.

ZACHARY ZWILLINGER: But it's there, it's everywhere I go! And it's not just *me* who's importing 1.3 million tons of sugar.

LAUREN: You've got a substantial stake in the market.

ZACHARY ZWILLINGER: We're a consumptive society. We *consume*. That's how we manage to stay economically strong. We spend and we spend and we eat and we eat and—don't you think there's something incredibly *normal* in all of this?

LAUREN: Falling in love with a hundred and twenty pounds of sugar and carbs and then eating her?

ZACHARY ZWILLINGER: Lauren, Americans eat and drink about five pounds of sugar a month.

LAUREN: We're talking a full-grown girl here, Zach. Not a hamster.

ZACHARY ZWILLINGER: Sugar *is* on the food pyramid.

LAUREN: "Use sparingly"?

ZACHARY ZWILLINGER: *(Groans.)* Ohhhh, I *use* them. I just *use* people.

LAUREN: Not technically "people."

ZACHARY ZWILLINGER: I feel so dirty. *(Beat, to self.)* I need to eat something . . . I'm SO hungry.

(Zachary Zwillinger wanders offstage, exits.)

LAUREN: Zach's loves frequently resemble this *(Slide of a soda can.)* this *(Slide of chocolate.)* and this *(Slide of a mound of sugar.)* Thus, whereas most people's food pyramids look like this *(Slide of the food pyramid.)* Zach's pyramid frequently resembles this. *(Slide of inverted food pyramid with sugar being the largest section, located at the top.)* Which is frustrating to me at least because his teeth look like this. *(Slide of Zach's perfect teeth.)* I think it's the fluoride. His dad's a dentist. *(Pause.)* But how did we get to this point? How did mere addiction become another form of cannibalism? It used to be the Gingerbread Woman, and when she went under, I figured that was that: he'd learned his lesson. I mean, anacondas only feed twice a year and they're . . . you know, *significant*. Sugar is not an essential nutrient, you *can* live without it. Zach, unfortunately, is a hopeless romantic and a quick eater. His heart and his stomach mended in less than two months. And along came the Sugar Plum Fairy. *(We enter into the past. The Sugar Plum Fairy enters, very much alive at this point in time.)*

LAUREN: He's going to eat you.

SUGAR PLUM FAIRY: Ohhh, but he has such PERFECT TEETH.

LAUREN: Teeth made for eating you.

SUGAR PLUM FAIRY: Not me. Not meeee. Strawberry Shortcake, she asked for it. With all that cake. And strawberries. I'm low-*caaaaaarb*. Twenty percent sucrose.

LAUREN: Suit yourself. *(Beat.)* He only brushes once a day!

(The Sugar Plum Fairy continues to smile, but once Lauren exits, she runs over to the edge of the stage to speak, in confidence, to the audience.)

SUGAR PLUM FAIRY: It's not that I don't love him. I consider myself a *trusting* person. But . . . *(Thinks.)* Did you ever watch *Gaslight*? It's kind of like that. Constantly wondering: Is Charles Boyer—or in this case, Zachary—attempting to murder me? And in the process making me question my own sanity?

ZACHARY ZWILLINGER: *(Enters with a glass.)* Milk, dear?

SUGAR PLUM FAIRY: *(To audience.)* But other than the wife murder thing, I've got all I could ask for. *(To Zachary Zwillinger, sweetly.)* Say something, Zachary. Say something.

(This is the game the two share. Zachary Zwillinger speaks the words deliberately with perfect enunciation. Each time he does so, the Sugar Plum Fairy rolls with delight at each beautifully pronounced word.)

ZACHARY ZWILLINGER: "Malapropism."

SUGAR PLUM FAIRY: Another. Another!

ZACHARY ZWILLINGER: "Presentation."

SUGAR PLUM FAIRY: Oh, Zachary!

ZACHARY ZWILLINGER: "Social movements in America."

SUGAR PLUM FAIRY: Ohhhhhh. *(To the audience.)* Such a BEAUTIFUL mouth.

ZACHARY ZWILLINGER: With one purpose only . . .

(Zachary Zwillinger embraces the Sugar Plum Fairy, and they begin making out. She breaks away abruptly.)

SUGAR PLUM FAIRY: Honey.

ZACHARY ZWILLINGER: Hmm?

SUGAR PLUM FAIRY: Did you just lick me?

ZACHARY ZWILLINGER: Darling?

SUGAR PLUM FAIRY: Did you just lick my—

(Zachary Zwillinger smacks his lips unconsciously, then looks up.)

ZACHARY ZWILLINGER: Your what, dear?

SUGAR PLUM FAIRY: Never mind. *(Silence, then.)* What do you want out of this relationship?

ZACHARY ZWILLINGER: What?

SUGAR PLUM FAIRY: What do you want with me?

ZACHARY ZWILLINGER: I don't want anything. I just want *you*. *(Beat, adds.)* *Here*. With me.

SUGAR PLUM FAIRY: Mmm, well, that's good. *(Silence.)* Zachary?

ZACHARY ZWILLINGER: Yes?

SUGAR PLUM FAIRY: Whatever happened to Strawberry Shortcake?

ZACHARY ZWILLINGER: Hmm?

SUGAR PLUM FAIRY: Strawberry Shortcake. You said she, uh, disappeared.

ZACHARY ZWILLINGER: She's gone now.

SUGAR PLUM FAIRY: Yes, dear. But . . . *how?*

ZACHARY ZWILLINGER: Dwelling on the past, sweet.

SUGAR PLUM FAIRY: Sweet?

ZACHARY ZWILLINGER: *Dear.* Darling. Pumpkin . . . Honey. Sugar pie. Peach. Cupcake. Tasty.

(As he says these words, Zachary Zwillinger licks his lips unconsciously.)

SUGAR PLUM FAIRY: Tasty?

ZACHARY ZWILLINGER: Say something, hon?

SUGAR PLUM FAIRY: Did you say tasty?

ZACHARY ZWILLINGER: Why would I say tasty?

SUGAR PLUM FAIRY: It just sounded like—well.

ZACHARY ZWILLINGER: Probably princess or something. *(Then, with an enticing level of excellent pronunciation.)* Paramour.

SUGAR PLUM FAIRY: *(Shudders with delight.)* Ohhh!

ZACHARY ZWILLINGER: Turtledove.

SUGAR PLUM FAIRY: Oh! Oh stop! Stop!

ZACHARY ZWILLINGER: Sweetheart.

SUGAR PLUM FAIRY: Oh, and to think they all warned me about you.

ZACHARY ZWILLINGER: Me?

SUGAR PLUM FAIRY: Well, you know, eating and all . . .

ZACHARY ZWILLINGER: Eating what? What would I be eating?

SUGAR PLUM FAIRY: Absurd. And with such PERFECT TEETH. Mmm, dessert?

ZACHARY ZWILLINGER: Yes. Um. Dessert.

(The Sugar Plum Fairy jetés innocently off the stage. Lauren then appears onstage.)

ZACHARY ZWILLINGER: I could fall in love with an apple if it were presented properly.

LAUREN: I know. Natural sugar.

ZACHARY ZWILLINGER: Really. Love is love is love.

LAUREN: You're avoiding the situation.

ZACHARY ZWILLINGER: How so?

LAUREN: It's inevitable.

ZACHARY ZWILLINGER: You don't know that.

LAUREN: You eat the Sugar Plum Fairy, you feel really bad about it, you get all heartbroken. Just AVOID it. Six billion people out there. *Trillions* of pounds of sugar. *(Beat.)* You know what's going to happen.

ZACHARY ZWILLINGER: But isn't that what makes love wonderful?

LAUREN: Funny, I could've sworn that's what makes love painful.

ZACHARY ZWILLINGER: The unpredictability? / The unexpected twists and turns it'll take? The recognition that even though something horrible and terrible is about to happen, life goes on and people live and love and make mistakes.

LAUREN: 'S not really unpredictability . . .

ZACHARY ZWILLINGER: Not that anything horrible and terrible is about to happen, of course.

LAUREN: Of course.

ZACHARY ZWILLINGER: You should try it some time.

LAUREN: Eating a boyfriend?

ZACHARY ZWILLINGER: No. Getting one.

LAUREN: And go through that drama?

ZACHARY ZWILLINGER: Tis better to have loved and lost—

LAUREN: Oh, shut up.

ZACHARY ZWILLINGER: It won't happen this time.

LAUREN: I bet.

SUGAR PLUM FAIRY: *(Offstage.)* Zaaaaaaaachary! Desserrrrrrt!

ZACHARY ZWILLINGER: Promise. *(Exits.)*

LAUREN: Me? I don't understand it. If it looks like a train wreck and talks like a train wreck and tastes like a hundred and twenty pounds of sugar, well, chances are you shouldn't let yourself fall madly in love with it. *(Beat.)* He's kind of like Elizabeth Taylor. "Just wanting to be loved!" Only difference is he can't eat Richard Burton twice.

(Fade out on Lauren. Tango music begins playing. We are back to the beginning, with Zachary Zwillinger and the Sugar Plum Fairy coming on in their mad hot tango.)

ZACHARY ZWILLINGER: Consummation.

(The Sugar Plum Fairy squeals with pleasure. Lights fade out as Zachary Zwillinger goes for the first bite.)

END OF PLAY

PLAYS FOR
THREE WOMEN

The Baby War

LAURA COTTON

Originally performed at Florida State University, July 21, 2007. Directed by Laura Cotton. Cast: Patricia Martin—Nina Rozin; April Westcott—Stephanie Blaire; Caroline Westcott—Theresa Avery.

CHARACTERS

> PATRICIA MARTIN, mid- to late forties, a glamorous, wealthy woman who is used to getting her way.
>
> APRIL WESTCOTT, sixteen years old, in the first few weeks of a pregnancy, bold and outspoken and unafraid.
>
> CAROLINE WESTCOTT, early forties, April's mother. A caring person who loves her daughter but does not always know what is best for her.

SCENE:

La Patisserie, a small café in the middle of a mall.

TIME

The present: around noon.

• • •

At rise: Patricia sits at a small table in the center of the stage. She wears a business suit and has a briefcase on the floor next to her. April and Carolyn enter. They are casually dressed. Patricia sees them and waves them over to join her.

PATRICIA: I'm so glad you two could come.

(April and Carolyn smile at her and sit down.)

PATRICIA: It's so nice to finally meet you, Carolyn. April has told me so much about you.

APRIL: I have?

PATRICIA: Of course you have.

(April gives her a confused look, then opens her menu.)

PATRICIA: Oh, you needn't look at that. All they have here is coffee and croissants. I already ordered for us.

APRIL: Thanks, but I don't eat croissants.

PATRICIA: Don't be ridiculous, everyone eats croissants. *(Clears her throat.)* Now, I'm sure you're both wondering why I wanted to meet you here today.

CAROLYN: I assumed it had something to do with April's pregnancy.

PATRICIA: Yes, that's precisely it. You see, when I first heard the news about April's . . . condition, I was stunned. I thought I'd raised Codie to be more careful about such matters. Needless to say, I didn't exactly react *well* to the news of the pregnancy. You probably already know this, April, but I threw Codie out of the house. He had to live at a friend's house for almost two weeks. *(Takes a sip of her coffee.)* Anyway, when I finally calmed down, I realized that this wasn't Codie's fault. Or April's, for that matter. I mean, yes, in a way it was, it would have been better if they waited till marriage for—for intercourse, but really, who does that nowadays?

APRIL: Actually, *I* wanted to wait. But Codie said we were going to get married in two years anyway, so what difference did it make?

PATRICIA: A world of difference, I'm afraid. Now, April, I'm sure you will agree with me when I say this baby marks the end of your life. You do agree, don't you?

APRIL: No.

PATRICIA: *(Completely ignoring her.)* Which is why I'm also sure you'll be quite relieved when you hear my news. *(A beat.)* You see, I've decided that I can't allow April to have an abortion.

APRIL: I wasn't planning on having an abortion.

PATRICIA: Of course you were.

APRIL: No, I wasn't.

CAROLYN: Are you sure, honey? You could just have a tiny one.

APRIL: A tiny abortion? What, are you out of your mind?

PATRICIA: In any case, I decided that it wouldn't be right for a girl so young to have such a dangerous medical procedure. I don't feel one way or another on the actual issue of abortion—far be it from me to judge the actions of others. I thought for quite a while on the subject and I decided—I decided . . .

APRIL: What?

PATRICIA: I've decided to raise the child. *(A beat.)* Myself.

APRIL: Do you honestly think I would let you—

PATRICIA: Now, now, you needn't pretend to argue with me. My husband Gary and I have managed to save quite a bit of money over the years—a lot of careful investing in stocks and bonds and such things—and we have more than enough to support the child. I will raise him like he is my own flesh and blood, which, in a way, I suppose he is. I know I'll be slightly older than most of the other mothers on the playground, but unlike many of *them*, I really want this baby. All April needs to do is to sign these papers.

(Takes some papers out of her bag and hands them to April. April and Carolyn stare at one another, taking this in. Finally, Carolyn speaks.)

CAROLYN: That's a wonderful idea!

APRIL: What?

CAROLYN: It's a fantastic solution! I was going to have to take care of the baby until you finished high school anyway, April. This really isn't any different.

PATRICIA: It's entirely different. You see, I'd like April to end all contact with the child.

CAROLYN: What's that?

PATRICIA: It's nothing against April personally, of course. It's just that in my research on adoption and mothers, I've discovered that it's far, far better if a child only thinks he has one mother. Another one just confuses things. Naturally, I'll tell him—or her—all about you later.

APRIL: When? When will you tell her?

CAROLYN: Her? Do you know the baby is going to be a girl?

APRIL: Well, no. Not for sure. But I'm getting a very feminine vibe. *(Looks at Patricia.)* Anyway, when will you tell her?

PATRICIA: Probably around seventeen. Maybe eighteen. It depends on how mature she is. If she's anything like her father is, I might not tell her at all.

CAROLYN: That sounds reasonable.

APRIL: So I would never even see my own daughter. Is that what you're saying?

PATRICIA: Of course you'll *see* her. I'll send you pictures, e-cards, videos—whatever you want. You just won't actually be able to spend *time* with the child. After all, we want to raise this child to have a strong morals and an understanding of right and wrong. We don't want her knowing that her mother . . . her mother had relations when she was a promiscuous teenager, now do we?

CAROLYN: She makes a very good point, April. I would rather not know if my mother had relations when she was a promiscuous teenager. I don't even like to *think* of my mother as a promiscuous teenager.

PATRICIA: I will give the child the best education this country has to offer. She'll go to all the right schools, take all the right classes, learn all the right things.

(Patricia and Carolyn get into a rhythm of talking back and forth very quickly, as if forgetting that April is there.)

CAROLYN: Can she learn French?

PATRICIA: Of course. I already have her on Vangarden Prep Preschool's waiting list. There, she'll learn French, Italian, Russian, Chinese, and Japanese. Perhaps just the tiniest bit of German, but not too much. We don't want her getting too aggressive now, do we?

CAROLYN: I always wanted to give April music lessons. Do you think the child can learn to play an instrument?

PATRICIA: No.

CAROLYN: Oh.

PATRICIA: But she will learn to ride a horse, and everyone knows that horse-back riding is far superior to any hobby except for tennis, golfing, and synchronized swimming, all three of which she will master at the age of eleven. After that, I plan to send her away to a boarding school from which she will not be released until the age of twenty-two. At that point, she will graduate with a bachelor's in history, a master's in English literature, and a Ph.D in cognitive psychology.

CAROLYN: Well, it sounds like you've given this a lot of thought. But I still have one major question.

PATRICIA: Ask away.

CAROLYN: Can she have access to a fitness center? April was a fat little kid and so was I. I think it runs in our family.

PATRICIA: *(Appalled by the idea.)* No one in my family has or ever will be fat.

CAROLYN: Well, you've convinced me. It sounds perfect. April, what do you say? Do you want Patricia to raise your child?

APRIL: No.

CAROLYN: No? No? Are you out of your mind?

PATRICIA: Perhaps she just needs some time to think about it.

APRIL: No. My answer is no.

CAROLYN: April, please. You're being just plain silly now. Patricia here is offering you an amazing opportunity.

APRIL: An opportunity I don't need.

CAROLYN: April, sweetheart, be reasonable. You don't want a child. Trust me.

APRIL: I *do* want a child. Codie and I both want one. And we've worked it all out. We've worked out what he calls our "master plan" for how we can afford to raise it.

PATRICIA: *(Cynically.)* And what, pray tell is that?

APRIL: You don't want to know.

PATRICIA: Actually, I do.

APRIL: You won't like it.

CAROLYN: Go ahead, April. Share it with us.

APRIL: Fine. But you can't tell me that it's ridiculous and stupid or anything. OK?

CAROLYN: I promise you that I won't.

APRIL: Patricia?

PATRICIA: I won't say a word. But if *you* think we might think it's ridiculous or stupid, don't you think there's a chance that it *is* ridiculous and stupid?

APRIL: No matter what I said, you'd think it was ridiculous and stupid.

CAROLYN: Please, April. Just tell us all ready.

APRIL: OK . . . Here goes. *(Takes a deep breath.)* We're going to raise the baby to be an Olympic athlete. Codie has already contacted Nike and they said they might be interested. Basically, we would start training the child as soon as she's born and Nike would make a documentary about it. My daughter's whole life would be on tape—like that movie, *The Truman Show*, only about an athlete.

(Silence.)

CAROLYN: I love it!

APRIL: *(Incredulous.)* You do?

CAROLYN: Are you kidding? It's ingenious. I wish I'd thought of it myself when you were little.

PATRICIA: You can't be serious.

CAROLYN: *(To Patricia.)* You're just jealous. Because you didn't think of it first.

PATRICIA: How dare you! Here I am trying to save your daughter from a life of financial hardship and self-sacrifice, and you have the audacity to tell me that I'm envious of her.

CAROLYN: Well, I think you are. *(To April.)* It's a marvelous plan, sweetheart. I'm so proud of you.

APRIL: Thank you, Mom. That means a lot to me.

(April hugs Carolyn.)

PATRICIA: What is wrong with you people? Can't you see how ridiculous this is? *(To April.)* Nike doesn't care about you. Nike is a huge, selfish company uninterested in the lives of boring, ordinary people like you. You have nothing to offer Nike. Nike is going to laugh in your face.

(April's cell phone rings. April answers the phone.)

APRIL: *(Speaking into her phone.)* Hello? Oh, hi Mr. Rodriguez. Yes, I'm the mother who called about the Nike documentary . . . Yes . . . Yes. I don't know. I was thinking maybe she could be a golfer . . . Oh, sure, yeah, a runner could be great too. We could put her in some little pink running shoes . . . Oh sure, yeah, yellow could be great too.

PATRICIA: *(Whispering.)* Tell him you already have a trainer for the baby.

APRIL: Huh?

PATRICIA: If this is really going to happen, I want to be a part of it.

CAROLYN: You see? I knew you were jealous.

APRIL: Thanks, Patricia, but no thanks.

PATRICIA: I'll pay you. Anything you want.

APRIL: Anything?

(Patricia nods.)

APRIL: *(Into phone.)* Sorry about that, Mr. Rodriguez. I was talking to Patricia. She's going to be the baby's personal trainer . . . Yes. Yes, she has excellent credentials. I think she trained Michael Jordan. And Natalie Portman. Yes, I know she's an actress, but she's also an excellent . . . an excellent . . .

PATRICIA: Swimmer.

APRIL: *(Into phone.)* Swimmer.

CAROLYN: She is?

(Lights fade.)

END OF PLAY

Sexual Perversity in Connecticut

MIKE FOLIE

Originally produced by Algonquin Projections, at the
Chernuchian Theatre, American Theatre for Actors,
New York City, June 15–17, 2007, as part of the 32nd annual
Samuel French Off-Off Broadway Short Play Festival. Directed
by Craig J. George. Cast: Clarissa—Haviland Morris;
Danielle—Vanessa Daniels; Jessica—Lily Mercer.
Also produced by NY Artists Unlimited, in association with
Montauk Theatre Productions/Shooting Star Theatre, at the
Players Theatre, New York City, September 10–29, 2007, as
part of the Bad Plays Festival 2007. Directed by Mary Lee
Kellerman. Cast: Clarissa—Kendal Ridgeway; Danielle—
Sarah Matthay; Jessica—Dina Drew.

CLARISSA, forties, a wealthy suburban housewife.
DANIELLE, early twenties, a young woman.
JESSICA, midthirties, Clarissa's neighbor.

SETTING

The living room of Clarissa's upscale home in Greenwich, Connecticut. The set can be suggested with just a few pieces of expensive-looking furniture. There should be a couch, a few chairs, an end table and/or a coffee table, and a well-stocked bar. Any other touches—art objects, lamps, etc.—that can be added to create an atmosphere of wealth and privilege are welcome but not necessary. Clarissa has more money than taste, but she has probably had the advice of a top-flight interior decorator.

TIME

The present.

• • •

Clarissa enters, followed by Danielle. Clarissa throws open her arms in a grand gesture, indicating the room.

CLARISSA: And this is the fucking living room.
DANIELLE: Oh, it's *you*, Clare, so very . . .
CLARISSA: Very what?
DANIELLE: Very, very . . . nice.
    (Pause.)
CLARISSA: You fucking bitch.
DANIELLE: What?
CLARISSA: Ten years ago, Dani—think about this!—ten years ago, when you were just this little piece of ass-twitching jail bait, stoking the pathetic fantasies of every lame-dick husband on East 89th Street—I trusted you with my fucking kids? Right? I trusted you with the two most precious things in my life. What could be more sacred than that?
DANIELLE: How are the kids?
CLARISSA: Ah, they're both such total fucking losers I want to slit my wrists.
DANIELLE: Well, you could see that coming.
CLARISSA: But you turned out all right, didn't you, sweetheart?
DANIELLE: I dunno. I'm sort of a whore.

CLARISSA: But you're an expensive whore, Dani. And that is why this thing with the "nice" . . .

DANIELLE: "Nice" is like—what?!—a four-letter word all of a sudden?!

CLARISSA: "Nice" can mean dainty, fastidious, finicky, fussy—miminy-piminy!

DANIELLE: Oh, fuck me! There's no such fucking word?

CLARISSA: You can look it up, Danielle. There are books and you can look that shit up.

DANIELLE: So have it your own way then! It's not nice!

CLARISSA: What is it, then?! It's not nice, what is it?

DANIELLE: It's . . . it's impressive.

(Pause.)

CLARISSA: That's right. (Slight pause.) Good girl. Help yourself to a drink.
(Danielle jumps up to make herself a drink.)

CLARISSA: And let me give you a little clue here, sweetheart—so that you have one to take home—impressive is the name of the game out here in Greenwich, Connecticut. Impressive is the raison d'-fucking-être.

DANIELLE: If it makes you happy, Clare, then you're happy.

CLARISSA: Because we are human beings here, Dani. Human beings. And do you know what that means?

DANIELLE: We have language?

CLARISSA: When I want that kind of bullshit I'll call up Noam-fucking-Chomsky and have him come right over with his—with his what?—with his fucking books and his pipe and sweater.

DANIELLE: We can think.

CLARISSA: We WANT, Dani! That's what makes us human beings. We want things.

DANIELLE: You want a drink?

CLARISSA: No. Yeah. Vodka.

DANIELLE: Vodka and what?

CLARISSA: And vodka, bitch.

DANIELLE: OK!

CLARISSA: And what do human beings want more than anything else in the whole world, Dani? What is the one thing that all human beings—in every fucking corner of the world—from here in the lush green hills of Connecticut all the way to the sorriest little poverty-wracked, shit-sore, piss-rot bog-hole of a village in some jungle crawling with fleas and dung beetles—what do all human beings want?

DANIELLE: Love?

CLARISSA: Give me a fucking break.

DANIELLE: Revenge!

CLARISSA: No! Well . . . yes! Revenge is good. But there's something else human beings always want more than anything else.

DANIELLE: What?

CLARISSA: We want other people to want what we have. That's what we all want, little Dani. Isn't that what you want?

(Slight pause.)

DANIELLE: I want to know what the fuck I'm doing here.

CLARISSA: I want you to fuck someone for me.

DANIELLE: Huh?

CLARISSA: You are familiar with the act?

DANIELLE: Who?

CLARISSA: This woman who'll be here any minute—Jessica. Jessie.

DANIELLE: That costs extra.

CLARISSA: Not her, numbnuts! Listen. Jessica . . . Fucking Jessie, who should only die of some disfiguring fucking disease. I want you to fuck her husband.

DANIELLE: Why?

CLARISSA: Because she's a stone-cold bitch and I hate her. And because she and I are the only two wives on this street got husbands who don't fuck around with other women.

(Danielle chokes on her drink and coughs.)

CLARISSA: You OK, pretty tits?

DANIELLE: Went down the wrong hole.

CLARISSA: As if you had one. I'd take care of it and fuck her fucking husband myself, but I can't. I'm too . . .

DANIELLE: Old?

CLARISSA: No! I'm too . . .

DANIELLE: Ugly?

CLARISSA: I'm too fucking principled.

DANIELLE: Forget it, Clare! I may be a whore, but there's some things even I won't do.

CLARISSA: Five thousand dollars.

DANIELLE: Ten.

CLARISSA: OK.

DANIELLE: Shit. Fifteen.

CLARISSA: Fuck you. You blew it. Ten.

DANIELLE: Let's have it.

CLARISSA: Here. Count it.

DANIELLE: How do I do it?

CLARISSA: I think you know how to do it, Dani.

DANIELLE: I mean, how do I get near the guy?

CLARISSA: For ten large you can figure that out for yourself.

(Sound of a doorbell.)

CLARISSA: Here's Jessie now. She's looking for a nanny for her ugly kids. You take it from there.

(Jessie enters.)

JESSIE: Fuck Neiman Marcus, fuck Neiman Marcus, fuck Neiman Marcus, fuck Neiman Marcus!

CLARISSA: Hey.

JESSIE: Fuck Neiman-fucking-Marcus!

CLARISSA: What'd they do to you, baby?

JESSIE: I go to return this silk blouse I only just bought last week . . .

CLARISSA: You want a drink?

JESSIE: No. Yeah. Scotch.

CLARISSA: Get Jessie a scotch, Dani.

DANIELLE: Scotch and what?

JESSIE: And scotch, bitch.

CLARISSA: Which blouse, the blue?

JESSIE: The red. Wouldn't take it back. Said I'd worn it and spilled drinks on it and shit.

CLARISSA: And had you?

JESSIE: Oh, who the fuck knows?

(Danielle gives Jessie her drink.)

JESSIE: Thanks, honey. So she gives me all kinds of attitude, the salesgirl. I'm in that store, what—two, three times a week. Plunking down the plastic. I'm, like, a hundred and fifty-fucking percent of that store's revenues. I HONOR them by shopping in that store. I swear to God, Clare, I bring them honor with my custom!

CLARISSA: You honor all of us, Jess.

JESSIE: You know, I know what you're saying and I know what you mean by that and fuck you I don't give a flying fuck because it's the goddamn truth! A lot of the bitches in this burb look down their noses 'cause it's a fucking—let's face it!—it's just a fucking chain like fucking Macy's! I mean, who cares they're from Texas?! Bunch of oil-soaked, big-hair bleached blondes driving black fucking Mercedes SUVs in cowboy boots!? I say to them: "This is Connecticut, you whore, where they fuck-ing invented money!"

CLARISSA: Damn straight.

JESSIE: People like that, you just gotta kill them. *(Pause.)* I honor them and they don't honor me. They should fucking die.

CLARISSA: I want you to meet someone, Jessie, this is . . .

JESSIE: Yeah, yeah, I know her. Dani, right? Hi, honey. Nice to see you again. So I say to this fucking excuse for a sales clerk, may her tits fall off, I say to her . . .

CLARISSA: You know Dani?

JESSIE: Yeah. She's your niece, right. I met her in the lobby of the Carlyle with your husband last week.

(Pause.)

CLARISSA: You fucking whore!

DANIELLE: Well . . . duh!

CLARISSA: You won't get away with this.

DANIELLE: Uh, I already did?

CLARISSA: And I thought we shared warmth.

DANIELLE: Nope. Just your husband.

(Clarissa stomps off.)

JESSIE: What did we say, ten thousand?

DANIELLE: Fifteen.

JESSIE: Worth every penny.

(Jessie pulls out a wad of bills and begins to count out money.)

DANIELLE: Clare said you're looking for a nanny.

JESSIE: Oh, I'll bet you're just wonderful with kids.

DANIELLE: I am.

JESSIE: Come anywhere near mine I'll slit your fucking throat.

(Jessie continues counting out money. Blackout.)

END OF PLAY

Sister Snell

MARK TROY

Originally performed at the Deaf West Theatre, Los Angeles,
May 2006, as part of the NoHo Theater & Arts Festival.
Directed by Mark Troy. Cast: Bernice Snell—
Francesca Ferrara; Charlotte Burdick—Beth Lucosius;
Voice of Mary—Nina Kate.

CHARACTERS

BERNICE SNELL, thirties, dressed like a nun, pretty, dark hair, somewhat cut-throat, but likeable.

CHARLOTTE BURDICK, twenty to thirty, very attractive, business attire, shy, nervous, like it was her first job interview.

MARY, any age, voice of authority, sarcastic, quick, very dry sense of humor (this role may be played with actress offstage, or onstage in a corner without pulling focus).

PLACE:

A corner office in a high-rise, Venice, California.

TIME

The present.

• • •

The offices of Poxner and Poser Architects. Mahogany desk, center; door at right. Bernice Snell enters. She is in a full nun's outfit with habit, guimpe, and coif. She rants to no one in particular.

BERNICE: Jesus Christ! Goddamn it—who do I have to sleep with around here to get anything done!? *Again.* St. Fabiola's is never going to find the recognition it deserves if this work does not get done. This work *must* get done! Hello? *(Into intercom on the desk.)* Mary, Jesus, and Joseph! Are you out there? Oh shit . . . Mary? Are you out there?!?

MARY: *(Offstage. Calmly.)* Yes, Ms. Snell.

BERNICE: Don't give me any attitude, Mary—what the hell is going on? Has the shipment of stained glass arrive at the construction site?

MARY: *(Offstage.)* Yes, Ms. Snell.

BERNICE: And there was no problem with the inventory?

MARY: *(Offstage.)* No, Ms. Snell.

BERNICE: Good. My skin crawls when there's problems.

MARY: *(Offstage.)* There was this one problem, Ms. Snell.

BERNICE: Jesus H.—what's the problem?

MARY: *(Offstage.)* The stained glass you ordered for St. Fabiola's is . . . is . . .

BERNICE: Well what the f— is it, Mary?

MARY: *(Offstage.)* It's Jewish, Ms. Snell.

BERNICE: I ordered *Jewish* stained glass for St. Fabiola's? Who am I—the devil?! A dybbuk? *(Sits, lights a cigarette.)* What am I supposed to do with Jewish stained glass?

MARY: *(Offstage.)* Yeah, that is a problem. Of course not as big a problem as the fact that they have Jewish stars all over them. And a likenesses of Moses. And King David. And a *dreidel.*

BERNICE: Shit. Would you shut up already. Where are my pills? *(Searching drawers.)* Where in God's name is the Zoloft? Mary? Are you out there?

MARY: *(Offstage. Even more calmly.)* Ms. Snell, the doctor refused to extend your prescription for the Zoloft.

BERNICE: Why would that A-hole do that?

MARY: *(Offstage.)* He'd never heard of anyone being on Zoloft since fourth grade.

BERNICE: Uh-huh, uh-huh, well what the hell does he know—the man hangs around sick people all day. He has no idea the pressures I'm under.

MARY: *(Offstage.)* You *were* married to him, Ms. Snell.

BERNICE: Uh-huh, uh-huh. Only briefly. I spent more time married to the pharmacist. At least with him, I knew I would come home to a nice meal and a big bowl of Zoloft! OK . . . get on the horn and get that distributor to take back those dreidels.

MARY: *(Offstage.)* What excuse shall I use, Ms. Snell?

BERNICE: Start with . . . the good patrons of Chicago's newest and most brilliantly designed downtown church, St. Fabiola, sees no need in bringing Jews into the congregation blah blah blah, and sign your own name. I don't want my name on such a blasphemous letter. I think I'm having an attack . . .

MARY: *(Offstage.)* You're not smoking in there, are you, Ms. Snell?

BERNICE: Don't be a stupid monkey, Mary. It's just my usual panic.

MARY: *(Offstage.)* Because if you started smoking again, you made me promise I would tell your psychiatrist.

BERNICE: Uh-huh uh-huh . . . Well he can go straight to hell.

MARY: *(Offstage.)* He cares about you.

BERNICE: Marry a man for six months, he wants to run your life. I'm not smoking! *(Puts out cigarette.)* Mary. Has the giant two-story cross arrived at the warehouse yet?

MARY: *(Offstage.)* Yes, Ms. Snell.

BERNICE: Good, good. At least we are on schedule with that! That cross is the cornerstone of St. Fabiola and brings with it the religious strength and virtuosity blah blah blah that is going to take me to the pinnacle of my career and put me in the history books of great architects.

MARY: *(Offstage.)* It's got an extra plank of wood attached to it.

BERNICE: Holy crap!

MARY: *(Offstage.)* They tell me that instead of the standard—one up and one across plank—this one has one up, one across, and another one up. It looks like the number four.

BERNICE: I'm fucked.

MARY: *(Offstage. Knowing the truth.)* So that's not how you designed it, Ms. Snell?

BERNICE: Where's my *Ritalin*?

MARY: *(Offstage.)* Uh-huh, uh-huh—all out.

BERNICE: How can a person be paranoid in this office without their drugs! Christ Almighty—this whole project is shooting down the toilet. Where's Joseph? I need Joseph. What's Joseph doing?

MARY: *(Offstage.)* He's working on the plans for the rec center, Ms. Snell.

BERNICE: And Jesus *(Pronounced Haysuse.)*? Get his butt in here. This place is falling apart. And my asthma is a real bastard today.

MARY: *(Offstage.)* Yes, Ms. Snell.

BERNICE: You're a crackhead, Mary, you know that?

MARY: *(Offstage.)* I do the best with what I've got, Ms. Snell.

BERNICE: Everybody who has ever worked for me has disappointed me. Is my appointment here yet?

MARY: *(Offstage.)* She's in the ladies' room. Throwing up.

BERNICE: About seeing me? I'm a pussycat.

MARY: *(Offstage.)* You're an evil C-word, Ms. Snell, that's your reputation.

BERNICE: Who in God's name is saying that?

MARY: *(Offstage.)* Who isn't?

BERNICE: I have an exemplary reputation. I'll freakin' break the bloody neck of anyone who says otherwise. Now you march yourself into that bathroom and stop that woman from vomiting in my building.

MARY: *(Offstage.)* Yes, Ms. Snell.

(Bernice reaches for a cigarette, then changes her mind.)

BERNICE: Six months. Six months I've been trying to find someone to paint that god-forsaken mural in the new church vestibule. The entire project depends on it. Damn it, all I get are *taggers* and leftists who have no idea what this magnificent church blah blah blah is going to do to my career!

(She squats to pick up a pencil on the floor as Charlotte Burdick enters in a business suit, carrying giant portfolio too large for her to maneuver. She sees Bernice on the ground looking like she's praying. Bernice turns.)

BERNICE: Yeah. What the balls are you staring at?

CHARLOTTE: I thought . . . I thought you were . . . praying.

BERNICE: Uh-huh. Uh-huh. I pray my tits look better in this outfit then they do. That's what I would pray for.

(She bursts out laughing in a delayed beat. Charlotte is genuinely scared.)

BERNICE: Well. Don't stand there like a stalker. Come in.

(Charlotte sits.)

BERNICE: *(Into intercom.)* Mary. See that we're not interrupted.

MARY: *(Offstage.)* Yes, Ms. Snell.

BERNICE: Damn. You just interrupted me! By saying that—you just. Never mind!

MARY: *(Offstage.)* Yes, Ms. Snell.

(Bernice rolls her eyes.)

CHARLOTTE: Charlotte Burdick, my pleasure.

(She reaches out to shake Bernice's hand.)

BERNICE: I do shake. A little germ-phobic. I use antibacterial cream. *(Into intercom.)* Mary? *(Nothing.)* Mary? *(Nothing.)* Oh crap. Mary—you can interrupt, you lazy bitch!

MARY: *(Offstage. Her usual droll.)* Yes, Ms. Snell.

BERNICE: Where's my antibacterial cream?

MARY: *(Offstage.)* Do you want me to run into the supply closet and get another quart?

BERNICE: Forget it. Later you'll lather up and give me a full body scrub.

MARY: *(Offstage.)* Goodie. I'll skip lunch, Ms. Snell.

BERNICE: Have a seat. I've been looking forward to seeing your work.

CHARLOTTE: You have? You don't know what that means to me . . .

BERNICE: I say that to everybody without meaning it, don't get your smile going and all.

CHARLOTTE: I want to thank you so much for this opportunity.

BERNICE: I don't have to tell you St. Fabiola is going to be one of the great churches built in the twenty-first century in America.

CHARLOTTE: I hear only good things.

BERNICE: Of course. I'm in charge.

CHARLOTTE: —Except for the *dreidel* incident.

BERNICE: *(With an evil glare.)* What do you know about the . . . *dreidel* incident?

CHARLOTTE: Well, I was throwing up in the ladies' room . . .

BERNICE: Minor misunderstanding between executive—me—and the suppliers. We're opening on schedule, Ms. Burdick, I can assure you of that.

CHARLOTTE: Absolutely. I didn't want to join Poxner and Poser Architects because they are on schedule anyway, Ms. Snell.

BERNICE: Why did you want to join Poxner and Poser Architects?

CHARLOTTE: I wanted to join Poxner and Poser Architects because of you, Ms. Snell. I just never knew you were a—

BERNICE: *(Interrupts.)* I suppose everyone wants to work with me.

CHARLOTTE: Unless they're afraid. I have followed your career from the beginning. From Columbia University to apprenticing at Schmidt and Young. Your very first design. The Harvey Meat Packing Building in New York.

BERNICE: Oh you liked that one?

CHARLOTTE: I wouldn't get my meat anyplace else. I lived in New York four years just to get my meat there. And I'm vegetarian. I'd go and admire the details. And your Donnavan Library in Indianapolis. I stole books. Just to sit there. St. Fabiola's . . . From what I've read, it's going to be your crowning achievement.

BERNICE: *If.* . . if I had had the perfect mural.

CHARLOTTE: I brought sketches.

BERNICE: I'll be kind as always.

(Charlotte opens her portfolio crashing things off the desk.)

BERNICE: Don't be nervous. *You're* only human. Let me see . . . Yes . . . *(Holds up one drawing.)* Uh-huh uh-huh. Interesting. I see you went with a religious theme.

CHARLOTTE: It's a church, *sister.*

BERNICE: Sister? That's cute. You call me Bernice. Hmm. I see you have here on this side . . . the hand of God.

CHARLOTTE: Reaching out . . .

BERNICE: Reaching out to . . .

CHARLOTTE: That's the man. Representing all mankind.

BERNICE: Very original. And . . . what's this in the corner?

CHARLOTTE: That's the devil.

BERNICE: I see. And the devil in the picture represents . . .

CHARLOTTE: The devil.

BERNICE: Uh-huh. Uh-huh. In the church, they might not want to go this way. I'm not sure, but I can see your train of thought.

CHARLOTTE: Thank you.

BERNICE: Let's look at the others, shall we? *(Picks up another one.)* Jesus in the manger.

CHARLOTTE: That's one of my favorite ones.

BERNICE: And he's a little baby, but he has his fist raised up.

CHARLOTTE: He's yelling at God.

BERNICE: That's a middle finger.

CHARLOTTE: He's really *peeved.*

BERNICE: Yelling at God with a middle finger—Little Jesus pissed off at something, is he?

CHARLOTTE: Upset about the inhumanity here on earth.

BERNICE: Voicing his opinion at such a young age—reminds me of *me.* Well it certainly is throwing the church a curve.

CHARLOTTE: He's perturbed about the evils. The hurricanes. The tsunamis. And . . . very upset about the voting on *American Idol.*

BERNICE: Well, that would piss off a young baby Jesus, true.

MARY: *(Offstage.)* Ms. Snell, may I interrupt a moment?

BERNICE: *(Into intercom.)* Damn you, Mary. Do not interrupt me under any circumstances.

MARY: *(Offstage.)* Word from the construction site, Ms. Snell. Father Johnson is very upset about the location of the confessionary. It's next to the men's room.

BERNICE: Well, why didn't you interrupt me, you cow? *(She looks over the plans.)* Christ. Well it's all purging, right? Tell the Father to keep his collar on, and I'll see what I can do.

MARY: *(Offstage.)* He's crying, Ms. Snell.

BERNICE: Crying? Who is he, the pope? OK, tell him to hold off on the *stigmata* and wait for me to get there! And I'm not to be interrupted again, Mary!

MARY: *(Offstage.)* Yes, Ms. Snell.

BERNICE: She did it again. She interrupted me.

CHARLOTTE: You're a little brash for a religious person.

BERNICE: Religion. That's a crock.

CHARLOTTE: But you're . . . you're a . . .

BERNICE: Look what they got me wearing. Stupid thing. You can't see my hips! Or my sexy ass. And I have a fantastic ass. *(She shows Charlotte, who turns away.)* Not an ass girl?

CHARLOTTE: I feel very uncomfortable hearing about sexy asses and while you are in your sacrament, Ms. Snell.

BERNICE: My what? I feel like a giant Mallomar in here. And you can't see my cleavage, which is a damn shame. Sometimes I hate this job.

CHARLOTTE: Being a nun?

BERNICE: Being an architect. I'm not a nun.

CHARLOTTE: You're—

BERNICE: Oh, you moronic undergrad. This was for a fund-raiser. You thought I was a *real* nun?

CHARLOTTE: Thank goodness.

BERNICE: I know nothing about being a nun, lady. Or about building a church for that matter. But I'm playing the game. Like you, I have risen to the charge. Brought my entire soul to the cause. *(She looks at another drawing.)* You've drawn the cross.

CHARLOTTE: Yes. Jesus was put on the cross. Did you know that?

BERNICE: In fact, however, your cross has someone else hanging from it.

CHARLOTTE: Regis Philbin.

BERNICE: That would be Regis Philbin.

CHARLOTTE: —Mr. Philbin represents our addiction to television. Our turning our backs on family and moral discussion in place of reruns and faux-reality programming.

BERNICE: And you think the bishop would like this in St. Fabiola?

CHARLOTTE: If he has any balls.

(Charlotte laughs—exactly as Bernice did earlier. Bernice sits.)

BERNICE: Is there anything you want to tell me about your work, Miss Burdick?

CHARLOTTE: *I'm an atheist!*

BERNICE: *(Sarcastic.)* I'm shocked.

CHARLOTTE: In fact . . . Not only am I sure there is no God, but I can prove it. Here you are dressed like a nun.

BERNICE: For a fund-raiser.

CHARLOTTE: If there was an Almighty, he would be very angry at you. It's blasphemy. Maybe strike you down for insulting nuns everywhere.

BERNICE: Oh, think?

CHARLOTTE: Your use of bad language . . . and using his name in vain. But he doesn't do anything.

BERNICE: I feel fine.

CHARLOTTE: He lets it slide.

BERNICE: Never felt better in my life. And I didn't even take my tricyclic antidepressant today.

CHARLOTTE: Doesn't even comment on it by making it rain hard or thun-
derclap.

BERNICE: *(Into intercom.)* Mary? Is the sky blue today?

MARY: *(Offstage.)* Clear skies, Ms. Snell.

(Bernice is about to speak.)

MARY: Winds south at ten miles per hour.

(Bernice is about to speak.)

MARY: Humidity fifty-nine percent.

(Bernice is about to speak.)

MARY: Dew point fifty-three degrees.

(Bernice is about to speak.)

MARY: UV Index. Two.

BERNICE: Shut up, Mary.

MARY: *(Offstage.)* Yes, Ms. Snell.

CHARLOTTE: Watch this. *(Looks up.)* I HATE YOU! *(At her.)* Nothing.

BERNICE: He's ignoring you completely.

CHARLOTTE: I draw pictures of his greatest patrons. His son even. I mock him
with my drawings. But he takes no revenge upon me. I'm still alive.
Healthy. I never go to confession. And I've wished bad things on many
other people.

BERNICE: You seem so innocent.

CHARLOTTE: I prayed that any other artist coming in for this very assignment
would be hit by a truck, or get a social disease so horrible that *I* would
get the job.

BERNICE: I coveted my neighbor. And my neighbor's neighbor—when my
neighbor wasn't home.

CHARLOTTE: I lie. I've cheated. I have not totally honored thy father or thy
mother.

BERNICE: I have in times, purposely dishonored both those freaks.

CHARLOTTE: And I don't keep the Sabbath.

BERNICE: We are actually taunting God.

CHARLOTTE: If there *was* a God.

BERNICE: —And if there was a God, he would bring his wrath down upon us
and teach us a good lesson.

CHARLOTTE: So there can't be. What's the purpose of having an all-powerful
one, if he never punishes?

BERNICE: Hey. I got another one. I got another test.

(She leans in and kisses Charlotte on the mouth.)

CHARLOTTE: OH my God—what was that?

BERNICE: HOMOSEXUALITY, BABY!

CHARLOTTE: I can't believe you just did that during a job interview. And dressed like a nun.

BERNICE: Oh, I can fix that.

(She starts to take her top off.)

CHARLOTTE: No!

BERNICE: It's sexual harassment. God has got to do something now.

(They both look up, but all is silent.)

BERNICE: You know I always thought . . . hey, there has to be a God, I mean, why else would everyone be so busy talking about him if he didn't exist? Now I'm thinking . . . if I haven't been struck down—the way I talk to people, the way I run my business, even how I've treated you here today —then it's a clear case for the absolute definitive conclusion that there is no higher power. Get your lips over here . . . I'm kissing you again.

(Bernice chases Charlotte.)

CHARLOTTE: I've never kissed a girl.

BERNICE: Me either. But I bet you if God *was* up there, he wouldn't make anything taste so good be so wrong?

CHARLOTTE: Stop!

(They both freeze.)

BERNICE: What? You wanna screw? That'll really piss him off.

CHARLOTTE: He's not going to be pissed off.

BERNICE: Then you believe he's up there?

CHARLOTTE: Look. If . . . if he is watching us, he wouldn't get angry because he made us this way. He made you a cantankerous hard-nose, difficult-to-deal-with, impossible job interviewee. And he gave me extraordinary talent for an art school dropout.

BERNICE: *(She sits.)* People *are* afraid of me. Afraid to speak up and get fired. Maybe I *am* a cold, hard person. Maybe I should soften. Charlotte. All those things we taunted God with . . . all those reasons he should punish us . . . what if, what if he brought you here to me today in order for me to *recognize* him? To know that the way I've been behaving is punishable. But instead of hurting me, striking me dead with a bolt of powerful lightning, he's letting me change. And grow. And love him. All by myself.

CHARLOTTE: No. He brought me here to get a job. I need work.

BERNICE: He's teaching me to be more human. To love his words.

CHARLOTTE: No. It's for my heath insurance.

BERNICE: I've seen the light.

CHARLOTTE: I've seen a dentist and I need a root canal I can't afford.

BERNICE: *(Covering up.)* Please forgive me, My Savior, for my inappropriate lack of dress code. His mighty hand could crush me—but instead, his mighty brain has given me free will.

CHARLOTTE: Are you sending me directly to human resources, because I can start today.

BERNICE: You've given me the Lord's word, Charlotte. It wouldn't be right if I hired you for such a menial task. *(Glances at the drawings.)* And with sketches like those. No . . . You've proven God is watching me. Religion is in my life now. In my blood, and permeating my entire office. No more sleeping around. No more cursing or treating my secretary Mary like dirt.

MARY: *(Offstage.)* Thank you, Miss Snell.

BERNICE: *(Run to the intercom.)* Shut your face, Mary, I'm being healed by the Lord.

MARY: *(Offstage.)* Yes, Ms. Snell.

BERNICE: *(To Charlotte.)* I realize now divorcing five men *was* inappropriate.

CHARLOTTE: No surprise St. Fabiola is the patron saint of divorced people.

BERNICE: I've been a loser and a whore.

CHARLOTTE: No.

BERNICE: Yes. Ask anyone.

MARY: *(Offstage.)* She's been a loser and whore.

BERNICE: See. And I *pay* her. *(Ushers Charlotte to the door.)* Charlotte Burdick . . . Go. Go out and spread your consecrated word. And maybe some day we can work on a project together where you don't insult the Big Guy Upstairs.

CHARLOTTE: Are you sure? I really need this job—

BERNICE: Uh-huh. *(And she practically pushes Charlotte out. Then moves to the intercom.)* Mary?

MARY: *(Offstage.)* Yes, Ms. Snell?

BERNICE: I'm heading back down to the fund-raiser. *(Fixing the habit.)* I must speak with Father Johnson. Fix the *dreidel* incident. I want to be nice, Mary. God won't let me be happy until I prove I am worth saving. I'm going to be kind and considerate. Loyal and supportive. And then someone can love me. And I can finally get off Simethicone—for my infuriating flatulence. Yes, Mary . . . I'm going to join the church!
(Bernice exits.)

MARY: *(Offstage.)* Yes, Ms. Snell? Ms. Snell? Joseph and Haysuse are back from the site. Are you there? She's out of the office, boys. Yeah. Another revelation. This week she wanted to be gay. Every week something else. She'll never change. She can't. Why do you think they threw her out of the nunnery?

(Lights slowly fade to black.)

END OF PLAY

PLAYS FOR
THREE MEN

Current Season

VANESSA DAVID

Produced by Toy Boat Productions at Coho Theater, Portland,
Oregon, December 27–29, 2007, for the Third Annual
Happy F@*#ing Holidays Show. Directed by Ryan Cloutier.
Cast: Prancer—Brandon Van Buskirk; Donner—
James Chance; Dasher—Marx Marvelous.

CHARACTERS

PRANCER, Merritt Parkway light-up reindeer.
DONNER, union-built light-up reindeer.
DASHER, alpha light-up reindeer.

SETTING

The front lawn of a house in suburbia.

TIME

The present.

. . .

At rise: Three actors dressed in black wearing reindeer antlers and wrapped in white Christmas lights. Posed on a lawn.

PRANCER: So, you guys, it looks like this is it! The big guy takes us down tomorrow.

DONNER/DASHER: Yep. Guess so.

PRANCER: It was really great working with you guys this season. I mean, yeah, we're in the shed together all year, but spending the holidays with you guys, out here on the front lawn, instead of out back in the woods looking down on the Merritt Parkway . . . what a lonely place that was.

DONNER: Wouldn't know. He didn't pick *me* to go out there. I don't know *why*. We come from the same *factory*, same *manufacturer*. I don't know what makes *you* better than *me*.

DASHER: He's not better than you, just *different*. He's facing out—you're facing down. I guess that's what the big guy wanted out there on the Merritt Parkway. C'mon now, it's our last night outside, let's make the most of it.

(Silence.)

DONNER: I'm glad I haven't seen them kids.

PRANCER: What kids?

DASHER: They're a year older now. Don't worry.

PRANCER: What kids?!

DONNER: None of your business!

PRANCER: What kids? We spent the last ten months in a six-by-eight shed and you never once mentioned any kids.

DONNER: Never mind the kids!

PRANCER: I want to see some kids! Have 'em climb on my back—that would be awesome!

DONNER: Oh, it would, huh?

DASHER: Why don't we change the subject—

DONNER: Screw you and them goddamn kids!

PRANCER: Shh! Watch your language!

DONNER: You wanna know what them kids did to me and him? They put us in all sorts of positions.

DASHER: You don't have to tell him—

DONNER: Sexual positions.

DASHER: OK! You've said enough. Now let's just—

PRANCER: What are they?

DONNER: All I know is they're humiliating! People would drive by and laugh at us. And point at ME! I was on the bottom.

PRANCER: But what does "sexual" mean?

DASHER: Well, actually, I heard the old man referring to them as homosexual. But I still don't know what it means.

PRANCER: Well, if people were laughing at it maybe it means "funny."

DONNER: Well, I don't want people to think I'm funny! I'm a serious light-up reindeer here! I was built for a specific purpose—to fulfill a basic human need. To celebrate the holiday season with light—light is color, light is life. Its white creates space, opportunity, beyond, infinity. Man's ability to capture light and shape it in order to create replicas of earth's life-forms, the land's own living creatures, and then to proudly place these sculptures of living light on his front lawn for all to see as a symbol of his stature, his place in life, in the world—a bold statement of opulence tempered with holiday traditions. I am a light-up reindeer and I refuse to be thought of as funny.

PRANCER: Wow. I guess I never thought of it like that. I kinda liked it when people would laugh at me in the woods above the Merritt. At least they saw me. I brought a little pleasure to their lives, some cheer—some holiday cheer. Isn't that what it's all about? If being in homosexual positions brings holiday cheer to the people, then I'm all for it. Bring on the kids.

DASHER: No! We only have one more night. Let's stay in the same position we've been in all season. For once!

DONNER: Wha'da ya mean for once, this is only our second year.

DASHER: Your second year. I had another light reindeer compadre two seasons ago. He didn't make it to New Year's Eve.

PRANCER: What happened?

DONNER: Those goddamn kids!

PRANCER: Where did you get that mouth?

DONNER: A union electrician. Where'd you get yours?

DASHER: BOYS!

DONNER: He's all, "where'd you get that mouth." Excuse me Mr. Looking Down on the Merritt Parkway.

DASHER: STOP IT!

PRANCER: Tell us what happened!

DASHER: Absolutely not! This is our last night on the outside. I want to stand here, plugged in, posed the same way the old man posed me in the beginning of the season. Nothing homosexual, nothing "funny," nothing broken or busted— *(Stops himself.)* I'm going to stand here quietly and enjoy the electricity going through me. *(Long silence.)* Ahh . . .
(Silence.)

PRANCER: So, did I miss anything else last year?

DONNER: What's the matter with you, can't you leave a reindeer alone?

PRANCER: Who, you?

DONNER: No, him. And me too! You've done nothing but run your possibly nonunion mouth since Thanksgiving!

PRANCER: Well we can—no one's home. The whole family's out shopping for one another, the whole neighborhood!

DONNER: Well here's a tip—just 'cause you've got the opportunity to talk doesn't mean you have to take it.

PRANCER: Well excuse me, Mr. Reindeer Etiquette. Spend one lousy season with another reindeer—you know everything about social interaction. You didn't even know about the other reindeer! You couldn't have talked *that* much!

DONNER: You know what? I'm over here with my HEAD pointing to the ground like I'm eating something—when, in fact, I don't even NEED to eat. I run on electricity, for God's sake. I don't even need to be makin' constant conversation—just to hear my own VOICE! Just to know that I'm here, on the lawn, that I'm real, that the big guy cares about me and that I'm an important part of the holiday season. I don't need to TALK ALL THE GODDAMN TIME TO KNOW THAT!
(Beat.)

PRANCER: Oh. You didn't have to be rude about it.

DONNER: There you go again—

DASHER: PLEASE! Please be quiet.

DONNER: Look. He's not gonna shut up until you tell your story—right? And then we're ALL gonna be quiet and enjoy our current. Right, Mr. Merritt Parkway?

PRANCER: Deal.

DASHER: No deal.

(Silence.)

PRANCER: C'mon. *(Pause.)* Please. *(Pause.)* Pretty please.

DONNER: Just tell the goddamn story and get it over with.

DASHER: *(Beat.)* I was right out of the box. Brand new. The old man put me out on the lawn. A few minutes later, he brought out the other guy. Looking down, just like you. We stood there forever before we spoke, days. We were both nervous, tentative . . . about the whole thing really. I mean, here we were, the first in the neighborhood. Light-up reindeer on the front lawn. Cars slowed down to look at us. People walking by would stop and stare. Some people liked us, but some people—well, some of the words people used to describe us. We could tell by the tone of their voice it wasn't good. When people pointed and laughed at us, it had nothing to do with Christmas cheer. It was stopping to piss on us, kick us over, hang their empties on our antlers—it was awful, humiliating, degrading. But every morning, the old man would be out here, putting us back up, cleaning us off. *(Pause.)* It must've started slowly, or I didn't notice, but one day, while being set up straight again by the old man, I saw he had started to lose it. The shine was gone, the finish. He couldn't really stand straight anymore, one of his antlers was cracked. The nightly attacks had taken their toll. He was never much of a talker, not like you Prancer, but he started to talk to me about the end—of the season, of his time on the lawn. It was slowly killing him, he said. His frame was broken in two places, twice epoxied by the old man. Some of his bulbs were busted, the tape holding his antler together had to be replaced, it was starting to overheat and the glue—it smelled. The old man took the tape off to replace it one day, after setting us up straight, yet again. And, the weight of the antler, well it just snapped—and then he kicked at Dancer. Screaming some kind of carnal, base, mammalian sound. It shook the universe, stopped time, and rendered me as useless as a light-up reindeer as I watched my only friend be destroyed by the very man that had given him reason to exist. And then as quickly as he'd lost it, his anger turned to pain, and he collapsed in the snow, sobbing and groaning and crying. It was almost pitiful. And then I realized, he saw everything as an attack on him . . . Every time something was done to us, it was done to him. These people were his neighbors.

How could they be so crude and callous during the height of the holiday season? What was it about them, about their character, what flaw did they possess? What did they find so threatening? Why did they find it necessary to lash out at their fellow man? At me. At my fellow reindeer. *(Pause.)* I never got any answers. He unplugged me and put me away right then. I never got to see New Year's Eve. And I never saw my reindeer friend again. I thought I'd be left in the shed forever, maybe I'd come out for a tag sale in the spring. But somehow the old man found it in his heart to take me out again and to buy me two new reindeer friends. And for that I am thankful. It's nice to have a purpose in life. A reason for being. I try to focus on that, the good stuff. I don't want to think about the bad. I don't understand it, and I may never understand.

PRANCER: Wow, man. I'm sorry.

DONNER: Well I'm glad you're here, Dasher. I'm honored to be here with you.

PRANCER: Well, yeah, me too!

DASHER: Well, now that I've told my story, let's all be quiet and ring in the New Year with the hum of electricity running through our frames.

DONNER: You got it, big guy.

PRANCER: Absolutely.

(Silence.)

DASHER: Oh, uh. Happy New Year.

DONNER/PRANCER: Happy New Year.

(Lights fade. Blackout.)

END OF PLAY

The Title Fight

IAN AUGUST

Originally produced by Poofyboo Productions at Chernuchin
Theater, New York City, June 6, 2006, as part of the 31st
annual Samuel French Off-Off Broadway Short Play Festival.
Directed by Ken Wiesinger. Cast: Teddy—Eben Gordon;
Milo—Shannon Michael Wamser; Dad—David Conley.
Also produced by EndTimes Productions at EndTimes
Underground at the Gene Frankel Theatre, New York City,
February 1–17, 2008, as part of Vignettes for the Apocalypse
2008, Second Annual One-Act Festival, where it was named
"Best Drama." Directed by Tony Macy-Perez. Cast: Teddy—
Alessandro Collo; Milo—Patrick McDaniel;
Dad—Jimmy Blackman.

Special thanks to Eben Gordon, David Ian Lee, Mike Folie, the support of the Quorum, the Stage One Writer's Group, Russell Dobular and EndTimes Productions, Ken Wiesinger, and, of course, my Emcee.

CHARACTERS

> TEDDY, late twenties, older brother.
> MILO, midtwenties, younger brother.
> DAD, fifties, dead.

SETTING:

> The backyard of the house the boys grew up in.

TIME

> The present.

. . .

The stage is bare except for two men: Teddy, the shorter of the two, in khakis and a button-up shirt; Milo, in ripped jeans and a T-shirt. Neither man wears shoes. They circle one another.

TEDDY: Are you ready?

MILO: Go for it.

TEDDY: 'Cause I'm not gonna pull any punches.

DAD: Boys, don't pull punches. When somebody whales on you, you whale right back on them. Did Patton pull punches?

MILO AND DAD: Did Schwartzenegger pull punches?

TEDDY: Schwartzenegger isn't a real person.

MILO: Don't be so stupid, of course he is.

TEDDY: I mean, he's not really a war hero or anything. It's a useless analogy.

DAD: I'm dead, I can make useless analogies.

TEDDY: You use that excuse all the time.

DAD: I'm dead, I can use excuses more than once.

TEDDY: Easy out.

MILO: So come on—I don't have all day.

(Teddy to the audience.)

TEDDY: There was a little patch of dead grass in the backyard, trampled yellow stalks. We went camping when I was a kid, pitched the tent right there, and spent one night in sleeping bags hitting each other with pillows and flashlights and steel-toed boots and around four in the morning, we got called inside.

(Lighting shift, the boys are younger—five and seven.)

DAD: Teddy! Milo! Come inside!

MILO: What is it?

TEDDY: Do you have more chips? We're hungry!

DAD: Get inside—your mother's going to the hospital.

(Lighting shift.)

TEDDY: That was the first time.

MILO: Remember that? She collapsed on the toilet, hit her head on the tub.

TEDDY: We didn't take down the tent for two months. By then, the grass underneath stopped trying to heal itself. It just gave up.

(Beat.)

MILO: You calling "uncle"?

TEDDY: Not on your life, pipsqueak.

MILO: So let's do this.

TEDDY: Fine.

DAD: Teddy, keep your hands level with your eyes—Milo, don't dance—nobody fucking dances anymore. It's a goddamned title fight, not a fucking ballet.

TEDDY: Yeah, Baryshnikov—

MILO: Who? You're such a faggot.

TEDDY: I'm just saying—

(Milo slaps Teddy.)

DAD: Fists! Dammit, use your fists! None of that open-handed bullshit.

MILO: Fists, right. Fists. Come here, you little bastard.

TEDDY: Go to hell.

(Milo to the audience.)

MILO: Already there and back. At home, on the stairs. She never cried, she had a weak heart but she never cried. I watched her stumble up the steps, holding onto the banister with two fingers from each hand. Knuckles white, skin pale, legs blue and veiny and weak. I propped her up with my shoulder.

(Lighting shift.)

DAD: Stop bugging your mother, she needs to do it on her own. Doctor's orders.

MILO: My hands are fine, Mom, just use mine.

DAD: What did I just tell you?

MILO: But she needs—

DAD: Milo!

MILO: But—

(Lighting shift.)

TEDDY: Stop using words. Stop speaking. You've got a vocabulary like a seven-year-old. I hate it when you speak.

MILO: Aaaaaasssss hooooole.

TEDDY: Is that a new one? Two syllables, that's a lot.

DAD: Boys, quiet down, your mother's trying to sleep.

(They stop sparring, the lights shift. Milo and Teddy are six and eight.)

MILO: Sorry, Dad.

TEDDY: Sorry, Dad.

DAD: Come here, boys, sit here. I need to talk to you.

TEDDY: What's up, Dad?

MILO: Teddy hit me with a book on the head. Should I hit him, Dad? Should I hit him back?

DAD: *(Exhausted.)* Sure, Milo. Give him a lick.

(Milo punches Teddy in the arm.)

TEDDY: Ouch! Jesus!

DAD: None of that!

TEDDY: Sorry.

DAD: Look boys, about your mother.

MILO: She's supposed to come to school tomorrow night.

DAD: Don't interrupt. Look, your mother is going to be away for a few weeks.

TEDDY: In the hospital?

DAD: Yeah. She needs some time away from you two. So I want you to be on best behavior. None of this running-around crap, and if there's a problem, you two work it out on your own. No yelling, no screaming, just go out to the dead patch in the backyard and solve your problem.

MILO: Solve the problem.

TEDDY: Dumbass—

(Teddy pushes Milo on the side of the head. Milo goes down. The lights return to normal.)

MILO: Cheap shot—Jes—Fuck!

TEDDY/DAD: There's no such thing as a cheap shot—

MILO: You never understood rules. Go for the chest, go for the legs, the arms—

MILO/DAD: Not the head. Too much explaining to the neighbors.

TEDDY: I understand just fine. But if I played by your rules, I'd always lose. You're too cutthroat. Any opportunity, you take it. Any opening, you go for it.

DAD: There's an opening! Milo! What the fuck are you waiting for? Christmas?

TEDDY: You've got no moral censor—you're just a ham-fisted ignorant hick!

DAD: Stop talking! Fight! Solve the problem!

MILO: I'm not smart as you, Teddy, I'm not clever. A man has to learn early on how to get what he deserves.

TEDDY: Take it.

MILO: You got the birthright, the opportunity—after that, what was left?

TEDDY: You had choices—

MILO: To what? *Do* what? I had nothing but my hands. You got soft, educated man. Real soft.

TEDDY: Shut up!

MILO: I never had a shot in hell—

(Lights shift again.)

DAD: Milo—turn off the TV—your mother's dead.

MILO: What?

DAD: Don't get soft on me, boy. Your mother's dead, and I don't have the money to waste on you going ahead with your schooling. If you think you can beat that out of your brother, have at him, but he's got a head start. I'm already invested in him.

MILO: So what am I supposed to do?

DAD: You're gonna work. You're almost a man, Milo, suck it up. No crying. You'll work for a living and you'll bring money home and you'll help me pay for your brother's education. He's got a shot.

MILO: He's got a shot.

DAD: Look, kiddo, if you want something, you go for it. You take it. Don't let no schoolin' stop you from taking what you deserve. Teddy!

TEDDY: Yes, sir?

DAD: Don't fuck up, buddy, or I'll have your brother kick your ass. Those are the rules.

(Lights shift.)

TEDDY: So I fucked up. Not everybody graduates from college. But I made my life—nobody handed anything to me on a plate. I worked for all that I have. I didn't let anybody tell me what to do.

MILO: Milo, send your paycheck to Teddy. Milo, gotta take a second job. Milo, come and help me fix this fucking alternator. Yeah, I had a lot of time to make *my* life.

DAD: You know what you boys need? A good boxing match. My pop used to send me and your uncle onto the street to duke it out. Made us stronger. Made us appreciate each other more. Learn to take opportunities as they come.

TEDDY: You worked with Dad—you were happy! How should I know you wanted to go to school?

MILO: I didn't have a choice! You had the choice! You had everything!

TEDDY: And that's it? This is why you want this—to fuck me over? Just a one-two punch in the ribs for big brother Teddy?

MILO: No more bullshit.

TEDDY: I guess not. So come on.

MILO: Sounds good to me.

(They circle one another through the next monologue, occasionally lashing out, never striking a blow.)

DAD: So I'm dead. Yep, I'm dead. Bet you can't even see me is how dead I am. It's been a short and terrible life. Wife up and left early—I'll be giving her a piece when I see her. Boys are failures. But then, boys are always failures. Think they can get your love and respect by hanging on every word you say. Truth is, I don't respect anybody who can't spit in my face.

TEDDY: I don't know what you want.

(Milo swings. Teddy ducks.)

DAD: So here goes:

MILO: Everything I never had.

(Teddy jabs. Milo hops out of the way.)

DAD: Listen up!

TEDDY: I don't owe you anything.

MILO: Like hell.

DAD: My Last Will and Testament.

(The boys stop, listen.)

DAD: My entire estate goes to *one* of my two sons. And boys—I'm dead. Solve your own damn problems."

(Milo and Teddy rush one another, wrestle each other to the ground. After a brief struggle, Milo pins Teddy to the ground. He draws back his right arm, prepares to punch Teddy in the face.)

TEDDY: Stop, Milo— Stop it! This is stupid— We don't have to do this.

MILO: I keep hearing his voice.

TEDDY: Me too.

MILO: It's freaking me out.

TEDDY: Jesus, Milo. If you want it so bad, take it.

MILO: What?

TEDDY: The car, the money, the house. I don't want it. I don't want any of it.

(Pause.)

MILO: Teddy.

TEDDY: What?

    (Pause.)

MILO: This is all I know how to do.

TEDDY: I know.

DAD: That's right, kiddo. Don't pull punches.

    (Lights go black as Milo punches down.)

END OF PLAY

PLAYS FOR
TWO MEN
AND
TWO WOMEN

Intervention

MARK LAMBECK

Produced by the Stratford Arts Guild in association with the
SquareWrights Playwright Group at Stratford Theater,
Stratford, Connecticut, September 14–15, 2007, as part of
Comic Timing, a one-act festival. Directed by Tom Rushen.
Cast: Julia—Teresa Kona-Leone; Mike—Robert Watts;
Amy—Linda Doheny; Craig—David Victor.

JULIA, early thirties, a pushy, female executive-type.

MIKE, late thirties, Craig's best friend and Julia's husband.

AMY, early thirties, Craig's loving wife.

CRAIG, late thirties, an accountant who is unaffiliated, the object of the intervention.

SETTING

Various street locations; no set required.

TIME

The present.

PROPS

JULIA, a shoulder bag and a cell phone.

MIKE, a cell phone.

AMY, a shoulder bag and a cell phone.

CRAIG, an attaché case.

• • •

At rise, Mike walks on downstage left with a cell phone at his ear. He continues walking in place once he reaches his mark.

MIKE: *(Into phone.)* Did you talk to Amy?

JULIA: *(Walks on downstage right with a cell phone, walking in place.)* He's coming.

MIKE: How'd she do it?

JULIA: She told him it was our anniversary and he had to help us celebrate at La Scala.

MIKE: Anniversary? *(Looks at phone, quickly presses a few buttons—-beeping sounds—till he gets to his calendar.).*

JULIA: I heard that!

MIKE: *(Finds calendar.)* But our anniversary's in June. *(Pause.)* Right?

JULIA: Are you trying to piss me off?

MIKE: No . . . I.

JULIA: I heard the beeping. I know you were surfing through your calendar to check the date.

MIKE: No. I wouldn't forget . . .

JULIA: *(Annoyed.)* Can we just focus on Craig for a minute, please?

MIKE: Sure. I'm with ya.

JULIA: I'm walking down Chapel headed toward Elm. Where are you?

MIKE: *(Still walking in place.)* I'm at Arbor heading toward Main. *(Pause.)* Look, are you sure we're doing the right thing?

JULIA: He's refused to join the rest of modern civilization. He's refused to adapt. He blew up at Amy when she even suggested it. She needs us there. We don't know how he's gonna react.

MIKE: What? Craig's not gonna get violent. I've known him since high school. Accountants don't throw punches.

JULIA: He got into a screaming match with Amy.

MIKE: We're all in this together. He knows we all love him. *(Pause.)* Plus, we can take him!

JULIA: I don't wanna take him. Craig's our friend. We're just looking out for his best interest. *(Intent.)* He has to understand that this intervention is for his own good. He can't go on refusing . . . Oh. Hold on, I have another call coming in. *(Presses buttons.)* Hello?

MIKE: *(Looks at phone, reads text message.)* Where are you two? With the letters R, U, and the number two. Gotta love text messaging.

JULIA: What? I can't hear you. What? Oh, hi Ian. Sorry. Bad connection. You're in the lobby? He hasn't left his office yet? What? You're breaking up. Move outside so you can get a better signal. Wait. Hold on a minute. *(Presses button.)*

MIKE: So what's the story?

JULIA: I have Ian on the other line. He's in the lobby at Craig's work.

MIKE: In the lobby? Man, is he crazy? He could be spotted.

JULIA: I know. I didn't even get to say anything yet. He keeps cutting out. Look, we're running out of time. He's still on the other line . . .

MIKE: I just got a text message from Chuck. He's at Point Zero wondering where we are. We were supposed to be the first ones there, and we haven't even gotten to our meeting point yet! Oh, hang on, honey, I'm getting another call. *(Pushes button.)* Hello?

JULIA: *(Pushes button.)* Are you there, Ian? Yeah. Better. Look, you gotta stay out of sight. He's gonna know something's up.

AMY: *(Enters upstage on a cell phone.)* Mike, where are you guys? I tried calling Julia but it went straight to her voice mail.

JULIA: Hold on a minute, Ian, I got a new voice mail. *(Pushes button.)*

MIKE: That's because she's on the other line with Ian. I have her on hold.

AMY: We're never gonna pull this. Craig's resisted for so long. I think he actually prides himself on being the last person in America who . . . Hold on. I have another call coming in. *(Presses button.)* Hello?

JULIA: He's what? Oh my God. Don't let him see you!

AMY: I know, Chuck. They're late. The plan is to intercept him on Main before he gets to La Scala. Just wait outside the restaurant—we'll see you. I have Mike on hold now. He's got Julia on the other line . . . Hello? Are you there? I'm losing you. Chuck? Hello?

JULIA: He what? Oh my God. How did that happen? Is he OK? No. Wait. I'm texting Mike right now. *(Presses buttons. Back into the phone.)*

AMY: Lost him. *(Presses button.)*. Hello? Mike? Are you there?

MIKE: Yeah. I'm here.

AMY: Chuck called to find out where everybody is. But I lost him.

MIKE: I know. He just texted me, "Where R – U – 2?"

JULIA: You know, they shouldn't be cleaning those floors till after six. They're lucky he didn't get hurt. He's not hurt, is he Ian?

AMY: I don't know why I let you guys talk me into this. Craig is adamant.

MIKE: Look Amy, it's under control. All the spotters are in place. Ian's at Craig's office. Chuck is at Point Zero. Julia's on her way, and I'm walking toward Main right now. Where are you?

AMY: I'm just turning onto Main.

MIKE: We'll meet you at the corner of Main and Hollister in *(Looks at watch.)* ten minutes.

JULIA: What? Say that again. I can't hear you.

AMY: I'm really having second thoughts. Craig's gonna think we're ganging up on him.

MIKE: We ARE ganging up on him! That's what you do in an intervention. Craig's my best friend. We only want to . . . Oh, hold on, Amy, I'm getting a text message. *(Puts her on hold. Reads.)*. Craig fell in the lobby. Got up. Looks OK. Oh, man! *(Presses button.)* Amy? OK, now don't panic . . .

AMY: You know it's never comforting to the person you're talking to when you tell them "don't panic."

MIKE: Apparently Craig fell in the lobby but he's fine.

AMY: Oh my God. What happened?

MIKE: Wait, there's another text message.

JULIA: OK, I'll check. You just sent it through?

MIKE: *(Reads.)* Uh, Amy, put me on hold and check your phone e-mail. Ian shot some video of Craig's fall on his cell and e-mailed it.

JULIA: *(Presses buttons. Looks at phone.)* Got it. Great action shot. You sure he's OK. Looks like a nasty spill.

AMY: Wait. Something's coming in. *(Pulls phone away, then back into it.).* It's an e-mail from Chuck. What's going on? Is Craig OK?

MIKE: Hang on, Amy. *(Holds phone away to look at it.)* OK, Chuck's e-mail has a link to the video footage Ian sent. Apparently, it shows Craig getting up and moving. Ya see? He's fine.

JULIA: *(Into phone.)* Nice video work, Ian. Did you send this to Amy? You know how she worries.

MIKE: Amy? Are you there?. Did you check out the video? Amy? Hello?

AMY: *(Looking at phone video.)* I can't believe Craig wore that red tie today. I told him to go with the blue. He never listens to me.

JULIA: That video footage is hilarious. *(Giggles.)* The way his portfolio flew up in the air like that and his leg bent under.

MIKE: Amy?

AMY: *(Presses buttons; listens.)* Hello?

MIKE: Man, I thought I lost you.

AMY: I'm here. I was watching the video.

JULIA: Good work, Ian. Now get out of there before he sees you. We'll call you later and let you know how it goes. *(Presses buttons.)*

MIKE: Hang on, I got another call coming in. *(Presses button.)* Hello?

JULIA: Mike? Good you're still there. Look, I got a voice mail from Amy.

MIKE: I know. I have her on the other line right now.

JULIA: Great! Conference me in.

MIKE: Hang on. *(Presses buttons.)* Hello? Amy are you still there?

AMY: I'm still here.

MIKE: Julia? Can you hear me?

JULIA: Loud and clear.

AMY: Hi, Julia.

JULIA: Hi, Ames. Where ARE you?

AMY: I'm on Main heading toward Hollister.

MIKE: That was fast. Me too.

JULIA: Amy, I know you're worried but it's gonna be fine. Mike and Chuck and me will be there with you.

AMY: What about Ian?

JULIA: He was just a spotter. I sent him home. We don't want to overwhelm Craig. That Ian . . . so quick with the camera work, huh?

MIKE: Fastest thumbs on the East Coast.

AMY: Oh . . . you guys. I knew I can depend on you. I'm so grateful . . .

JULIA: What are friends for?

MIKE: Oh, man! I think I see him coming. *(Pointing to distance.)* Way down the street. Where are you now Amy?

AMY: *(Coming up behind him on phone; taps Mike.)* Turn around.

MIKE: *(Yelps and literally jumps.)* Ahhhhh . . . Jesus!

JULIA: What's going on?

MIKE: Amy's here. We can see Craig down the street. Where are you?

JULIA: I'm on Hollister. I'll be there in a minute.

MIKE: *(To Amy.)* Should we duck behind a bush or something?

AMY: Craig just came from work—he's still deep in thought.

MIKE: Right, he won't even see us until he's practically on top of us.

JULIA: *(Exits stage left.)* OK, I see you guys on the street. Look left.

(Mike and Amy both look left. They start waving.

AMY: *(Waving.)* Hey, Julia!

MIKE: Here he comes.

CRAIG: *(Enters limping – almost walks into Mike.)* Oh excuse . . . Mike? Amy? I thought you guys were gonna meet me at La Scala. *(Looks at watch.)* Am I late?

AMY: *(Takes his arm.)* No, sweetie. *(Rubs his back.)* You're fine.

MIKE: Everything's gonna be fine.

CRAIG: *(Confused.)* What?

JULIA: *(Enters stage right coming up behind Craig.)* We're here for you, Craig. You know how much we all care about you.

CRAIG: Julia? What are you talking about?

MIKE: It's time you faced reality, Craig.

JULIA: You can't hold out any longer. You HAVE to give in.

AMY: Oh, sweetie. I love you! It's for your own good.

MIKE: We all love you, man!

JULIA: *(Opens purse, takes out a cell phone.)* Here. Take it. It's yours.

CRAIG: What? NO!

MIKE: You're the last man in America without a cell phone.

JULIA: Did you really think you could hold out forever?

CRAIG: NO! I won't take it.

JULIA: Grab him!

(Mike and Amy both grab Craig as he struggles to pull away.)

JULIA: *(Putting cell in Craig's hand.)* Your number is 918-2773.

CRAIG: NO! *(Gets loose; drops portfolio and puts his hands over his ears; yells.)* NO! *(Looks at Mike, then Amy.)* My God. How could you?

MIKE: We could because we're your friends, man.

AMY: I'm your wife. I love you.

JULIA: This is an intervention, Craig.

CRAIG: But an intervention is for someone who's addicted to something. YOU'RE the ones addicted to cell phones. Everyone's obsessed! *(Raising his voice.)* People walking down the street with earpieces looking like they're talking to themselves. Car crashes because drivers are on hands-free systems. The other day I was in the men's room and the guy in the next stall was making a business deal on his cell while . . . multitasking!

AMY: Sweetie, it's time.

CRAIG: My God—even my own wife.

AMY: Please Craig. I worry about you when you go on those bike rides alone without your wallet, without ID. What if you were hit by a car?

MIKE: With a cell phone, you could call for help.

JULIA: You could program in an ICE.

CRAIG: An Ice?

MIKE: I-C-E. In case of emergency. They could speed-dial Amy.

AMY: It's for your own safety.

JULIA: What if you broke down on the road and couldn't call Triple-A?

CRAIG: No! It's a cult. You're the ones who need an intervention!

MIKE: What if you were running late and were supposed to meet Amy at her mother's, but you were stuck in traffic—while she worried.

AMY: Or if I needed you to pick up a pizza for dinner.

MIKE: Or I cancelled our squash court because I twisted my ankle and you were already heading for the Y.

CRAIG: No. I can't do it!

JULIA: What if Amy sent you to pick up her favorite shampoo and there you were, in the personal-care aisle, looking over rows and rows . . .

MIKE: Shelves and shelves . . .

JULIA: Of hair products but you couldn't remember the one she wanted!

AMY: All you'd have to do is call.

CRAIG: But what about the monthly bill? Roaming charges. Minutes that should have rolled over but didn't. Contracts that lock you in for two years even if the service sucks. Erroneous charges they won't remove. *(Hyperventilating.)* Text messaging fees!!!

MIKE: *(Patting Craig.)* Take a deep breath, buddy. We've all been there.

JULIA: It's part of being a member of a technologically advanced society.

MIKE: Yeah, you don't wanna be an outcast, man.

(Cell rings. Amy, Julia, and Mike dive for their phones.)

JULIA: *(Holding up her phone victoriously.)* It's me. Hello? Not now, Ian. I'll call you when it's over. *(Hangs up.)*

AMY: *(To Craig.)* It's so humiliating when I can't reach you at a moment's notice. At work, my coworkers look at me with pity when I have to leave a message on the land line at your office.

JULIA: I hear they're reviewing legislation mandating everyone over the age of six carries a cell phone. For emergencies.

MIKE: So kids won't get nabbed by psychos.

JULIA: Our government can't be responsible if someone can't reach 911.

CRAIG: *(Starts breaking down.)* Oh my God. I can't. I just . . .

JULIA: It's all about accessibility.

MIKE: Yeah, man, don't you want to be accessible?

(A cell phone rings again. Julia, Amy, and Mike all dive into their purses/pockets to retrieve theirs again.)

JULIA: *(Holding up phone.)* It's me! *(Presses button.)* Hello? Chuck? Yes. It's done. No. He's actually holding it in his hand.

CRAIG: *(Looks at the phone in his hand.)* My God, I'm holding it in my hand.

JULIA: We'll be there in a few minutes. What? You're breaking up.

AMY: *(Comforting Craig.)* Oh, sweetie, you'll grow to love it. You'll grow to depend on it just like the rest of us.

JULIA: Ian posted the video of Craig's fall on YouTube? *(Looks at the others excitedly.)* It's already gotten over a thousand hits?

MIKE: Hey, man, you're a star.

CRAIG: Oh my God. Ian was there? How did he . . . ?

AMY: Call your mother. I'll show you how to program in her number.

JULIA: Chuck, I gotta go. I promised Ian I'd call him when it was over.

(A cell phone rings again.)

MIKE/AMY: *(Together. Answering their phones.)* Hello?

(Blackout.)

END OF PLAY

PLAYS FOR
THREE MEN
AND
ONE WOMAN

Guys, Only Guys!

JEROME PARISSE

Original production performed at Gasworks Theatre,
Melbourne, Australia, January 22–26, 2008, as part of the
Pink Shorts Festival. Directed by Mark Wilson.
Cast: Gabriel—Ian Carlsson; David—Lance Twentyman;
Frank—Kliment Poposki; Sarah—Galit Klas.

For John.

<small>CHARACTERS</small>
  <small>GABRIEL</small>, male, the archangel of resurrection, majestic, soft spoken.
  <small>DAVID</small>, thirty-something, slim, a little unruly.
  <small>FRANK</small>, male, an angel, helper of Gabriel.
  <small>SARAH</small>, female, an angel, helper of Gabriel.

<small>SETTING</small>
  Gabriel's office, somewhere between death and life.

<small>TIME</small>
  The present.

●   ●   ●

The stage is in darkness and light music can be heard in the background. Lights come up. An archangel is sitting at a desk with a computer in front of him. He is Gabriel. He is busy typing. Someone knocks at the door. Gabriel stops what he is doing. He speaks very softly.

GABRIEL: Come in.
  (A man enters the stage and looks cautiously around. He is David.)
GABRIEL: Don't be afraid. Please, come in.
  (David takes a few steps forward, unsure.)
DAVID: Hi.
  (David stops. Gabriel points at the chair in front of his desk.)
GABRIEL: Please, take a seat.
  (David sits down and looks around. Gabriel smiles at him.)
GABRIEL: No need to be nervous. Relax. *(Gabriel looks at his computer screen.)*
  Your name was David Williamson, is that right?
DAVID: Yes, it was.
GABRIEL: You've asked to see me. Does this mean you're ready?
DAVID: I am.
GABRIEL: I hope you realize reincarnation is not for the fainthearted . . .
DAVID: I do.
GABRIEL: Once you've made your decision, there's no turning back . . .
DAVID: I completely understand . . . I'm ready.

GABRIEL: Excellent. *(Gabriel types something on his keyboard and looks at the screen, frowning.* Um . . . My records tell me you've . . . how shall I put it . . . behaved inappropriately during your previous life . . .
(David stares at his feet.)

GABRIEL: You beat your wife and got drunk most weekends . . . And you let her down at the time she needed you most, when she was diagnosed with breast cancer! . . . There's even a mention of tax evasion and road rage. What on earth do you think you were doing, David?

DAVID: I'm sorry.

GABRIEL: I'm not sure you realize how serious this is. It's been a long time since I've seen something so . . . so . . . . so . . . I can't even find the right word!

DAVID: I've changed.

GABRIEL: We shall see.

DAVID: I have. I promise.

GABRIEL: All right then. To make up for your former shortcomings, you will be given a hurdle in your next life.
(Gabriel picks up a box from underneath his desk and presents it to David.)

GABRIEL: Pick a piece of paper from this box, please.
(David tries to see what's inside.)

GABRIEL: I didn't say you could look inside!
(David puts his hand in the box. He picks a folded piece of paper and looks up at Gabriel, who nods. David slowly opens the piece of paper and reads it.)

DAVID: *(Very excited.)* GAY!!!

GABRIEL: Yes?

DAVID: IT SAYS GAY!!!

GABRIEL: And why are you so happy, if you don't mind me asking?

DAVID: *(Handing over the piece of paper to Gabriel.)* Look, it says I'm going to be gay!

GABRIEL: *(Reading the piece of paper.)* It seems so. *(Pause.)* But only if I agree to it.

DAVID: Please!

GABRIEL: I'm not totally convinced this is right for you.

DAVID: Oh, come on! I deserve a chance . . .

GABRIEL: Do you really think being gay is such a good thing?

DAVID: I've been told it's the best!

GABRIEL: I'm not sure I'm with you . . .

DAVID: Well, first there's the dance parties. I've heard the gay ones are amazing. Thousands of topless guys sweating next to each other, with great music and visual effects. And a gay friend of mine told me gay guys are the best kissers. They do it for hours, tongue and everything—

GABRIEL: *(Making a face.)* Everything!?

DAVID: Yes! And of course, they're great at . . . well, you know . . . because . . . well, you know what I mean, don't you?

GABRIEL: I have absolutely no idea what you mean.

DAVID: They . . . well, they know what it feels like to have their cock sucked . . . so, of course they know how to do it best . . . It's not like girls chewing it off like a stick of celery . . . It's the real thing!

GABRIEL: OK, OK, OK, that's enough. I get the message. *(Pause.)* Don't underestimate the difficulty of being gay, though. You'll have to come to terms with your sexuality during your teen years. You will fear being abandoned. You may actually even be rejected by your friends or family—

DAVID: I'm not afraid! I want to prove myself this time.

GABRIEL: Well—

DAVID: Please! Please!

GABRIEL: All right. But first I want to make sure you realize what you'll be facing. Frank, Sarah!

(Two angels appear. They're Frank and Sarah.)

FRANK/SARAH: Yes, sir?

GABRIEL: Could you please show David here what it means to be gay? You first, Frank.

(Gabriel leaves his seat to Frank, who takes his wings off before sitting down. Spotlight on Frank and David. Gabriel and Sarah watch them from the side.)

FRANK: David, I'm sure you know why I've asked you to come and see me this morning . . .

(David looks at Gabriel with a question mark on his face. Gabriel nods, telling David to go with the flow and play the part.)

DAVID: Um . . . not really, no . . .

FRANK: You don't? OK, listen. I'm not going to beat around the bush. I'm sorry to have to say this to you, but I'm afraid you can't be working for us anymore. As soon as we finish this conversation, I'd like you to clear your desk and leave.

DAVID: But that's—

FRANK: Stop by the HR department on your way out. They've prepared your pay check. And as a *goodwill* gesture, we'll pay you the long service leave you've accumulated, even if we don't have to, because you've only been working for us three years. But we'd like this to be an amicable parting of ways.

DAVID: But . . . why? You've never had to complain about my work. My customers are happy!

FRANK: Your customers, yes.

DAVID: So, what's the problem?

FRANK: It's not just about the customers . . . It's . . . it's the rest of the staff, too.

DAVID: I don't understand . . .

FRANK: I've had some complaints . . .

DAVID: Complaints? Who from? What about?

FRANK: From everyone. Your behavior . . . is somewhat . . . unorthodox. Listen, I'll be frank, we don't want people like you in this company. It's bad for business.

DAVID: But—

FRANK: I have nothing against you of course, but I can't tolerate such abnormalities in my staff.

DAVID: You can't do that! I'm calling my lawyer!

FRANK: Just you try, asshole! I've got the best lawyers in town; they'll crush you like there's no tomorrow. Forget about getting another job! Do you hear me?

(David takes his head in his hands.)

GABRIEL: Thanks, Frank. Sarah, your turn.

(Sarah takes her wings off and takes David in her arms. Gabriel and Frank watch from the side.)

SARAH: I love you, David. I love you so much.

DAVID: Sarah . . .

SARAH: I want to marry you.

DAVID: I like you too, Sarah, but I don't want to get married. It's . . . . it's not what I want.

SARAH: It's OK, honey. We can live together for a while and get married when you're ready.

DAVID: I'll never be ready. I don't want a relationship, I—

SARAH: I love you so much. You're the one I've been waiting for all my life.

(David pushes himself out of her arms.)

DAVID: Sarah, I can't . . . . I don't love you . . . . I'm . . . I'm gay.

SARAH: You're funny! You need more time, that's it? You need time . . . Of course.

DAVID: Sarah, I'm gay.

SARAH: *(Pause.)* You're kidding, right?

DAVID: No. I like men. I'm sorry.

SARAH: You, little piece of shit!!! I knew something was not quite right from the start. I could feel it . . . That's disgusting! How could you? You filthy bastard! Shame on you!

DAVID: Sarah!

(Sarah stomps out. Then she has second thoughts and turns around. David looks scared, but she hugs him to the point of making him suffocate.)

SARAH: Don't you worry, darl. It's just a phase. I'll help you change. I'll show you what it's like to be with a girl. You've probably never had the right kind of experience. With me, everything will be fine.

GABRIEL: Thanks, Sarah. Last one: the parents.

(Frank comes to Sarah's side. He is visibly furious. Sarah looks torn. They face David. Gabriel watches from the side.)

FRANK: *(To David.)* I don't want to hear this!

SARAH: *(To Frank.)* Please . . .

FRANK: I didn't raise my son to be a faggot!

SARAH: *(To David.)* What are the neighbors going to think?

DAVID: Who cares about the neighbors?

FRANK: You've got to see a doctor.

DAVID: Dad, I'm not sick. I'm gay, that's all.

FRANK: Well, you've got to stop that.

DAVID: I can't. It's who I am. I didn't choose to be gay. I was born like that.

SARAH: What's the family going to think?

DAVID: Mum!

FRANK: You're not my son anymore. Get out of my house!

SARAH: Frank, please!

DAVID: But, Dad—

FRANK: Get out immediately before I kick your ass! And don't ever come back—unless you're cured.

(David starts to leave, looking very sad. Sarah is sobbing.)

GABRIEL: Thank you, Frank and Sarah, thank you very much. That'll do.

(Frank and Sarah pick up their wings under one arm and leave the stage. Gabriel sits at his desk and makes a gesture for David to sit down too.)

GABRIEL: So, do you still want to be gay?

DAVID: Well . . . yes, I think so.

GABRIEL: You are pretty determined, aren't you?

DAVID: Well . . . it's just that gay guys don't have to worry about going back home to their wives every night. They don't have to listen to endless complaints about kids, periods, washing, cooking, or what to wear. No headache excuses in bed either . . .

GABRIEL: What about love?

DAVID: Isn't love universal? That's what you angels keep telling me. *(Pause.)* I just want to be with guys. Just guys. For once!

GABRIEL: Just guys?

DAVID: Yes! Guys and only guys!

GABRIEL: Very well. You've convinced me. Let's find out the details of your next incarnation.

(David rubs his hands, grinning. Gabriel types something on his keyboard and looks at the screen.)

GABRIEL: You will live in Sydney, Australia . . .

DAVID: Fantastic!

GABRIEL: You will work as a nurse in a hospital . . .

DAVID: Cool.

GABRIEL: And your name will be Rachel.

DAVID: But you said I was going to be gay!

(Gabriel has a broad smile on his face.)

GABRIEL: Yes. You are going to be a lesbian.

END OF PLAY

PLAYS FOR
TWO MEN
AND
THREE WOMEN

The Birthday Knife

JEROME PARISSE

Originally produced by Fire Rose Productions at Secret Rose
Theatre, NoHo Arts District, North Hollywood, California,
October 18–November 10, 2007, as part of ACToberFest.
Performed by New Renaissance Theatre. Directed by
Jenny Byrd. Cast: Michael—Ron Moon; Vanessa—Marie
Lively; Hunter—Ben Fuller; Sandy—Dana Jenkins;
Rachel—Amy Poncher.

CHARACTERS

> VANESSA, late twenties, works as a TV news presenter, pretty and fairly
> casual.
>
> MICHAEL, early thirties, Vanessa's boyfriend, easy-going.
>
> HUNTER, thirty-something, Rachel's new boyfriend, dressed somewhat
> formally.
>
> SANDY, twenty-something, a friend of Vanessa.
>
> RACHEL, another friend of Vanessa.

SETTING

> Vanessa's living room.

TIME

> Saturday morning.

•   •   •

*Lights come up on stage. There is a sofa with a coffee table and an armchair.
The phone rings. Vanessa enters to pick up the phone. She sits on the sofa.*

VANESSA: Hello, this is Vanessa speaking.
> . . . Oh, hi Sandy, how are you?
> . . . Thanks!
> . . . It's only been a month, you know . . . One mistake, that's all it takes.
> . . . Shush!
> . . . Excellent! What time can you be here?
> . . . OK. See you tonight. Lots of love.
> *(Vanessa hangs up. Michael enters.)*

MICHAEL: Who was that?

VANESSA: Sandy.

MICHAEL: What did she want?

VANESSA: Confirming tonight. She's coming at eight to help me get ready.

MICHAEL: Great! *(He kisses her.)* Excited?
> *(Vanessa nods. She pulls him toward her and kisses him.)*

MICHAEL: I'm going to get the paper. Need anything?

VANESSA: No, thanks. Actually, could you buy some orange juice? We've
> run out.

MICHAEL: OK. I won't be long.

VANESSA: See you soon.

(Michael exits. Vanessa grabs a magazine from the coffee table and starts reading. Hunter enters a few seconds later. Vanessa thinks it's Michael and doesn't look up from her magazine.)

VANESSA: Forgot something?

HUNTER: Good morning.

VANESSA: *(Starting and getting up.)* Who are you?

HUNTER: Hello!

VANESSA: Who *are* you?

HUNTER: My name's Hunter. And I'm very well, thanks for asking . . .

VANESSA: How did you get in here?

HUNTER: Michael let me in. He said he was going out to get some stuff and I could come in.

VANESSA: Ah . . . all righty . . .

HUNTER: Mind if I sit down?

VANESSA: No . . . of course not . . .

(Vanessa sits back on the sofa and Hunter sits opposite her in the armchair.)

VANESSA: Are you a friend of Michael?

HUNTER: No. Well . . . yes and no . . . *(Pause.)* I'm actually more a friend of yours to say the truth.

VANESSA: A friend of mine? I don't understand . . .

HUNTER: OK. What about this: I spend half an hour with you every day!

VANESSA: Half an hour with me . . . ? Ah . . . OK, got it! Sorry, I'm a bit slow on the uptake.

HUNTER: No worries . . . I've been dying to meet you in person for a very long time!

VANESSA: *(Laughing.)* I'm just a TV news presenter, you know. Nothing to write home about.

HUNTER: You must be joking! Channel one, six o'clock news! How much better could it be? You're too modest.

VANESSA: I've only just started.

HUNTER: You're so good-looking, so professional, so . . . perfect . . . yes, perfect! It sounds corny, I know, but everything you do is so right! I mean it.

VANESSA: I'm doing my job, that's all . . . But thanks anyway. You said you're a friend of Michael?

HUNTER: When I saw you do it the first time, I thought . . . that's *it*! Those shows you were hosting before were OK, but they weren't doing you any justice. Six o'clock news, wow! I'm sure you'll get the seven-thirty job pretty soon!

VANESSA: It's not that easy, you know. There's a lot of politics involved. It's not just about skills . . .

HUNTER: Come on! You're a natural! It'll be piece of cake for you.

VANESSA: I wish I could be so sure . . . You've got no idea how hard it is.

HUNTER: Nobody can do it like you, I swear. You remember last week on Tuesday night . . . when you were talking about the G8 summit and they got all mixed up and showed the video of the gorillas? You handled the situation perfectly. You didn't look fazed at all. I would have cracked up or something, but you, you just apologized and moved on . . . Remember?

VANESSA: Do I? Do I remember?! I thought I was going to die. The technicians were in stitches, I could hear them behind my back. And I had to keep a straight face all the time. But that's part of the job. One mistake, that's all it takes . . .

HUNTER: You were perfect. Per – fect! I've watched it many times, I can't fault you.

VANESSA: You've watched it many times?

HUNTER: I taped it.

VANESSA: Excuse me?

HUNTER: I can't always be there! Stuff to do, people to see. So I tape the news every night. No big deal . . . And that way, I can watch you as often as I want—and on weekends too, when you're not on air.

VANESSA: You're pulling my leg, aren't you?

HUNTER: Do I look like it?

(Pause.)

VANESSA: What do you . . . what do you do for work?

HUNTER: How's Caroline?

VANESSA: Who's Caroline?

HUNTER: Your sister, who else?

VANESSA: Caroline's very— Hold on! How do you know my sister's name?

HUNTER: I read your interview in *Newsweek* the other day. You mentioned your sister . . .

VANESSA: Oh, that's right . . . I had forgotten . . . *(Pause.)* Sorry, you were saying about your job . . .

HUNTER: I'm glad you've got such a good relationship with her. There's nothing like sisters, I say. But you've outperformed her by far . . .

VANESSA: We're different, that's all.

HUNTER: You can say that again! Like chalk and cheese! She must have got her dark hair from your dad—

VANESSA: There's no picture of her in the magazine!

HUNTER: I did my research. It's amazing what one can do with the Internet these days . . .

VANESSA: I wonder what Michael's doing . . . He said he wouldn't be long . . .

HUNTER: I'm sure he'll be here soon.

VANESSA: You still haven't told me what you do . . .

HUNTER: *(Smiling widely.)* Look at you, of course. What else?

VANESSA: I mean, what do you do for work?

HUNTER: Why is it that people always want to know what I do for work? *(Pause.)* Got a job for me in television? I'd be a fantastic assistant, you know. I'd make you coffee, manage your diary, take your calls, make sure nobody pisses you off . . .

VANESSA: I've already got an assistant, thanks. You don't have a job?

HUNTER: Let's talk about something more interesting, shall we?

(Hunter gets up and sits next to Vanessa on the sofa. She gets up quickly.)

VANESSA: Michael will be back any second now!

(Hunter gets up and reaches the door before Vanessa has time to reach it. Hunter glances outside.)

HUNTER: Not here yet . . . He's probably met some friends on the way.

(Vanessa sits in the armchair. Hunter stays up, not too far from the door, close enough to block the passage if necessary.)

HUNTER: So . . . how's your relationship with Michael? Couldn't find much about it on the Internet . . . I figured it may be a sign . . . *(Pause.)* No, you're right. None of my business. Let's talk about something else. How was dinner with Caroline last night?

VANESSA: Again! How do you know about it?

HUNTER: I saw you two go in *The Wild Duck.* I've heard it's a damn good place.

VANESSA: You *saw* us?

HUNTER: Yep. *(Pause.)* OK, I had sort of been following you . . .

VANESSA: You've been following me!? You're . . . You're . . . . That's insane!

HUNTER: It's a pretty normal thing to do for a fan, you know. Did you enjoy the pork medallions?

VANESSA: That's enough! I don't like the idea of you spying on me. Or anybody else for that matter . . . And I never asked you to come in—

HUNTER: Michael did.

VANESSA: He's never mentioned your name before.

HUNTER: Guess what? I love pork medallions too. When I was working as a butcher in Randwick, I used to cut them beautifully. Not too thick, not too thin, very juicy . . . my customers loved them . . . I was the eastern suburbs pork medallion expert! I even got a decoration for it. I'll show it to you one day . . .

(Vanessa gets up and starts pacing the room nervously.)

VANESSA: I don't mean to be rude, but I've got stacks of things to do.

HUNTER: Fifty thousand!

VANESSA: Fifty thousand what?

HUNTER: Pork medallions! I've cut fifty thousand pork medallions in my life! I've made the calculation myself: thirty medallions on average per day, six days a week, for five years . . . that's it! It adds up to fifty thousand . . . Isn't it amazing?

VANESSA: It's a . . . a staggering number . . . I'm very impressed.

HUNTER: Thanks!

VANESSA: But I've got lots to do . . .

HUNTER: I won't stay long.

VANESSA: And I've got a phone call to make.

(Vanessa goes to grab the phone, but Hunter hurries to grab it before her. In the process, a large knife falls from his jacket. Vanessa freezes and stares at the knife.)

VANESSA: What's that?

HUNTER: A knife.

VANESSA: I . . . I can see it's a knife. But . . . what are you doing with a knife of this size in your pocket?

(Hunter picks up the knife and plays with the handle, the blade, very slowly and intentionally. Vanessa can't keep her eyes away from the knife.)

HUNTER: It's the knife I used to cut my pork medallions with. Such a beautiful beast, isn't it? Look at how sharp the blade it. And it feels so right in my hand. *(Pause.)* A knife is a man's best friend, I say.

(Vanessa keeps an eye on the knife and another one on the phone.)

VANESSA: I thought beer was a man's best friend.

HUNTER: Are you talking about Michael?

VANESSA: Leave Michael out of this.

(Hunter places the knife on the coffee table.)

HUNTER: Why are you so restless?

VANESSA: I'm not . . . I mean, I don't know. It's just that . . . I'm busy, you see, I—

HUNTER: I know. Why do you think I came to see you today of all days? *(Hunter starts singing.)* "Happy birthday to you! Happy birthday to you! Happy birthday, dear Vanessa! Happy birthday to you!"

VANESSA: Thanks . . . I . . . I don't want you to leave . . . but . . . I'd better start getting ready . . .

HUNTER: The party is not before tonight.

VANESSA: Yes, but I've got lots to prepare.

HUNTER: You didn't look very busy when I came in.

(Hunter looks away for a second or two. Vanessa grabs the knife and hides it behind her back. She slowly makes her way backward toward the sofa. Hunter hasn't noticed she's got the knife.)

HUNTER: I say, you deserve something special for your birthday . . . What about a kiss from me?

VANESSA: No.

HUNTER: No?

VANESSA: We don't know each other . . . It wouldn't be . . . it wouldn't be correct.

HUNTER: Correct? What a curious word to use! Who knows what's correct these days?

VANESSA: Trust me, I know.

HUNTER: I trust you. *(Pause.)* Can I kiss you?

VANESSA: Don't even think about it!

(Hunter moves toward Vanessa, who takes refuge behind the sofa, the knife still hidden behind her back.)

HUNTER: Hmm . . . Is this a way of behaving towards a fan?

VANESSA: Leave my house immediately!

HUNTER: OK. If that's your wish, I'm going to leave. But not before I've given you a kiss. Just a kiss. Nothing else.

VANESSA: No way.

HUNTER: On the cheeks . . . All correct, as you say. And it's my birthday present, remember . . .

(Hunter joins Vanessa behind the sofa to give her a kiss. Vanessa pushes him away with a scream. Short struggle. They fall. Vanessa gets up. Hunter's dead, the knife in his body. Vanessa looks at the body and moves away from the sofa.)

VANESSA: Oh! . . . Oh! . . . Oh my God! Oh my God!

(Michael enters, followed by Sandy and Rachel. They're carrying a huge present wrapped in paper with a ribbon and a big knot. They're singing "Happy Birthday to You, Happy Birthday to You, Happy Birthday, Dear Vanessa, Happy Birthday to You." Vanessa looks at them, in a daze. They give her a kiss and sit on the sofa. Hunter's body is entirely hidden by the sofa.)

VANESSA: Michael? Sandy?

SANDY: Happy birthday, darling.

MICHAEL: Where's Hunter?

VANESSA: Hunter?

MICHAEL: Rachel's new boyfriend.

VANESSA: Rachel's new boyfriend?

RACHEL: Isn't he great? We only met two weeks ago. He's so gorgeous . . . I'm in love, big time! The joke wasn't his idea, it was Michael's. Wasn't it, Michael?

MICHAEL: Yep!

RACHEL: You didn't mind, did you? I wasn't too sure about it, but Michael thought it could be fun . . . *(Pause.)* Where is he anyway?

VANESSA: Where's who?

RACHEL: What do you mean, who? Hunter, of course!

MICHAEL: Yes, where is he, Vanessa? I let him in. Don't tell me the bastard didn't have the guts to do it!

VANESSA: Michael . . .

SANDY: Vanessa, are you OK?

MICHAEL: *(Pointing at the present.)* And he's got the knife! Without the knife, we can't open your birthday present . . .

(Lights fade except a spotlight on Vanessa. Spotlight fades.)

END OF PLAY

PLAYS FOR
THREE MEN
AND
THREE WOMEN

Cabfare for the Common Man

MARK HARVEY LEVINE

First Equity production at the Phoenix Theatre, Indianapolis, May 2005, as part of Cabfare for the Common Man: An Evening of Plays by Mark Harvey Levine. Directed by Bryan D. Fonseca. Cast: Jon Lindley, Megan McKinney, Sara Riemen, Deborah Sargent, Michael Shelton, Bill Simmons.

MAN, thirties, the common man.

CABDRIVER, thirties to fifties, gruff.

MOM, forties to fifties, a mom.

DAD, forties to fifties, married to Mom.

FRIEND 1, male, youthful.

FRIEND 2, female, just as youthful.

SEXY GIRL, sexy, and a girl.

ANOTHER SEXY GIRL, equally sexy and girl-like.

MALE COLLEGE FRIEND, like Friend 1, but more collegiate.

FEMALE COLLEGE FRIEND, hauntingly similar to Friend 2.

WOMAN, thirties, flighty.

ANOTHER WOMAN, thirties, controlling.

WIFE, thirties, not so flighty or controlling.

SETTING

A bed. Also, a cab. Simultaneously.

TIME

The present.

•   •   •

Man lies in bed, asleep. Cabdriver is perched at the end of his bed, holding a steering wheel. The play should be done mostly at breakneck speed.

CABDRIVER: Where ya headed?

MAN: *(Bolting straight up in bed.)* What?

CABDRIVER: Where ya goin'?

MAN: *(Not expecting a cabdriver in his bed.)* I don't know . . .

CABDRIVER: Fair enough!

(The Cabdriver starts the meter, and the cab ride begins. Various objects whiz past them, creating the sense of motion. The first objects are sweet and childlike—simple landscape drawings, happy street signs, friendly people. Mom and Dad get in on either side of him.)

MOM: Hiya, cutie!

DAD: Heya, pal!

MAN: Who are . . . ?

MOM: We're Mom—

DAD: and Dad. We'll be with you the wholllle time.

MOM: Look at all the things to see!

DAD: *(An encouraging punch on the shoulder.)* Uh?

MOM: Isn't it exciting?

DAD: Uh?

    (More things fly by: mailboxes, cows, baseball players, cereal boxes, dogs.)

MAN: Wow . . . !

DAD: The sun's rising!

MOM: The birds are singing!

DAD: Isn't it great?

MAN: Can we go faster?

MOM: *(Proud.)* Faster!

DAD: That's my boy!

MOM: They always want to go faster!

MAN: Faster!

CABDRIVER: You got it, kid.

    (The cab zooms forward. Suddenly, a little turbulence. They bounce.)

MAN: Whoa . . .

CABDRIVER: Childhood's always a little bumpy.

MOM: Don't worry!

DAD: You'll be fine.

MOM: You've got us!

DAD: And your friends, too!

MAN: Friends?

    (Two Friends get in, full of energy.)

FRIEND 1: Hey!

FRIEND 2: How's it going?!

FRIEND 1: Can we ride along?

MAN: *(Of course!)* Are you kidding?

FRIEND 2: Let's ride together!

MAN: You guys are with me to the end!

FRIENDS/MAN: *(A toast.)* To the end!

MAN: Faster! Faster! I can't wait to get— Where is the end?

FRIENDS: *(Variously.)* I don't know! Ya got me! Who knows?

MAN: How do I know when I've arrived?

DAD: Oh you'll know.

MOM: You'll be great!

DAD: You will be great.

MOM: When you arrive.

DAD: We've got big plans for you, buddy boy! Big plans!

(Suddenly there's a horrible crash. Everyone is knocked around.)

MAN: What happened?

CABDRIVER: We hit puberty! Hang on, let me look at the damage . . .

(Mom, Dad, and the friends get out to look, too. Two Sexy Girls slink into the cab.)

SEXY GIRL: Hi there.

ANOTHER SEXY GIRL: Mind if I brush my leg against you?

SEXY GIRL: Mind if I brush my hair near you?

ANOTHER SEXY GIRL: Mind if I develop firm yet perky young breasts?

MAN: Um . . .

(Mom and Dad get back in the cab and throw out the girls.)

MOM: Get out! Get out!

DAD: There'll be plenty of time for that later.

MOM: Much much later.

(The friends climb back in.)

FRIEND 1: Well, it looks like you dented your ego.

FRIEND 2: Your self-esteem's all smashed to hell.

FRIEND 1: And your skin's messed up.

MAN: Never mind, let's just go! Go! Go!

(The objects zoom by again. Comic books, guitars, and tennis shoes fly by.)

MOM: Turn here.

(They turn hard. The Man bumps his head.)

MAN: Ow!

DAD: And head towards Engineering Heights.

MAN: Wait a minute—

DAD: Take the Marching Band Expressway.

MAN: Dear God, no!

MOM: It's a safer choice, lambchop.

DAD: This time of day, absolutely.

MAN: This is my cab ride . . .

DAD: Yeah, but we know this area.

MOM: We've been here before.

DAD: And besides, we're paying for it.

MAN: I want to go somewhere else!

DAD: Well, you're not going to.

MOM: Sorry, sweetie pie.

(They come to a screeching stop.)

MAN: Where are we?

CABDRIVER: High school graduation!

DAD: Everyone out for pictures!

(All except the Man tumble out of the cab and form a typical graduation-picture pose. The Man turns to the Cabdriver.)

MAN: Go! Go!

(The parents and friends recede in the distance.)

MAN: Ha!

(Two College Friends get in. They're wearing black and are very serious.)

FEMALE COLLEGE FRIEND: Hey.

MALE COLLEGE FRIEND: How's it going.

FEMALE COLLEGE FRIEND: Can we ride along?

MAN: Sure! Come on in!

(They ride along. More things fly past: paper, boom boxes, works of art, pizzas.)

MALE COLLEGE FRIEND: This is all total bull, you know.

FEMALE COLLEGE FRIEND: We're not going anywhere.

MALE COLLEGE FRIEND: We're going somewhere, everyone else isn't.

FEMALE COLLEGE FRIEND: We need new cabs.

MALE COLLEGE FRIEND: We'll drive our own cabs!

FEMALE COLLEGE FRIEND: To the end!

COLLEGE FRIENDS AND MAN: *(A toast.)* To the end!

MAN: Faster! Faster! I can't wait to get—I still don't know where the end is . . .

MALE COLLEGE FRIEND: We need new ends!

FEMALE COLLEGE FRIEND: Beer?

MAN: No, thank you.

MALE COLLEGE FRIEND: Drugs?

MAN: No, thanks.

FEMALE COLLEGE FRIEND: Sex?

MAN: Don't mind if I do.

FEMALE COLLEGE FRIEND: Not with you!

(The two College Friends fall back on the bed, making out.)

MAN: Driver . . . Turn here.

(The Cabdriver turns sharply, and the College Friends roll off.)

MAN: Keep driving. Keep driving.

CABDRIVER: You're the boss.

(Night falls. Lights from other cars play along their windshield. Laundry baskets go by. People with parkas and Walkmans on. A procession of telephones.)

MAN: *(Looks behind him.)* What do you think happened to my parents?

CABDRIVER: Oh, you're way past them now.

MAN: What about my friends?

CABDRIVER: Say, which way here?

MAN: What?

CABDRIVER: Fork in the road. Which way you wanna go?

MAN: I don't—I don't know . . .

CABDRIVER: *(Points right.)* Full-time job. It's safe, flat, but a little boring. It'll get you there, but it'll take more time. Mostly freeways and billboards, though.

MAN: OK . . .

CABDRIVER: *(Points left.)* Follow your dream. Steep hill, roadblocks, landslides, lotsa guys crash and burn. You might not get there at all. But it's supposed to be a pretty drive.

MAN: Wow.

CABDRIVER: So what'll it be, kid?

MAN: Um . . . Left! No right! No lef—

CABDRIVER: Pick one!

MAN: What if we go straight?

CABDRIVER: I don't know what's there—

MAN: What if we chance it?

CABDRIVER: There's no map!

MAN: Do it!

> *(The cab lunges forward. It's now very dark. And scary. Newspapers fly by. Coffee machines. Blind men with blankets. Limping computers. The wind howls.)*

CABDRIVER: Well, now you're lost.

MAN: OK, slow down a sec . . .

CABDRIVER: Can't slow down.

MAN: Just let me get my bearings.

CABDRIVER: Sorry, kid.

MAN: Look! Up ahead!

CABDRIVER: What?

MAN: It's a woman! Stop!

WOMAN: *(Climbing in.)* Hi!

MAN: Hi, I'm lost!

WOMAN: I'm lost too. Wanna be lost together?

MAN: Yes!

WOMAN: Doesn't that sound romantic?

MAN: Lost!

WOMAN: Together!

MAN: *(Puts his arm around her.)* You and me!

WOMAN: Can I show you my pet snakes?

MAN: Um . . .

WOMAN: I got them from this guy I was in a religious cult with . . .

MAN: Um . . .

WOMAN: Oh, I'm not in the cult anymore. Trust me, after shock therapy, you lose all interest in alternative philosophies.

MAN: OK, you need to get out of the cab now.

(She exits. Another Woman appears.)

MAN: Hi, I'm lost.

ANOTHER WOMAN: *(Climbing in.)* Oh, I'm not.

MAN: You're not?

ANOTHER WOMAN: No, I know which way to go.

MAN: Oh, thank God. *(Puts his arm around her.)* You and me!

ANOTHER WOMAN: Take the Domestic Parkway. It's a safer neighborhood.

MAN: Um—

ANOTHER WOMAN: And head towards Unrelenting Drive. It's quicker.

CABDRIVER: This time of night, absolutely.

MAN: Wait, wait, this is my cab ride . . .

ANOTHER WOMAN: Yeah, but I know this area. I've been here before.

MAN: I want to go somewhere else.

ANOTHER WOMAN: Well, you're not going to.

MAN: Yes, I am, actually.

ANOTHER WOMAN: OK, stop the cab! I'm outta here.

(She gets out.)

MAN: Drive!

ANOTHER WOMAN: *(Shouting after him as she recedes.)* Loserrrrr!

MAN: Maybe she's right . . .

(It starts to rain. The Cabdriver puts his windshield wipers on.)

MAN: Where am I going? How will I know when I get there?

CABDRIVER: I don't know, pal. I can't even see where we're at . . .

MAN: Wait, there's another person up ahead!

CABDRIVER: That's how you got in trouble the last two times.

(They stop. The Wife peers in.)

MAN: Hi, I'm lost.

WIFE: Everybody's kinda lost.

MAN: Need a ride?

WIFE: Not particularly.

MAN: Want one anyway?

WIFE: OK. Just for a little bit.

MAN: Drive, cabbie!

(*Pause.*)

WIFE: So, didja hit puberty?

MAN: Oh my God, I slammed into it!

WIFE: They should have a warning sign.

MAN: Flashing lights.

(*They laugh.*)

WIFE: This is nice.

MAN: (*Puts his arm around her.*) You and me.

WIFE: (*Puts her arm around him.*) Me and you.

MAN: I'm still a little lost, though. Hey, maybe you know . . .

WIFE: What?

MAN: How will I know when I've arrived?

WIFE: I don't think you ever do.

MAN: You never know?

WIFE: You never arrive.

MAN: Never?

WIFE: No . . . but isn't it a nice trip? Look, it stopped raining . . .

MAN: Never!?

WIFE: The sun's coming up.

MAN: Never.

WIFE: The birds are singing.

MAN: They are?

WIFE: Listen . . .

(*He listens. The Wife lies down in bed, asleep. We hear the sound of a baby crying. Everything but the Cabdriver goes away. The Wife groggily wakes up.*)

WIFE: The baby . . .

MAN: It's OK . . . I'll go check . . . You sleep.

WIFE: OK . . .

(*She plops back down again. Man gets up, but then turns to the Cabdriver.*)

MAN: Hey.

CABDRIVER: Yeah?

MAN: Keep the meter running . . .

(*He exits. Lights fade.*)

END OF PLAY

PLAYS FOR
FOUR MEN
AND
ONE WOMAN

A Case of Anxiety

MARK HARVEY LEVINE

First produced in the Gardner-Webb University New Plays
Festival, April 2006. Directed by Aaron Delane Wilkinson.
Cast: Robert—Caleb Moore; Marissa—Stacie Worrell;
Inspector—Karl J. Mosbacher IV; Gorilla—Nathan Klein;
Pirates—Mark Houser, Josh House, Traci Beckett, Jen Wiles.

CHARACTERS

> ROBERT, midthirties, glass is half empty.
> MARISSA, midthirties, glass is half full of wine.
> INSPECTOR, thirties to fifties, straight out of Agatha Christie.
> GORILLA, straight out of the jungle.
> PIRATES, at least three, maybe more.

SETTING

> A living room in a modest apartment.

TIME

> The present: morning.

.   .   .

> *Robert enters, wearing a robe and brushing his teeth. He is half asleep. He yawns. He brushes. Marissa enters.*

MARISSA: Mornin' sweetie.

ROBERT: *(He is very hard to understand as he is brushing his teeth.)* Mnnin'!

MARISSA: Hey, whatcha doing after work? I thought maybe we'd go out to eat tonight.

ROBERT: *(Brushing.)* Wll—

MARISSA: Unless you have any plans . . .

ROBERT: *(Brushing.)* Wll, I hv to mrbisot d' fromjin, sbrab d' blammel vivteen times and den cmpleetly refrub d'entire flobberrgggghhh—
> *(Suddenly, he chokes on his toothbrush. He makes a few gurgling sounds, desperately trying to extract the toothbrush. He falls over, dead, on the floor.)*

MARISSA: Robert . . . ? Robert! Oh my God! Are you . . . Are you—
> *(A British Inspector, straight out of Agatha Christie, bursts through the front door calmly sucking on a pipe.)*

INSPECTOR: Dead? I'm afraid so, ma'am.
> *(Marissa cradles Robert's head in her lap and cries out to the heavens, very movie-of-the-week.)*

MARISSA: WHYYYYYYYYYY!?

INSPECTOR: *(Bracing his foot on Robert's stomach, he pulls the toothbrush out of Robert's mouth; it makes a popping sound.)* Improper toothbrush grip, most likely. You've got to really hold on to the handle. A loose brush, an ill-timed yawn, and Bob's your uncle.

MARISSA: He was so young . . . What's to become of me?

INSPECTOR: There, there, my dear. Why don't you come away from this horrible sight? Let's get you a soothing cup of tea.

(He leads her out the door.)

MARISSA: *(As they exit.)* Thank you . . . you're very kind . . .

(As they exit, Robert gets up and continues to brush his teeth, but now holding onto the brush very tightly with both hands. He exits to the bedroom/bathroom area. He reappears immediately more fully dressed and pulling a sweater over his head. He gets tangled in the sweater, struggles mightily, and falls down dead. Marissa once again enters from the bedroom.)

MARISSA: Robert! Oh my God, no! No!

INSPECTOR: *(Entering once again through the front door.)* Sorry to say, yes. Suffocated in his own sweater.

MARISSA: I begged him to get a cardigan.

INSPECTOR: Precisely. A small crew neck, a wrong turn at the sleeve, and the squirrel's up your smokestack.

MARISSA: Are you sure?

INSPECTOR: Oh, this sort of thing happens quite often. Although I am going to have to take you in for questioning.

MARISSA: Of course. I understand.

(The Inspector shepherds her through the front door. Robert immediately sits up, puts on his sweater very carefully, and then starts putting on his shoes. He suddenly stiffens, cries out, and falls over dead. Marissa once again enters from the bedroom. This time there is more than a hint of annoyance in her voice.)

MARISSA: Oh, Robert, not again.

INSPECTOR: *(Entering as before.)* I'm afraid so, ma'am.

MARISSA: But how?

INSPECTOR: *(Lifting Robert's foot.)* Tarantula in the penny loafer! The foot slides in, the fangs come down, and the bobbin's off the wicket.

MARISSA: Was it . . . murder?

INSPECTOR: Most likely not. But I'm going to have to . . . investigate you. *(Sexily.)* Thoroughly.

MARISSA: Ooo.

INSPECTOR: If you'll come with me.

(The Inspector puts his arm around Marissa and leads her out the front door. Robert again sits up. He removes his shoes, shaking each one carefully before putting it back on. This time Marissa enters from the bedroom casually, yawning.)

MARISSA: Morning, honey . . .

ROBERT: Morning . . .

MARISSA: You want something to eat before you go?

ROBERT: I'm just going to grab some toast . . .

(He exits to the kitchen area.)

MARISSA: *(Realization hits her, she speaks and moves in "slow motion".)* Nooooo!
(But it's too late. We hear a zapping sound and the lights flicker. Robert staggers in holding a piece of burnt toast. He falls down dead at Marissa's feet.)

MARISSA: *(Very annoyed.)* Oh for God sakes . . .

INSPECTOR: *(Entering on cue as always.)* Yes . . . a faulty wire, a thick slice of
sourdough, and the lemur's up the stump.

MARISSA: You always know what to say.

INSPECTOR: Just doing my duty, ma'am.

MARISSA: No, it's more than that . . . I can see it in your eyes . . .

INSPECTOR: Please ma'am . . .

MARISSA: Call me Marissa.

INSPECTOR: Marissa . . . I've got to keep my professional detachment.

MARISSA: You love me. Admit it.

(They embrace. Robert sits up on this.)

INSPECTOR: *(Very dramatic.)* I'm not allowed. You're a suspect. I took an oath.

MARISSA: *(Even more dramatic.)* Oh, to blazes with your oaths! Look me in the
eyes and tell me you don't love me!

ROBERT: Hey!

INSPECTOR: Damn it, Marissa . . . I . . . I can't . . .

ROBERT: Hey! Marissa!

MARISSA: I'm sorry, Robert. But I need . . . stability.

ROBERT: You're my wife!

MARISSA: I want someone who's . . . a little more alive.

ROBERT: It's called being cautious! I'm careful!

MARISSA: I need someone who isn't dying all the time!

ROBERT: You want alive? I'll give you alive!

*(He lunges at the Inspector, but the Inspector pulls out a gun and levels it at
Robert.)*

INSPECTOR: Careful, old bean. One false move, a twitch on the trigger, and
it's surrender, Dorothy.

ROBERT: *(Holding up his hands.)* All right. Marissa—look. I know I worry too
much. I go straight to the worst-case scenario.

MARISSA: It's always a step away from disaster with you.

ROBERT: This is Los Angeles! You can get killed by mudslides, earthquakes, stray bullets—

(There is a shot. The Inspector looks down at his gun.)

INSPECTOR: *(Sheepishly.)* Sorry . . . finger slipped.

(Robert falls down, dead.)

MARISSA: *(Rotely, no feeling whatsoever.)* Oh Robert. Oh no. Oh God.

INSPECTOR: Well, this appears to be an open and shut case. I'm pretty sure I did it. But I'm going to have to question you anyway. Shall we?

MARISSA: Take me away, Inspector. Take me back to Scotland Yard and work me over.

INSPECTOR: Right-o.

(Robert gets up again.)

ROBERT: Not so fast! You're not going anywhere!

INSPECTOR: I'm not?

ROBERT: No, no, you are, *she's* not. You're leaving. I've had enough dying. I'm going to live from now on. You'll see, Marissa. I'm not going to be afraid! Except I'm afraid you're no longer needed, Inspector. Cheerio and tah tah!

(Robert opens the door to let the Inspector out and is immediately attacked by a giant gorilla who bursts into the apartment. [If you can't find a gorilla with an Equity card, someone in a gorilla suit will be fine. If you can't find a gorilla suit, a particularly large and hairy actor will do the trick.] The gorilla picks Robert up and tosses him around.)

INSPECTOR: Escaped gorilla! I've seen this all too often.

MARISSA: *(Sighs.)* It's sad, really.

INSPECTOR: Yes, one unlocked cage, one enraged primate, and pop goes the garbanzo.

(The gorilla begins twirling Robert around. He speaks to Marissa and the Inspector whenever he comes around to them.)

ROBERT: Just because I'm— *(Twirl.)* —careful doesn't mean— *(Twirl.)* —I'm not alive. *(Twirl.)* It just means— *(Twirl.)* —that I look ahead. *(The gorilla begins shaking him violently, making his voice come out quavery.)* And yes, when I look ahead sometimes I see bad things. Fires. Muggers. Heart attacks!

(Suddenly the gorilla grabs its chest, has a massive heart attack, and falls down dead.)

INSPECTOR: Oh, good show! A high-potassium diet, a burst of activity, and—

ROBERT: *(Cutting him off.)* All right already! *(To Marissa.)* OK, so I plan. I'm a planner. But I can also dream! I have dreams for us, Marissa. Best-case scenarios! I see us happy. And it's that . . . vision . . . of happiness I want to protect.

MARISSA: Maybe you could stop protecting it and start having it a little.

ROBERT: I want to! I want to be . . . carefree and spontaneous. But . . . I can't help thinking what might happen.

MARISSA: What might happen is I could walk out that door.

(As they speak, the gorilla sits up. The Inspector guides the gorilla out the door.)

INSPECTOR: Back to the zoo with you. A quick trip in the cab, a nice tranquilizing dart, and Nelly's in the basket . . .

(The gorilla and the Inspector exit.)

ROBERT: This is a dangerous world. You have to be prepared.

MARISSA: There's such a thing as being too prepared. There's such a thing as being so careful you miss the fun. You're going to miss me, Robert. I'm fun. And you're gonna miss out on me 'cause you're afraid we're going to be . . . I dunno . . . attacked by pirates . . .

ROBERT: I wish you hadn't said that.

(With a mighty "arrrrrgh!" a band of pirates bursts through the door, window, bedroom—everywhere. They chase Robert around.)

MARISSA: You're so busy protecting us, Robert, that you forgot to enjoy what it is you're protecting.

ROBERT: *(Dodging pirates.)* I know, I know . . . and I'm planning to change.

MARISSA: Huh. You're planning to change. I don't want you to plan, Robert. Just . . . change.

ROBERT: *(Running for his life.)* It's . . . hard to do.

MARISSA: Do it because it's hard.

ROBERT: Um . . . OK . . . I'll try . . . but we could end up in trouble.

(Robert punches one of the pirates, takes his sword, and begins to fight all the others, Errol Flynn style.)

MARISSA: Do it anyway.

ROBERT: I mean . . . sometimes a plan is good.

MARISSA: Sometimes it isn't. Do it for me.

ROBERT: For you? For you, I'd do anything.

(Robert fights three pirates with one sword, defeating them all.)

MARISSA: Well, that's why I married you.

ROBERT: It's not going to be easy. I may backslide.

(Robert falls back and ends up in a "clinch" with a pirate. He pushes the pirate off.)

MARISSA: I'll help you. We'll face it together.

ROBERT: That sounds . . . reasonable . . .

(Marissa grabs a fallen pirate's sword and joins Robert.)

MARISSA: Starting now.

ROBERT: "Now" seems good. Let me pencil you in for "now."

(Working together, Robert and Marissa kill all the pirates. They stand exhausted but happy.)

MARISSA: So, mister . . . what are you doing after work?

ROBERT: I have no plans.

(Blackout.)

END OF PLAY

Fear of Spheres

LISA LOOMER

Originally produced by Artwork Enterprises at the
Craterian Ginger Rogers Theater, Medford, Oregon,
January 14, 2008. Directed by Christopher Acebo.
Cast: Tim—Josh Houghton; Dan—Sam King;
Joaquin—Juan Rivera LeBron; Alice—Eve Smyth;
Therapist—David Thompson.

CHARACTERS

TIM, sixteen-year-old boy, very tall and skinny, with a lisp.

DAN, middle-aged, working guy.

JOAQUIN, twenties, a handsome Latino.

ALICE, forties.

THERAPIST, a man with a calm demeanor.

SETTING

A bare room with a large blue ball.

TIME

The present.

• • •

Lights come up on five people sitting in a semicircle, staring at a large blue ball. From stage right to stage left, they are: Tim, Dan, Therapist, Joaquin, and Alice. After they stare at the ball for several beats, the Therapist speaks.

THERAPIST: Good morning, everyone. Good to see you.
   (He takes in the group. Smiles.)
THERAPIST: You are all here today for one reason. You are dealing with something which afflicts men and women . . . young and old . . . with no regard to wealth or social status. You're all here for the same reason. *(Beat.)* Spheraphobia. Do you know what that means?
   (Dan's hand shoots up in the air.)
DAN: Fear of b-b-balls?
THERAPIST: Yes, Dan. Fear of balls. Actually, fear of anything . . . *(Carefully, gently.)* Spherical. Anything that goes round and round. Fear of spheres. *(Looks at Dan and Tim.)* Some of us are afraid of big balls . . .
   (Looks at Joaquin.) Others are afraid of Ping-Pong balls. Some of us have been hurt by balls. *(To Alice.)* Some have lost balls . . . But I believe that in sharing our stories, we can heal. So. Who would like to begin?
   (Dan shoots up his hand again, but the Therapist ignores him, looking at the others. Finally, Tim, a boy of sixteen, speaks.)
TIM: I'll share. Uhm, my name is Tim.
ALL: Welcome, Tim.
TIM: Thank you. Uhm . . . Let's see . . . Well, I guess you could say there were a lot of balls in my family. Everybody played some kind of ball . . . Base-

ball, soccer, dodge ball, you name it. And since I was five eight in the third grade . . . My mom signed me up for, what else? *(With loathing and resentment.)* Basketball. *(Yells.)* And I hated it!

(Joaquin busts out Tourette's-like.)

JOAQUIN: *(Singing, shaking.)* "Goodness, gracious, great balls of fire!"

THERAPIST: *(Finger to his lips.)* Joaquin. *(To the others.)* As some of you know, Joaquin suffers from the uncontrollable urge to sing "Great Balls of Fire." Just try to ignore it.

JOAQUIN: Sorry. I'm so sorry.

THERAPIST: That's all right. You're safe here.

(He puts a comforting hand on Joaquin's thigh. Then realizes and quickly takes it away.)

THERAPIST: Go on, Tim.

TIM: So anyway, my mom forced me to play basketball. Like three times a week.

DAN: B-b-bitch.

THERAPIST: No cross talk, please.

TIM: So I like got back at her by refusing to eat anything round. I stopped eating eggs. I stopped eating meat balls. Matzoh balls . . . I wouldn't eat anything off a plate if the plate was round . . . BECAUSE I HATED BASKETBALL! I hated that creepy leathery feel . . . I hated the color— like liver! I hated the way the ball got caught in the net—like it was being choked by spiderwebs—

THERAPIST: Talk to the ball, Tim. Tell the ball how you feel.

(The therapist holds the ball so Tim can talk right to it.)

TIM: *(Scared, to ball.)* I—don't want to play with you.

THERAPIST: Louder.

TIM: I don't want to play with you!

THERAPIST: Louder, Tim!

TIM: I hate you! I HATE YOU! You're not my thing!

JOAQUIN: *(Singing and shaking.)* "Goodness, gracious, great balls of fire!"

ALICE: *(To Joaquin.)* It's OK, hon . . .

THERAPIST: What did you want to do, Tim? What did you want to play?

(Tim hugs the ball.)

TIM: *(Crying.)* I . . . I wanted to juggle. I don't hate balls. I just wanted to juggle. But she wouldn't let me.

THERAPIST: Thank you, Tim. Joaquin, would you like to go next?

JOAQUIN: *(Collecting himself.)* OK. OK. My name is Joaquin.

ALL: Welcome, Joaquin.

JOAQUIN: And my problem is the moon. See, where I come from, everybody thinks the moon is sooo romantic. They get out their guitars . . . They write poetry . . . They get all into magical realism and shit. Well, I'm sorry man, the moon just creeps me out, OK? Like the sun? It comes up, it goes down. That's cool. I can deal with that. The moon? One night it's just a little slivery thing. And then it keeps growing and growing . . . And before you know it? Bam. Shining through the window . . . Like a searchlight . . . Following you all over the place—

(The Therapist holds the ball high, in front of Joaquin.)

THERAPIST: What do you want to say to the moon?

JOAQUIN: *(To the ball.)* Stop watching me, man! Stop following me! *(Paranoid; to the ball.)* No, that wasn't me under that balcony. No, you didn't see nothing—'cause I wasn't there!

(He lets out a slew of bits of songs, Tourette's-like: "Blue Moon," "When the moon hits the sky like a big pizza pie, that's amore," "Bad Moon Rising." He begins "Moon River," but panics and stops.)

JOAQUIN: *(To the ball, paranoid.)* I never sang that song. I never sang to that girl. I don't even know "Moon River"!

THERAPIST: *(Doesn't buy it.)* I think everyone knows "Moon River," Joaquin . . .

DAN: *(Sings badly.)* "Moon river, wider than a mile . . ."

JOAQUIN: Shut up, will you?

OTHERS: *(Sing.)* "I'm crossing you in style, someday . . ."

(They continue, directing the song at Joaquin who cowers.)

"You old faker, you heartbreaker—"

(Joaquin breaks down and sings to the moon, the ball.)

JOAQUIN: *(Sings.)* "Wherever you're goin', I'm goin' your way . . ."

(Joaquin cries, hugging the ball. Alice tries to comfort him, but the Therapist gets in between them and wrenches the ball away.)

THERAPIST: Would you like to go next, Alice?

(He places the ball near her, menacingly near.)

ALICE: Me? Oh, no, no, I'm just visiting. I don't really have a problem with balls.

(Alice gently kicks the ball with her foot and it rolls across the stage, terrifying the others who scream and jump onto their chairs for safety. Finally, one is able to speak.)

DAN: I'll talk. I'm Dan. I guess you could say I have a problem with a lot of b-b-balls—

THERAPIST: Multiple spherical disorder . . .

DAN: But the ball I really hate? The one I'd really like to smash? The ball that drops at the end of the year. *The* ball. The ball that drops in Times Square. Every. Single. Year. I feel like that thing is dropping right on my goddam head. I mean, you go to work, you come home and watch TV . . . Seed the lawn . . . Clean the gutters . . . Put on the snow tires . . . Take off the snow tires . . . Put on the snow tires . . . And before you know it, there it is again. *(Frightened.)* Ten! Nine! Eight—!
   (The others join in, seeing the ball in their minds.)
DAN/OTHERS: *(Frightened.)* Seven! Six! Five! Four! Three! Two! One!
DAN: Ready or not . . . Whammo.
THERAPIST: What do you want to say to the ball, Dan?
DAN: Slow down! I didn't stop smoking yet! Stop! Give a guy a chance! I'm not ready, you, you, you— *(Dan flips out, kicking and punching the ball, rolling over and under it on the floor, fighting for his life.)*
JOAQUIN: Goodness gracious, great balls of fire!
   (Dan winds up on the floor, spent.)
THERAPIST: It's OK, Dan, it's OK now. Alice? Would you like to—
   (The Therapist places the ball in front of her.)
ALICE: *(Lightly.)* Oh no, no, thanks, I'm fine.
   (But Alice never looks at the ball. Ever.)
DAN: Oh, come on, Alice, get real.
JOAQUIN: *(Mocking.)* She's just visiting.
TIM: We all have fears of spheres, Alice.
ALICE: Oh, not me. I play tennis. I play a little raquetball. I'm fine.
THERAPIST: Then why can't you look at the ball?
JOAQUIN: Eye on the ball, Alice!
ALICE: No.
DAN: You can do it.
ALICE: *(Laughs.)* I don't need to look at it, I know what it is. It's a Pilates ball. Big deal. Look . . . *(She goes to the ball, without looking at it, sits on it, and starts to bounce.)* See? Nice ball. Bouncy, bouncy. *(Bouncing, laughing.)* You know what scares me? What wakes me up at three AM? The sheets! I'm afraid of the sheets 'cause there's asbestos in the sheets that could give cancer. And I'm afraid of organic cotton sheets 'cause I could be burned alive. I'm afraid of driving to work and ruining the environment . . . and I'm afraid of staying home and losing my job.
   (Percussion begins to accompany her, in the style of the Beat poets.)
ALICE: I'm afraid of voting for Hillary 'cause people hate Hillary for not crying sooner . . . And I'm afraid someone's gonna shoot Obama. I'm afraid

my kids will stop reading—and I'm afraid I'll never learn to use an iPod. I'm afraid I'll never see Paris . . . and I'm afraid of traveling with an American passport.

(The percussion grows more intense. Tim starts to juggle.)

ALICE: I'm afraid of reality . . . but more afraid of reality shows. *(Beat, bouncing.)* I'm afraid of the whole ball of wax.

THERAPIST: Keep bouncing, Alice. Keep juggling, Tim. Sing, Joaquin!

JOAQUIN: *(Sings "Moon River.")* "Two drifters, off to see the world, there's such a lot of world to see . . ."

ALICE: I am afraid, of the whole ball of wax.

THERAPIST: Can you dance, Sam, while the ball comes down? Maybe mambo?

DAN: I can try . . .

(Dan does the mambo, as Tim juggles. And Joaquin sings faster, and the drums get louder, as Alice bounces to, "I'm afraid of the whole ball of wax." And the Therapist nods and takes it all in, as it reaches a crescendo.)

JOAQUIN: *(Singing.)* "Rainbow's end, my Huckleberry friend . . . Moon River and meeee—!"

ALICE: *(Overlapping.)* . . . The whole ball of wax.

(Blackout.)

END OF PLAY

RIGHTS AND PERMISSIONS